PROFIT FROM
LEGAL
INSIDER TRADING

PROFIT FROM LEGAL INSIDER TRADING

Invest Today on Tomorrow's News

Jonathan Moreland

DEARBORN™
A **Kaplan Professional** Company

This publication is designed to provide accurate and authoritative information in regard to the subject matter covered. It is sold with the understanding that the publisher is not engaged in rendering legal, accounting, or other professional service. If legal advice or other expert assistance is required, the services of a competent professional person should be sought.

Associate Publisher: Cynthia A. Zigmund
Senior Managing Editor: Jack Kiburz
Interior Design: Lucy Jenkins
Cover Design: Jody Billert, Billert Communications
Typesetting: the dotted i

Published by Dearborn, a Kaplan Professional Company

Printed in the United States of America

00 01 02   10 9 8 7 6 5 4 3 2 1

Library of Congress Cataloging-in-Publication Data

Moreland, Jonathan.
    Profit from legal insider trading : invest today on tomorrow's news /
Jonathan Moreland.
      p.   cm.
    Includes bibliographical references and index.
    ISBN 0-7931-2723-8 (pbk.)
    1. Investment analysis   2. Corporation reports.   3. Insider trading in
securities.   4. Investments.   I. Title.
HG4529.M67   2000
332.63'2042—dc21   00-009302

Contents

Acknowledgments

Thanks to my own personal insiders—Beatrice, Anne-Gail, Gail, Wally, Leslie, Gwen, and Craig—for support during the drawn-out process of finishing this book.

Thanks also to so many who shared knowledge, stories, insights, and time: John Heine, John Spears, Glenn Curtis, David Sterman, Tom Britt, Aaron Edelheit, Anthony Marchese, Luciano Siracusano, David Geracioti, Gordon Anderson, Bernie Faulk, Richard Dann, Carr Bettis, Marc Strausberg, Barbara Palumbo, Henry Wilf, Peter Romeo, and many others.

I also specially acknowledge the help of Paul Winn for his assistance with writing the book. Your hard work is really appreciated.

Introduction:
The Information Flow
to Know

Every day, investors have the opportunity to put their money into more than 15,000 U.S. stocks. But such a huge opportunity is also hugely confusing. How do you start narrowing down your investment choices?

Value investors may start by looking for stocks with low price-earnings or price–book value ratios. Growth investors likely head to the quarterly financial results in a newspaper looking for stocks with great year-over-year earnings comparisons. Momentum investors probably prefer to look at the list of percentage gainers and stocks with large trading volume increases. But all of these investors could increase their returns if they started their stock picking by looking at the same information flow: insider trading.

It should come as no surprise to anyone that insider trading occurs every day in the stock market. What might surprise investors is that much of it is done with the full knowledge and sanction of the U.S. Securities and Exchange Commission (SEC). So blatant are these insiders, they actually tell the SEC what they do. Theirs isn't the sort of insider trading that made Ivan Boesky infamous. He profited from trading on *material, nonpublic* information provided to him by a network of informants. The activity I refer to is the trading by directors and executives in their own company's shares. This insider trading is not only legal but is reported by executives to the SEC via a document called a *Form 4.*

This legal—and public—insider data, and that provided by other SEC documents, are a highly worthwhile source of investment ideas no matter what investment style you favor. Insider data is also invaluable for following stocks you already own. After all, who's in a better position to know a company's prospects than its own management? Corporate insiders obviously have access to the same level of material and nonpublic information that sent Mr. Boesky and his friends to jail— only they are allowed to act on it in many cases!

Obvious abuses by corporate insiders such as purchasing large amounts of shares just before their company is acquired at a premium, still aren't allowed, of course. Many publicly traded companies also have internal guidelines that only allow their executives to trade during certain windows of time. But an executive can hardly forget what he saw in the last sales report or heard in the last strategy meeting when he is on the phone to his broker buying his own company's shares. There is likely plenty of important, nonpublic information that is helping him make an investment decision.

By analyzing the Form 4s filed at the SEC, you may not know all that these insiders know, but you can certainly know what they do. And this information may be just as good. In a victory for common sense, numerous academic studies have proved that the insider data filed at the SEC is useful for garnering excess returns in stocks. A more important testimony comes from institutional investors, many of whom have successfully used the SEC's insider data to help in making investment decisions for years.

In fact, professional investors have enjoyed timely access to the SEC's insider trading data for decades. They could afford to pay the hundreds of dollars per month it used to take to access the up-to-date detailed electronic databases of private firms that specialize in aggregating Form 4 and other insider trading data from the original paper forms filed with the SEC. Until recently, by the time individual investors got hold of the affordable printed versions of the data from the SEC itself, institutions had already traded on the information. Perversely, over the past 25 years or so, the data that was meant to level the playing field for individual investors has only been providing institutional investors another leg up.

But the Internet and the SEC's EDGAR project for filing various SEC forms electronically are leveling the uneven playing field. Though it still costs more money than most individuals probably care to pay for the most detailed and timely insider data, the cost is coming down quickly.

It won't be long until this important data will be as commonplace for individuals to review as a company's quarterly earnings.

Using the Form 4 and other insider data as an investment tool is more involved than blindly mimicking the trades of a chairman, however. Some signals and patterns are important, whereas others are just time-wasting noise. This book shows you the nuances of interpreting insider trading data so you'll be prepared to profit from the flood of information that is on its way. We don't advocate using insider data as the only information needed to make an investment decision, but it is a time-saving first screen to determine what stocks should be analyzed further. It can also be a comforting sign—or a red flag—for a stock you already have in your portfolio.

HOW THIS BOOK IS ORGANIZED

Chapter 1 explains what insider data is while Chapter 2 differentiates legal and illegal insider trading activity. Both of these background chapters include a dash of history about how insider regulations and data evolved in the United States.

Chapters 3 through 11 answer the important questions of how the various insider documents filed at the SEC can help investors make money. Special emphasis is given to Form 4 documents, which are the most important insider data forms filed at the SEC. Form 144, Schedule 13D, Schedule 13G, and Form 13F are also analyzed for profitable information, as are corporate buybacks.

In Chapter 12, I discuss the availability and evolution of insider data in important capital markets outside the United States.

Once armed with the knowledge of how to use insider data, Chapters 13 through 15 tell you where to get it. Free services are identified, and paid-for data are assessed for usefulness.

At the end of each chapter, a summary of important points is listed to assist readers who are in a hurry or who need a quick recap. The insider data presented at my firm's Web site <www.insidertrader.com> is used as the source for the data in the text's examples, not only because of my familiarity with our service, but because I feel that our service is an excellent source of data for anyone with an Internet connection.

1

What Exactly Is Insider Data?

WHY INSIDER DATA EXISTS

When the U.S. Congress of 1934 legislated the Securities and Exchange Commission (SEC) into existence to protect individual investors, it realized that corporate executives had an unfair advantage when trading their own company's shares. But the congressmen also realized they could not ban such transactions. Even then, shares were used as incentives for employees, and who would start a public company without being able to participate in its success?

In lieu of banning insider transactions, Congress dictated disclosure. If insiders did trade, they would have to fill out a form and tell the world about it. "Disclosure is the fundamental principle of regulating securities markets at the federal level," according to John Heine, deputy director of public affairs at the SEC. Heine also points out that the regulators who drew up the Securities Act of 1933 (the 1933 act), and the Securities Exchange Act of 1934 (the 1934 act) appear to have been greatly influenced by Louis Brandeis, a prominent securities lawyer at the turn of the 20th century who later became a Supreme Court Justice. Mr. Brandeis's view on combating securities fraud was summed up as follows: "Sunshine is the best disinfectant." Disclosure of transactions was seen as the necessary sunshine.

Section 16 of the 1934 act attempts to reign in some of the blatantly unfair trading practices used by some corporate insiders of the day. It

1

was developed after what was apparently very candid testimony about trading abuses, as congressional records from 1934 show:

> Among the most vicious practices unearthed at the hearings before the subcommittee was the flagrant betrayal of their fiduciary duties by directors and officers of corporations who used their positions of trust and the confidential information which came to them in such positions to aid them in market activities. Closely allied to this type of abuse was the unscrupulous employment of inside information by large stockholders who, while not directors and officers, exercised sufficient control over the destinies of their companies to enable them to acquire and profit by information not available to others.[1]

Disgruntled shareholders did sue to try and stop insiders' abuses, but they rarely got justice. Shareholders didn't necessarily lose because of lack of proof of manipulation, either. There was just an entirely different mindset in the early 1900s about insiders using their unfair advantages. A court ruling from a dismissed insider-trading case in 1916 sums up the prevailing attitude of the day:

> "The officers are not bound to acquaint a stockholder willing to sell his shares with facts which would enhance the price of the stock. The officers are trustees for the shareholders only as to the management of the corporation and not in their private dealings."[2]

Though such a ruling would seem unlikely today, similar regulatory apathy is actually still the norm in most non–U.S. stock markets. (See Chapter 12 for the state of insider trading regulations around the world.)

But obvious abuses and growing public outcry in the United States after the 1929 crash forced the federal government to regulate the overly free U.S. market. Congress first passed the 1933 act to set guidelines on registering securities for sale. One year later, the 1934 act regulated how securities were traded once issued. The job of the newly formed SEC was to develop rules to carry out the intent of the acts, and then enforce them. Overseeing the taming of the market was Joseph Kennedy, the SEC's first chairman, future ambassador to England, and patriarch of what became a political dynasty. In the early 1930s, how-

---

1. S. Rep. No. 1455, 73d Cong., 2d Sess., at 55 (1934).
2. Aaron Feigen with Don Christensen, *Investing with the Insiders Legally* (New York: Simon and Schuster, 1988), 29–30. (This book is out of print, and Feigan has unfortunately passed away.)

ever, he was best known as a successful businessman who many felt had firsthand knowledge of (and benefit from) the stock market abuses he was hired to combat.

THE DEFINITION OF *INSIDER*

A first step for the U.S. Congress of 1934 was to develop a definition of *insider.* The SEC had to know whom to police, and the people being watched over needed to know that they were now expected to play by new rules. According to the 1934 act, an insider is an officer or director of a public company, or an individual or entity owning 10 percent or more of any class of a company's shares. The definition in all its legal verbiage is presented in Appendix A. There are even more words spared on how to more specifically define *officer* and *beneficial owner* in Rule 16a-1 of the Code of Federal Regulations. This lovely piece of prose is excerpted in Appendix B.

Most readers should be content with the knowledge that the definition of an insider is intended to cover the people who have the most knowledge of the inner workings and future prospects of a publicly traded company.

REPORTING REQUIREMENTS

Once you're pegged as an insider, the SEC becomes very interested in how you may be benefiting from the unfair advantage you have when trading your own company's shares. The concept of *disclosure* mandated in the 1934 act was put into practice by section 16(a) of the act, which requires insiders to report their stock holdings and trading activity on Forms 3, 4, and 5.

Insiders must make an initial statement of holdings within ten days after gaining their insider status even if they don't yet own any shares in the company in which they have become an insider. This is done via the SEC's *Form 3.*

Subsequent changes in ownership must be received at the SEC on a *Form 4* by the tenth day of the month following an insider's trade. Any trade by an insider in the month of October, for instance, must be reported to the SEC by November 10. Like all the SEC's filing deadlines, the tenth day of the month is not the date a Form 4 should be postmarked by. It is the date when the SEC is supposed to actually have the form in its hallowed halls. This filing deadline seems arbitrary today, but it was mandated in 1934 to account for the U.S. Postal Service's capabilities then. Presumably, it was geared to allow insiders the ability to do all their paperwork at the end of the month and still get it to the SEC on time. The filing deadline is just one of numerous aspects of insider trading laws that could use some updating.

To help guard against any funny business just before someone becomes an insider, trades made up to six months prior to achieving insider status must also be reported on a Form 4 soon after filing Form 3. Filing requirements linger for another six months after insiders lose their status as well, thus helping to stop such abuses as a director's giving up his or her seat on a company's board just in time to buy the company's shares before an imminent merger.

Insiders must also file a *Form 5* within 45 days after their company's fiscal year-end to disclose transactions that are required to be reported under section 16(a) of the 1934 act but aren't required to be shown on a Form 4. These include dividend reinvestments, certain transactions by market makers, and certain merger-related trades, among others. Any Form 4 transactions not previously reported must also be included on this form.

A Form 5 not only has to be filed by anybody considered an insider at fiscal year-end but also by anyone who was considered an insider for any part of the previous year. This is another way the SEC attempts to stop people from popping back and forth between being or not being an insider just to skirt filing requirements.

FORM 4: INSIDER BUYING AND SELLING

Of the three forms discussed above, Form 4 is generally considered the most important source of useful insider information and is the main focus of this book. While Forms 3 and 5 record a snapshot of an insider's holdings of the company's shares, Form 4 informs investors how insiders came to hold their position. It is the dynamic piece of insider data that gives the best window into the feelings insiders have about the prospects of their respective firm's shares.

The basic statement of holdings illuminated in Forms 3 and 5 seem mundane in comparison with the information accessible on Form 4— so much so that Forms 3 and 5 can generally be passed over in favor of spending whatever time and resources you have on prospecting through the more useful Form 4 data. Form 4 lists the name of the insider, his or her relationship to the company, and the number and price of the shares traded. It also gives the dates of an insider's trades, the insider's total holdings after the transactions, and whether the trades were open market, related to the exercise of stock options, or traded under some other special circumstance. Numerous different trades can be listed on one Form 4, the front and back of which is presented in Figure 1.1.

Besides being quite detailed, Form 4 is also timely. With the deadline for filing being the tenth of the month following the transaction, an insider's trade should take 41 days at most to reach the SEC—and that's only if the insider trades during a 31-day month. Form 4s can, of course, be filed immediately, and some do reach the SEC within days of the trades they show. However, there is always a predictable bulge in the number of filings around the tenth of the month as insiders rush to meet the deadline. In general, approximately one-third to one-half of Form 4s filed in any given month are filed in the days around the tenth of the month.

Insiders don't wait until the last minute to be sneaky. The deadline surge is more the result of procrastination than anything else. The fact is that filling out a Form 4 and all the other SEC documents is just annoying paperwork for insiders, most of whom are busy executives. The burden is typically passed to an overloaded secretary or company lawyer to complete, and the forms are seldom a high priority for the secretary or lawyer either. This may explain why some (anecdotal evidence suggests around 5 percent) of the Form 4s filed with the SEC are not filled out correctly and require some interpretation. Indicating a share purchase that should have been a sale, typing in the wrong transaction price or the amount of total holdings—virtually every field on the form can fall prey to human error. Mistakes seem to be made as much by highly paid legal counsel as by overworked secretaries.

Another subset of filings also reaches the SEC late. In any given week, a small percentage of Form 4s with trade dates that are months or even a year old betray the tardiness of insiders or their charges. Again, this is more likely the result of a mistake than intended deceit. (Let's face it, any insider trade that is really illegal is not going to be reported at all to the SEC.) Late filers generally don't get more than a slap on the wrist from the SEC if no harm seems to be done. But much worse can, and does, happen to the tardy (see Chapter 2).

Fortunately, the vast majority of insiders are both diligent and accurate when filing their Form 4s, and they supply the market with high-quality investment information every time they trade their own company's shares in the open market.

FIGURE 1.1 Front and Back of SEC Form 4

FORM 4

☐ Check this box if no longer subject to Section 16. Form 4 or Form 5 obligations may continue. *See Instruction 1(b).*
(Print or Type Responses)

UNITED STATES SECURITIES AND EXCHANGE COMMISSION
Washington, D.C. 20549

STATEMENT OF CHANGES IN BENEFICIAL OWNERSHIP

Filed pursuant to Section 16(a) of the Securities Exchange Act of 1934, Section 17(a) of the Public Utility Holding Company Act of 1935 or Section 30(f) of the Investment Company Act of 1940

OMB APPROVAL
OMB Number: 3235-0287
Expires: September 30, 1998
Estimated average burden
hours per response 0.5

1. Name and Address of Reporting Person*

(Last) (First) (Middle)

(Street)

(City) (State) (Zip)

2. Issuer Name and Ticker or Trading Symbol

3. IRS or Social Security Number of Reporting Person (Voluntary)

4. Statement for Month/Year

5. If Amendment, Date of Original (Month/Year)

6. Relationship of Reporting Person(s) to Issuer (Check all applicable)

____ Director ____ 10% Owner
____ Officer (give title below) ____ Other (specify below)

7. Individual or Joint/Group Filing (Check Applicable)
____ Form filed by One Reporting Person
____ Form filed by More than One Reporting Person

Table I - Non-Derivative Securities Acquired, Disposed of, or Beneficially Owned

1. Title of Security (Instr. 3)	2. Transaction Date (Month/Day/Year)	3. Transaction Code (Instr. 8)		4. Securities Acquired (A) or Disposed of (D) (Instr. 3, 4 and 5)			5. Amount of Securities Beneficially Owned at End of Month (Instr. 3 and 4)	6. Ownership Form: Direct (D) or Indirect (I) (Instr. 4)	7. Nature of Indirect Beneficial Ownership (Instr. 4)
		Code	V	Amount	(A) or (D)	Price			

Reminder: Report on a separate line for each class of securities beneficially owned directly or indirectly.
* If the form is filed by more than one reporting person, *see* Instruction 4(b)(v).

(Over)

SEC 1474 (7-96)

FIGURE 1.1 *(Continued)*

FORM 4 (continued)

Table II - Derivative Securities Acquired, Disposed of, or Beneficially Owned
(e.g., puts, calls, warrants, options, convertible securities)

1. Title of Derivative Security (Instr. 3)	2. Conversion or Exercise Price of Derivative Security	3. Transaction Date (Month/Day/Year)	4. Transaction Code (Instr. 8)		5. Number of Derivative Securities Acquired (A) or Disposed of (D) (Instr. 3, 4, and 5)		6. Date Exercisable and Expiration Date (Month/Day/Year)		7. Title and Amount of Underlying Securities (Instr. 3 and 4)		8. Price of Derivative Security (Instr. 5)	9. Number of derivative Securities Beneficially Owned at End Of Month (Instr. 4)	10. Ownership Form of Derivative Security: Direct (D) or Indirect (I) (Instr. 4)	11. Nature of Indirect Beneficial Ownership (Instr. 4)
			Code	V	(A)	(D)	Date Exercisable	Expiration Date	Title	Amount or Number of Shares				

Explanation of Responses:

** Intentional misstatements or omissions of facts constitute Federal Crime Violations. *See* 18 U.S.C. 1001 and 15 U.S.C. 78ff(a).

Note: File three copies of this Form, one of which must be manually signed. If space is insufficient, *see* Instruction 6 for procedure.

Potential persons who are to respond to the collection of information contained in this form are not required to respond unless the form displays a currently valid OMB Number.

_____   _____
**Signature of Reporting Person   Date

FORM 144: INTENT TO SELL

Form 144s are considered harbingers of future selling activity by insiders and are even called "intent to sell" documents or "planned sales" when presented by some data services. These colloquialisms are misleading, however, and are far too simplistic descriptions that only confuse the uninitiated about the intelligence that can be garnered from the forms. For numerous reasons (explained in Chapter 7), Form 144s are not perfect harbingers of future selling activity. Still, they are worth keeping an eye on. Technically speaking, filing a Form 144 is the final part of a process that exempts a holder of unregistered shares from registering them with the SEC before they are sold in the open market.

Form 144s were mandated by the SEC in 1972, when it passed Rule 144 to help clarify the Securities Act of 1933. According to the 1933 act, stocks, bonds, and other securities must be registered with the SEC before being issued to the public. Registration requirements include filing documents at the SEC that disclose the type of security being offered, how it will be distributed, and substantial financial information about the company behind the security.

Investors in a public offering of stock see all this information in the prospectus that is sent to them by the Wall Street firm underwriting the security. With disclosure like this, the 1933 act satisfies its stated purpose: "To provide full and fair disclosure of the character of the securities sold in interstate commerce and through the mails, and to prevent fraud in the sale thereof."

But the SEC isn't so anal in its mandate to protect individual investors that it cannot see that this amount of disclosure doesn't make sense all the time.

There are also numerous exemptions from registration that allow companies to issue small amounts of shares directly to somebody as part of a private placement, a stock bonus, or a pension or profit-sharing plan, or for a number of other reasons. The SEC's exemptions give a nod to the reality that companies issue shares outside of large public offerings and that requiring the extensive registration disclosure in all instances would be a gruesome burden.

And if registering small, private issuances of shares is too onerous for the company, the people who receive these unregistered shares certainly can't be expected to do the paperwork when they finally sell the shares in the open market. Under Rule 144 of the 1933 act, they are relieved of this burden. As the SEC's own text of Rule 144 explains, this rule is designed to prohibit the creation of public markets in securities of issuers concerning which adequate current information is not available to the public. At the same time, where adequate current information concerning the issuer is available to the public, the rule permits the public sale in ordinary transactions of limited amounts of securities owned by persons controlling, controlled by or under common control with the issuer and by persons who have acquired restricted securities of the issuer.

Basically, if the seller of a small number of unregistered securities isn't considered an underwriter, the seller is exempt from registering them. Exemption from registering shares doesn't necessarily mean holders have carte blanche to trade as they please, however. If there are fewer than 500 unregistered shares to be sold and the total value of the shares is less than $10,000, they can be sold at will. But if both of these minimums are not met, the SEC's Rule 144 holds up numerous hoops for sellers of unregistered shares to jump through. These requirements aren't nearly as onerous as registering the shares, but they are burdensome enough to make sure that a company doesn't undertake a "stealth" offering of its shares by issuing them in dribs and drabs.

The four conditions Rule 144 lays out are as follows:

1. The unregistered shares have to have been held by the selling party for at least one year. It was originally two years, but the SEC lessened the holding period with a 1990 rule change.
2. The sale must be made through a brokerage firm.
3. Information must be freely available to the public about the issuer of the securities.
4. The number of shares being sold cannot represent more than 1 percent of the issuer's shares outstanding and must also be less than the average weekly trading volume of the shares over the preceding four calendar weeks.

If these criteria are met, a person may file a Form 144 with the SEC giving notice of their intent to sell a specified number of unregistered shares within the next three months.

THE "SMART MONEY" FORMS

Some large investors and investment groups may not be considered insiders according to the SEC's criteria, but that doesn't mean they don't have an advantage. Large shareholders often manage to get better information about a company than mere mortals with a few thousand shares. Because they have more money riding on the firm, large shareholders understandably make it their business to dig up all the information they can. The actions of this "smart money" are worth keeping an eye on.

Schedule 13D

This SEC document is filed by holders of 5 percent or more of any class of a company's outstanding shares. When a person or entity first reaches the 5 percent ownership level, a 13D must be filed within ten days. And it is important that the intention of the investment must also be stated on the form. Subsequent trades must be promptly stated on an amended 13D.

Schedule 13D was first mandated in 1968, when Congress passed changes to the 1934 act designed to require disclosure by parties affecting the change of ownership of companies by acquiring shares. Schedule 13Ds used to be among the most monitored SEC documents around. In the midst of the mergermania of the 1980s, a 13D was often the first indication that a company was being taken over. Raiding firms would discreetly acquire 4.9 percent of their targets' shares before pouncing across the 5 percent ownership barrier that required a 13D to be filed. Cover blown, the large investor declared its intention to take over the company whether management went along or not. A fight for the remaining shares often ensued, and professional arbitrageurs bet heavily on the outcome.

Although the importance of 13Ds has waned somewhat in recent years (as explained in Chapter 8), they remain a decent source of information about the trading activities of many larger investors.

Schedule 13G

Not all the smart money around wants to take over the firms it buys ownership in. The great influx of money into mutual funds, for instance, has turned mutual fund managers into major owners of many companies. The bylaws of their funds certainly don't allow them to make a grab for power. The SEC exempts such passive, large investors from the burdensome reporting requirements of Schedule 13D but does make them fill out Schedule 13G instead.

Schedule 13Gs were mandated in 1977 and must be filed 45 days after the end of each calendar year by passive investors owning 5 percent or more of a company's outstanding shares. One 13G must be filed for each company in which 5 percent or more is owned. This less-frequent filing is certainly a relief from paperwork for passive investors, but it also mitigates the usefulness of the data to investors given that it is dated and only represents holdings rather than transactions. Nevertheless, Schedule 13Gs certainly offer some useful information.

Form 13F

A better source for finding out what equities mutual fund companies like is Form 13F. This is a quarterly SEC report of equity holdings submitted by institutional investment managers having assets under management of $100 million or more. Included in this category of managers are certain banks, insurance companies, investment advisors, investment companies, foundations, and pension funds. The resources of all these institutions certainly give them credence as smart money, whose actions could yield valuable information.

Though they supply similar information, Form 13Fs and Schedule 13Gs are different animals. A subset of the filings may seem redundant to individual investors, but the forms resulted from different regulatory goals. The definitions of *passive investors* who fill out 13Gs and *investment managers* who must file 13Fs are definitely not the same. And while the 13G is company specific, the 13F is filer specific. One 13G must be filed for each company in which a large investor owns more than 5 percent, whereas a 13F simply lists all of the investment manager's holdings. If you are particularly enamored of a certain institution's investment skills, Schedule 13Fs make it easy to monitor what its smart money is invested in—or, rather, where it was at the end of the last quarter.

Chapter 1   AT A GLANCE

1. Better information about securities and disclosure of insiders' trades was deemed necessary to help prevent abuses that contributed to the 1929 market crash.

2. The Securities Act of 1933 states that securities must be registered to be traded.

3. The Securities Exchange Act of 1934 states that insiders must report holdings and trades in their respective company's shares. The Securities and Exchange Commission (SEC) was born to oversee the new regulations. Forms 3, 4, and 5 are mandated by this act.

4. **Insider:** An officer or director of a public company or an individual or entity owning 10 percent or more of any class of a company's shares.

5. **Form 4:** Reports changes in an insider's holdings and is the most important source of useful insider trading data.

6. **Form 3:** Initial statement of holdings by insiders.

7. **Form 5:** Yearly statement of holdings by some insiders.

8. **Form 144:** Notice of intent to sell unregistered shares; first mandated in 1972 as an exemption to the 1933 act.

9. **Schedule 13D:** Filed by holders of 5 percent or more of any class of a company's shares outstanding; mandated in 1968 as a change to the 1934 act and designed to require disclosure by parties who may materially change the ownership of a company.

10. **Schedule 13G:** Filed yearly by passive investors owning 5 percent or more of a company's outstanding shares; mandated in 1977 as a change to the 1934 act.

11. **Form 13F:** Filed quarterly by institutional investment companies having assets under management of $100 million or more and lists all equity holdings; mandated in 1977 as a change to the 1934 act.

2

Legal versus Illegal
Insider Trading

Even though Form 4s have been around for over 60 years, many investors just becoming familiar with them are still surprised this information exists. Most investors are happily surprised that such obviously useful information is finally becoming affordable enough for them. However, others question how useful the data can be given that acting on material, nonpublic information is illegal. For if the insiders really did trade on material, nonpublic information, wouldn't they be put in jail? In theory, insiders shouldn't act on material, nonpublic information. In practice, they do.

Even as the U.S. Congress of 1934 was legislating its rules against illegal insider trading, it realized that the disclosure it was mandating wouldn't completely stop the practice. As government records from 1934 state:

> Because it is difficult to draw a clear line between truly inside information and information generally known by better-informed investors, the most potent weapon against abuse of inside information is full and prompt publicity.
>
> The (Congressional) Committee is aware that these requirements are not air-tight and the unscrupulous insider may still, *within the law,* use inside information for his own advantage. It is hoped, however, that the publicity features of the bill will tend to bring these practices into disrepute and encourage voluntary maintenance of

proper fiduciary standards by those in control of large corporate enterprises whose securities are registered on the public exchanges. (emphasis added)[1]

The emphasis on "within the law" is ours, but the wording shows that lawmakers were being realistic with their expectations of what the new regulations would accomplish. It doesn't imply that insiders are allowed to use material, nonpublic information. It does imply, however, that because it is so hard to prove that information is material and nonpublic, insiders will likely get away with using it.

It's not that insiders necessarily act unscrupulously (although some most certainly do). More to the point is that insiders can hardly clear their minds of all they know about their company when they are on the phone with their stockbroker. Seeing a sales report, discussing new product strategies in meetings, talking in the halls with someone on the research and development team—all of these bits of information allow insiders to form an opinion of how prospects look for their company. Is any one of these pieces of information material and nonpublic? Maybe, maybe not. If so, it would be difficult for the SEC or the U.S. Justice Department to prove.

But insiders need not be privy to company secrets to trade well. Even if none of the above data inputs is material, nonpublic information, putting them all together can paint a very obvious investment conclusion. Insiders can easily argue they were simply acting as a better-informed investor, and not an illegal insider trader. What distinguishes these two? A rather large gray area.

CASES IN POINT

The fact is that the U.S. Congress, the Justice Department, and the SEC have never actually inked specific definitions of what makes an insider's trading illegal. It has been left to lawyers arguing actual cases to build a body of case law in determining when an insider (or anyone else trading securities in the United States) is wearing a white hat or a black hat.

Watershed cases whose decisions formed the backbone of today's body of case law include the following: *Chiarella v. United States* (1980),

---

1. H.R. Rep No. 1383, 73d Cong., 2d Sess., at 13 (1934).

Dirks v. SEC (1983), and *United States v. O'Hagan* (1997). All of these cases were tried by the SEC and U.S. Justice Department lawyers under their authority to enforce the broad antifraud provisions of Rule 10b-5 of the Code of Federal Regulations. The broadness of Rule 10b-5 resulted, no doubt, from a realization that specific definitions of illegalities would be virtually impossible to formulate. Also, a specific list of illegal trading practices would quickly become obsolete as the securities markets evolved. The result was the short-but-sweet rule presented in Figure 2.1, which ensures a lifetime of employment for lawyers arguing the cases to define its very general terms.

Case law has reached some consensus in differentiating legal and illegal insider trading activity—but, again, only a general one. The three things that must be proved in order to label insider trading activity illegal are that

1. trading occurred;
2. the trade occurred while the person was in possession of material, nonpublic information; and
3. the person who did the trading had access to the information as a result of a relationship of trust or fiduciary duty that was subsequently violated by the trading. In other words, the information was misappropriated.

The term *material, nonpublic information* also has a working definition. Basically, it is any information about a company not disclosed to the marketplace but which, if disclosed, would likely affect significantly

---

FIGURE 2.1 Rule 10b-5. Employment of Manipulative and Deceptive Devices

---

It shall be unlawful for any person, directly or indirectly, by the use of any means or instrumentality of interstate commerce, or of the mails or of any facility of any national securities exchange,

a) To employ any device, scheme, or artifice to defraud,
b) To make any untrue statement of a material fact or to omit to state a material fact necessary in order to make the statements made, in the light of the circumstances under which they were made, not misleading, or
c) To engage in any act, practice, or course of business which operates or would operate as a fraud or deceit upon any person, in connection with the purchase or sale of any security.

---

the market price of the securities of the company or would be considered to do so by a reasonable investor.

The three-point framework of prosecuting insider fraud cases and the definition of *material, nonpublic information* helps to clear up the gray area a bit, but the wiggle room for insiders is clearly visible between all the vagaries that the SEC and Justice Department must prove in court. Cases have been decided on whether a relationship of trust existed. Others focused on whether such a relationship was violated by a trade. Proving that information was material and nonpublic is just as hard. Agreeing on what a reasonable investor would think or what a significant movement is in a security is also hardly set in stone.

The vagaries in the law don't deter the SEC from policing transactions closely for insider trading violations. John Heine, deputy director of public affairs for the SEC, reports that 6 percent of the SEC's legal actions in 1998 involved cases of insider fraud. That is a healthy concentration considering all that the SEC keeps its eyes on. The agency is hardly on a witch hunt, however, and doesn't prosecute insiders just for trading well. "The securities laws are not designed to punish people for making money," points out Heine. "If anything, they are meant to foster commerce."

A POWERFUL, LONG ARM

When the law does come down, both civil and criminal penalties can result. The SEC litigates the civil suits, and the U.S. Department of Justice handles the criminal side of the cases.

On the civil side, the SEC can impose cease and desist orders, injunctions, and monetary penalties. The fines start at $5,000 for any vanilla type of violation but rise to $50,000 per violation if it is proved that the insider showed deliberate or reckless disregard of the regulatory requirement. The SEC can even argue in court for fines of up to $100,000 per violation if a significant risk of substantial loss to others could have resulted from a fraudulent action. In addition to disgorging any gains from fraud, an insider trader may be fined further up to three times the amount of the gains.

Criminal penalties for fraudulent securities transactions (whether by insiders or not) can be much worse. Monetary fines of up to $1 million are possible, as is a jail term of up to ten years.

Once out of jail, an insider trader's travails may still not be over. The SEC has the right to ban particularly onerous offenders from serving as an officer or director of any publicly held company or from engaging in the securities business completely. The company employing an insider trader may also find itself liable for its employee's actions. Under the Fraud Enforcement Act of 1988, a company must show that it has internal compliance measures in place to guard against 10b-5 violations, a requirement that has prompted companies to formulate internal policies to guard against such violations.

Most publicly traded companies, for instance, have windows for their insiders when they are allowed to trade. A window typically closes a month or so before the end of the company's fiscal quarter and stays closed until a few days after the company releases the quarter's earnings to the public. This is the company's way of removing any insiders' temptation to trade on the material, nonpublic information of how much money the company made or lost in the quarter. The existence of internally established trading windows also explains why insider activity at a company can occur in clusters.

A company that imposes trading windows on its insiders also typically will close them if any important corporate action is pending, such as a merger or acquisition. This is something to keep in mind when reviewing a company's insider transactions because at times the lack of any filings can tell you something.

NONCOMPLIANCE

The SEC also watches if insiders are filing their various forms correctly and promptly, as section 16(a) of the 1934 act mandates. Not to do so makes even the most legitimate of insider trades illegal. Being late with a Form 4 may not seem as harmful as being declared a fraudulent insider trader under Rule 10b-5, but the criminal penalties and civil fine schedule are the same for both.

"Prior to 1990, the enforcement of 16(a) by the SEC was sporadic and not very successful in fostering compliance with the provision," asserts Peter Romeo, an ex-SEC lawyer now practicing in the private sector. "With the signing into law on October 15, 1990, of the Securities Enforcement Remedies and Penny Stock Reform Act of 1990 [the 1990 Reform Act], however, the Commission obtained additional powers that now make it relatively easy to enforce Section 16(a)."[2]

---

2. Peter Romeo, *Comprehensive Section 16 Outline* (San Francisco: E.P. Executive Press, April 1997), 9.

In practice, however, the SEC has not used its new teeth to generate much income for the government. As of March 1997, the SEC tried to impose monetary penalties only nine times on late filers. It won in each case but appeared to settle for less money than it could have gotten under the letter of the law.[3]

The SEC won't admit that there is any grace period, say, a few days or a month, during which a late filing is accepted without any action. But there is probably some internal SEC policy that recognizes there are better ways to spend its limited enforcement resources than to go after minor procrastinators.

Criminal penalties for late filing are even more rare. "In the more than 60 years that Section 16 has been in existence, there have only been three reported instances of criminal actions under Section 16(a)," according to Peter Romeo. "All involved egregious reporting violations that were part of a larger scheme of unlawful activity."[4] Again, the Justice Department is the agency responsible for bringing criminal charges.

The SEC has been much more active in imposing the collateral consequences it gained the right to use under the 1990 Reform Act. Companies whose insiders file forms late or incompletely must disclose the executives' transgressions in their 10-K and annual proxy statement. The SEC can also ban people from serving as an officer or director of a public company or in the securities industry altogether if it deems their section 16(a) violation to be particularly egregious.

That's some serious teeth, which has prompted companies to play a more active role in making sure that their insiders comply with filing requirements. Making disclosures of tardiness in the 10-K is, after all, embarrassing, and losing the services of an officer or director because of an SEC ban isn't anything to write shareholders about either. The increase in companies' participation in what are really individuals' responsibilities is credited with significantly increasing the timeliness and accuracy of Form 4 filings since the 1990 Reform Act was passed.

It will be interesting to see if future legislation further pressures companies to police the data filings of its insiders. As originally legislated, Form 4s were meant to be an individual's responsibility. This is a major reason why it is not mandatory for Form 4s and Form 144s to be filed on the SEC's Electronic Data Gathering, Analysis, and Retrieval (EDGAR) system, as it is for company filings like 10-Ks and 10-Qs.

---

3. Ibid.
4. Ibid.

"We had our hands full handling questions on how to use EDGAR from the 15,000 or so companies that were made to use it in the mid-1990s," says one SEC employee, who wished to remain anonymous. "There are at least ten times as many individual insiders, and we don't have the personnel to handle their service needs if they were made to use the system."

But if the trend to make companies more liable for their insiders' filings continues, the same people who are now sending their company's 10-Ks to EDGAR may become responsible for sending Forms 4 and 144 there too. This has already become standard practice at many bigger companies that have resources to throw at their compliance departments, and more to lose if their insiders' do something wrong.

Most companies don't baby-sit their insiders, however, and the vast majority (anecdotal evidence suggests upwards of 90 percent) of the Form 4s received at the SEC arrive by mail. The legislative path to mandate EDGAR filing of these forms seems clear, though. And if that came to pass, perhaps the SEC would also reduce the deadline for filing the forms to just a few days after an insider trades.

A COUPLE OF DEFINITES

With such a vast gray area between legal and illegal insider trading, it's good to know that two types of insider transactions are easily spotted and definitely non grata: short-swing transactions and short sales. Short-swing transactions refer to short-term speculation by insiders in their own company's shares, which is specifically defined by the 1934 act as comprising a purchase and then a sale (or sale, then purchase) of a company's shares within a six-month period. Short selling is when investors sell borrowed stock in the open market with the expectation of replacing the shares at a lower price some time in the future.

Section 16(b) of the 1934 act requires insiders to return any profits made from short-swing transactions, while section 16(c) bans short sales by insiders altogether. Both of these measures were taken after Congress concluded that the disclosure mandated by section 16(a) was not enough to deter insiders' potential abuse of these types of transactions.

Banning short sales by insiders was a specific response to insiders' use of "bear raids" in the early 1900s to line their pockets. In a bear raid, insiders would sell their own firm's shares short and then spread false bad news about the company to drive the price down. After covering their short positions for a profit, insiders would profit again by buying their now artificially low-priced shares and talking the price back up by discounting the false rumors they themselves had spread. "Several major fortunes were made literally overnight using tactics just like these," wrote Aaron Feigan in his 1988 book *Investing with the Insiders Legally.* "Few people thought there was anything wrong with these activities. It was just part of the game."[5]

The need to ban short-swing transactions stemmed from the rampant abuse of such short-term speculative trading before the 1929 stock market crash. During congressional hearings in the 1930s, insiders freely admitted to using confidential information for short-term profits. "Congress determined that the best method of dealing with these practices was the enactment of a flat rule taking the profits out of a class of transactions in which the possibility of abuse was believed to be intolerably great."[6]

There are, however, certain exemptions to the short-swing rule. Insiders exercising stock options often buy shares at below-market prices from their company and immediately sell them in the open market for a profit. That is fine. Acquiring stock as part of a company benefit plan also doesn't trigger the short-swing restrictions on insiders. The in-and-out (or out-and-in) trades referred to by section 16(b) are the open market kind.

The wording of section 16(b) is curious, however. Short-swing transactions by insiders are not banned per se; only profiting from them is. Because the transactions are not illegal, no criminal penalty attaches if insiders make them. There are likewise no civil fines. The penalty is simply to require that the insider must give any profits from the trades back to the company behind the stock.

If an IBM insider profits from short-swing trading, for example, IBM can demand the money. IBM must file the suit in court to receive the profits within two years of the activity. If IBM doesn't move fast enough, any IBM shareholder can file the suit in court to recover the profits on behalf of the company. In neither case does the SEC get involved.

With nothing to gain, section 16(b) has basically stifled short-swing transactions by insiders, but not completely.

---

5. Aaron Feigen with Don Christensen, *Investing with the Insiders Legally* (New York: Simon and Schuster, 1988), 29.

6. Peter Romeo, *Comprehensive Section 16 Outline* (San Francisco: E.P. Executive Press, April 1997), 120.

In April 1997 a director at Xircom, Kirk Mathews, thought his shares were quite a bargain after they traded below $10 in reaction to a disappointing earnings release (see Figure 2.1). His 510,000 share purchase was large in its own right and also in relation to the amount of shares he had at the time. It showed a lot of confidence in Xircom's prospects and also turned out to be a good short-term buy, as the shares traded back to over $15 within a month. Mathews obviously showed a lot of savvy and once again showed why Form 4 data is so useful to monitor.

FIGURE 2.1 Form 4 History for Xircom (Nasdaq: XIRC)

Insider Name	Title	Trans Type	# of Shares	Trans Date(s)	Trans Price(s)	Total Holdings	D/I Own
Bass, Robert W.	VP	B	500	4/28/97	8.94	NA	D
Holliday, Randall H.	VP	B	1,000	4/25/97	9.19	NA	D
Mathews, J. Kirk	DIR	B	510,000	4/25/97–4/17/97	8.57–11.12	687,702	D
Holliday, Randall H.	VP	S	1,500	2/14/97	25.00	796	D
Holliday, Randall H.	SEC	B*	1,500	2/14/97	10.38	NA	
Biba, Kenneth J.	DIR	S	5,000	2/13/97	26.25	45,200	D
Bass, Robert W.	VP	S	2,000	2/7/97	28.25	100	D
Bass, Robert W.	VP	B*	2,000	2/7/97	10.00	NA	
Russo, Carl E.	EX VP	S	10,000	2/4/97	27.00	NA	D
Russo, Carl E.	EX VP	B*	10,000	2/4/97	11.00	NA	
Holliday, Randall H.	VP	S	5,000	1/30/97	25.25	796	D
Schroeder, William J.	DIR	S	5,000	1/24/97	27.53	15,000	D
Gates, Dirk I.	CB	S	50,000	1/22/97	26.70	1,171,700	I
Devis, Marc	VP	S	25,831	1/22/97	26.58	NA	D
Devis, Marc	VP	B*	25,831	1/22/97	10.00	NA	
Mathews, J. Kirk	DIR	S	50,000	1/21/97	30.25	178,702	D
Rosenberger, William F	PR	S	12,500	1/21/97	29.75	NA	D
Gates, Dirk I.	CB	S	20,000	11/29/96	20.00	1,223,200	I
Devis, Marc	VP	S	61,470	11/21/96–11/1/96	19.00–20.13	NA	D
Degennaro, Steven F	CFO	S	24,587	11/19/96	18.50	1,905	D
Holliday, Randall H.	VP	S	1,500	11/11/96	18.88	796	D
Russo, Carl E.	EX VP	S	624	11/1/96	20.13	NA	D
Schroeder, William J.	DIR	S	5,000	11/1/96	20.06	20,000	D
Brown, Thomas V.	VP	S	1,145	11/1/96	20.13	NA	D
Bass, Robert W.	VP	S	1,149	11/1/96	20.13	100	D

Transaction Type Codes: B=Form 4 Buy, S=Form 4 Sale, B*=Option-Related Form 4 Buy.
Ownership Codes: D=direct, I=Indirect. For all other codes, see the full Key Figure 3.2 on page 27.

Unfortunately for Mathews, he had shown similar prescience just three months before, selling 50,000 shares in the open market in January 1997 as they spiked over $30 in reaction to Intel's taking a stake in the company. By selling, then buying Xircom's shares in the open market in just a three-month period, Mathews had made short-swing profits. Two other vice presidents, Robert Bass and Randall Holliday, had done the same. Although these two both exercised and sold options in February 1997, that wasn't the problem. It was the open market sales of Holliday in both February 1997 and November 1996 and Bass's sales in November 1996 that activated the short-swing rules.

Xircom acted quickly. Its internal processes found the insiders' oversights in early May 1997, and a demand to relinquish profits was made to the insiders shortly after. A press release was issued by the company later in May about the whole affair, by which time the profits had already been recovered. Neither the SEC nor the Justice Department was involved at any time.

For anyone following Form 4s, however, the fact that Xircom's insiders had to give back the profits hardly negated the good information the forms delivered. Although the price of Xircom's shares drifted down in the second half of 1998 after its short-term recovery, it never fell back to the price at which the executives bought the shares. A year later, Xircom's shares were at $18—double the price at which insiders bought and at least 50 percent higher than the price when their Form 4s reached the public domain.

Xircom's insiders effectively called the bottom for their stock while properly pointing out that it was a good short-term and longer-term investment. If Kirk Mathews trades Xircom again, I would certainly take it as a sign that I should consider following his lead.

DON'T LOOK A GIFT HORSE IN THE MOUTH

The Xircom example is hardly an exception. Even with numerous laws in place to combat insider trading and the SEC and U.S. Justice Department doing their best to enforce them, there are still a remarkable number of examples of insiders trading well—too many to dismiss executives' transactions as merely lucky. Academic studies (see References at end of book) confirm that insiders have a knack for calling their stocks' movements, nor would professional investors be paying what they do for timely insider trading data unless they thought the data gave them useful signals.

Yet most of the prescient insiders never hear a peep of inquiry from the authorities. Is the SEC just missing something? Are all the profits made by these officers just ill-gotten gains from trading on material, nonpublic information? Possibly. Some of the officers are certainly trading on information they shouldn't be using, but, as I've pointed out, proving fraud is not easy. Most insiders are probably making their money by acting as better-informed investors, however, and there is nothing illegal with that.

For investors, the more pragmatic answer to the question of whether the insider trading indicated on a Form 4 is legal or not is: Who cares? As long as the information on a Form 4 is useful in helping us make money, we should leave the legal worries to the insider who made the trade and simply use the information for ourselves. The laws and enforcement in place should catch most of the serious offenders and prevent the securities markets from deteriorating into their pre-1929 state of unfairness. And in any case, the really unscrupulous insiders trading blatantly on material, nonpublic information are not taking the time to fill out a Form 4 to document their illegal trades.

For any insiders who do fill out their Form 4s properly, I actually hope that they *are* pushing the limits of legality and making the most of their unfair advantage in trading their own company's shares. Gaining a little advantage is why investors follow this data. We may not know what the insiders know, but as long as we know what they do, we can use the insider data filed with the SEC to alert us to when a stock-moving event may be brewing at a company.

Chapter 2 — AT A GLANCE

1. In practice, insider trades filed at the SEC may be based on material, nonpublic information.

2. No definition of illegal insider trading exists; precedents set by actual cases guide enforcement.

3. Illegal insider trading may result in both civil and criminal penalties, but such consequences are rare.

4. Legislation appears to be trending toward making companies more responsible for the accuracy and timing of their insiders' filings.

5. Insiders are not allowed to sell their own company's shares short.

6. Insiders are not allowed to buy and sell (or sell and buy) their own company's shares within a six-month time period.

3

Analyzing Form 4 Transactions: Getting Started

OVERVIEW

"It . . . was envisioned by Congress that the reported trades by insiders would provide investors with useful information on which to base investment decisions by giving them an idea of the purchases and sales by insiders which may in turn indicate their private opinion as to the prospects of the company."[1] If this was the purpose of mandating such "useful information," why do so few individuals use insider data in their investment strategies? The simple answer: It has been too expensive to get timely data until recently. Chapter 15 explains where to get this newly affordable data so you can finally play on a level playing field with the institutional investors who have long paid through the nose for this important information.

But now that individuals are able to join the club, they must learn the rules. Using Form 4 and other insider data as investment tools is more involved than buying when a chairman buys and selling when he sells. Some signals and patterns are important, whereas others are time-wasting noise. Just as you have to look at the footnotes of an income statement to determine how "real" a company's earnings are, a little investigation of insider trading is necessary to determine if it's really significant.

---

1. H.R. Rep. No. 1383, 73d Cong., 2d Sess., at 13 (1934).

As explained in Chapter 1, Form 4 information filed with the SEC supplies the most important insights into insiders' sentiments and is the main focus of this book. Perhaps the nicest thing about incorporating Form 4 and other insider data into your investment strategy is that its interpretation is primarily a matter of using common sense. It's a matter of putting yourself in the insiders' shoes and asking yourself: What would make me buy or sell like the insider did? Would I have to be bullish, bearish, or something in between to have made the trade? But as Will Rogers said (and more than once, no doubt): "Nothing needs to be taught like common sense."

Keeping in mind the rules of thumb for analyzing Form 4 transactions in Figure 3.1 will get you started quickly and keep you from wasting time. Each rule is explained in detail in the chapters that follow along with explanations of certain nuances of insider transactions.

FIGURE 3.1 Rules of Thumb for Analyzing Form 4s

---

1. *Screen Out the Noise*
   - Focus on open-market purchases and sales.
   - Remember that option-related trades are less significant than open-market trades.
   - Don't get confused by "funny data."

2. *Judge Relative Importance*
   - Purchases are easier to interpret than sales.
   - Size matters.
   - Transactions by hands-on insiders are more important than transactions by other insiders.
   - Initial purchases by new insiders are less important than purchases by long-time insiders.
   - Trades of direct holdings are more important than transactions of indirect holdings.

3. *Recognize Patterns*
   - Look for clusters of activity.
   - Throw out bad clusters.
   - Check credentials.
   - Nothing can mean something.
   - Don't waste time with conflicting data.

4. *Take Other Considerations into Account*
   - Insiders tend to be early.
   - Don't pay much more than insiders did.
   - There's more buying at smaller companies.
   - Insider activity is not a technical indicator.

I often use excerpts from a particular company's insider data history to help explain my points. These histories are taken from my firm's site InsiderTrader.com. To conserve space, numerous abbreviations of transaction types and titles of insiders, and other codes are used. These notations are usually intuitive, but a full key to all abbreviations and codes used in figures is given below in Figure 3.2.

FIGURE 3.2 Key to Abbreviations Used in Figures

Transaction Codes
B—Open-Market Form 4 Buy
S—Open-Market Form 4 Sale
B*—Option-Related Form 4 Buy (These shares are often sold right away, as indicated by a Form 4 sale of the same amount of shares by the same insider shortly after the B* transaction date.)
JB—Non-Open-Market Buy (Indicates trades related to gifts, dividends, 401(k) or IRA distributions, or other types of private transactions. The price of the shares traded may not be a market price.)
JS—Non-Open-Market Sale (Indicates trades related to gifts, dividends, 401(k) or IRA distributions, or other types of private transactions. The price of the shares traded may not be a market price.)
PB—Private Form 4 Buy (Used specifi-cally when a company sells shares directly to the insider. The price of the shares traded may not be a market price.)
PS—Private Form 4 Sale (Used specifi-cally when an insider sells shares back to the company. The price of the shares traded may not be a market price.)
3—Form 3 Filing
144—Form 144 Filing
13D—Schedule 13D Filing
13G—Schedule 13G Filing

Relation of Insiders to Their Respective Companies
B/O—Beneficial Owner of 10% or more of a class of a company's shares
CB—Chairman
CEO—Chief Executive Officer
CFO—Chief Financial Officer
COCB—Co-Chairman
CO CEO—Co-CEO
COO—Chief Operating Officer
CT—Controller
DIR—Director
EX DIR—Executive Director
EX OFF—Executive Officer
EX VP—Executive Vice President
OFF—Officer
P—Private or Shareholder
PART—Partner
PR—President
SEC—Secretary
SEC/TR—Secretary/Treasurer
SR OFF—Senior Officer
SR VP—Senior Vice President
TR—Treasurer
TTEE—Trustee
VCB—Vice Chairman
VP—Vice President

Holding Type
D—Direct
I—Indirect: Shares held by a family member, ESOP, trustee, or general partner
D/I—Combined Direct and Indirect

FOCUS ON OPEN-MARKET PURCHASES AND SALES

Most individuals buy and sell their stocks in the open market. They find the bid and asked price for the shares through their personal or on-line brokerage service and execute their trades by the same means in the open market. But insiders have numerous other methods for acquiring or disposing of shares, some of which are not in the open market and therefore aren't registered in the trading volume and other statistics gathered by the exchange on which the stock trades. The SEC has had to accommodate this reality on the forms it uses for gathering data.

When Form 4s were first collected in 1936, the SEC gave insiders eight different transaction codes to use when filling them out: gifts, stock dividends, inheritance, conversions, redemptions, transfers, and distributions. The lack of any of these special codes on the old forms indicated that the trade was open market.

Things are more complicated today. As the securities markets and regulatory environment evolved over the decades, the few initial codes became increasingly inadequate for telling the whole story of what was behind an insider's buying and selling. After much tinkering over the years, the SEC now gives insiders a choice of 20 different transaction codes in four different categories to put on their forms. Figure 3.3 lists the transaction codes in the SEC's *Official Summary of Security Transactions and Holdings,* a monthly printed tome of insider data published by the U.S. Government Printing Office (discussed further in Chapter 13.) Because insiders are banned from short selling their company's shares, as explained in Chapter 2, selling these shares short is one transaction type you won't see.

The list of transaction types may seem a little overwhelming, but don't despair. Most investors will find that just looking at transactions with the P and S codes is enough. These codes include the open-market purchases and sales, respectively, that relay the strongest indication of insiders' sentiment. Don't be thrown off if you see a B (for buy) rather than a P on an insider history that is on the Internet or some printed source. Some vendors use that notation instead, as do the examples in this book.

Although diligent research may now and then yield an interesting insight from SEC forms containing other transaction types, the information is usually not worth the effort, especially when compared with the much meatier bits of information that can be gleaned from open-

---

FIGURE 3.3 Transaction Codes Used on SEC Forms 3, 4, and 5

General Transaction Codes
P—Open market or private purchase
S—Open market or private sale
V—Transaction voluntarily reported earlier than required

Rule 16b-3 Transaction Codes
A—Grant, award, or other acquisition pursuant to Rule 16b-3(d)
D—Disposition to the issuer or issuer securities pursuant to Rule 16b-3(e)
F—Payment of exercise price or tax liability by delivering or withholding securities incident to the receipt, exercise, or vesting or a security issued in accordance with Rule 16b-3
I—Discretionary transaction in accordance with Rule 16b-3(f) resulting in acquisition or disposition of issuer securities
M—Exercise or conversion of derivative security exempted pursuant to Rule 16b-3

Derivative Securities Codes (except for transactions exempted pursuant to Rule 16b-3)
C—Conversion or derivative security
E—Expiration of short derivative position
H—Expiration (or cancellation) of long derivative position with value received
O—Exercise of out-of-the-money derivative security
X—Exercise of in-the-money or at-the-money derivative security

Other Section 16(b) Exempt Transactions and Small Acquisition Codes (except for Rule 16b-3 codes above)
G—Bona fide gift
L—Small acquisition under Rule 16a-6
W—Acquisition or disposition by will or the laws of descent and distribution
Z—Deposit into or withdrawal from voting trust

Other Transaction Codes
J—Other acquisition or disposition (described transaction)
K—Transaction in equity swap or instrument with similar characteristics
U—Disposition pursuant to a tender of shares in a change of control transaction

---

market transactions. Investigating these other types of trades more often reveals that the insider got a more advantageous price for the shares, was lent money for the transaction, or benefited from some other factor that mitigated the insider's risk of losing money.

This doesn't mean that insiders are doing anything sneaky or illegal; it just means that they are taking advantage of some special perk their position allows. But anything about an insider's trade that mitigates his or her risk also lessens the trade's importance as an indicator to investors of the insider's true sentiment. The more an insider's transaction resembles what the average investor must do to trade the shares, the more significant the transaction is likely to be.

This is just common sense, really. If insiders can buy their company's shares at 15 percent below the market value directly from the company without paying commissions and trading costs (as some companies' purchase plans allow), they can still make a nice profit even if the stock price moves only sideways over the next year. The stock could even move down in price by 10 percent, and the insiders would still not lose money. Such an advantage obviously influences insiders' risk/reward calculations and their decision of whether to buy.

On the other hand, when insiders buy their company's shares in the open market, they have to make the same risk/reward calculations individual investors do. They must figure in the trading costs of paying commissions and buying at their stock's ask price. A decision that buying shares on the open market is worth the risk even with these costs is a much stronger signal to us that we should consider acting likewise.

Some non-open-market transaction codes aren't easy to decipher even if you wanted to try to make use of the information. Transaction code F, for instance, means: "Payment of exercise price or tax liability by delivering or withholding securities incident to the receipt, exercise, or vesting of a security issued in accordance with Rule 16b-3."

What a morass of legalese. There is no doubt a good reason why this transaction code was added to the list by the SEC, but it doesn't seem that an insider called his broker and inquired about the bid and ask price of the shares.

Although an argument could be made for investigating non-open-market trades if you have a large number of shares in a company, that's probably overkill. The time you invest investigating is not likely to yield any information you can use to make money.

If you are using insider trading data to prospect for new investments, you definitely should not go any deeper than straightforward open-market purchases and sales. Your time is valuable, so don't waste it. Focus on open-market Form 4 transactions.

Thankfully, most data vendors clearly demarcate open-market from non-open-market trades, making it easy to screen out this noise in the Form 4 data. In the figures used in this book, transaction type "B" denotes an open-market purchase, while a "B*" indicates an option-related purchase. A "JB" indicates one of the other purchase types that isn't particularly significant. Gifted shares make up much of the other purchase types, and the reasons for gifts are usually more related to tax planning by the insider than on an analysis of future value.

REMEMBER THAT OPTION-RELATED TRADES ARE NOT TOO SIGNIFICANT

After narrowing your attention to open-market transactions, it's time to filter out another major source of noise in insider trading data: option-related trades. Insider data vendors and newsletters mark options-related purchases and sales with a little "o" indicator, an asterisk (*), or other such marker. The SEC's monthly publication, the *Official Summary of Security Transactions and Holdings,* has a separate column that includes a Y (for yes) if the trade is option related.

Of the nearly 400,000 Form 4 transactions filed during the three-year period 1997–1999, 16.5 percent were option-related purchases.[2] That's a lot of noise to clear out.

Public companies commonly grant stock options to employees as a type of incentive pay. An employee is given the right to buy shares from the company at a set price, which is usually the market price on the day the options are granted. If the stock subsequently goes down in price, the options aren't worth a thing, and insiders don't exercise them. But if the stock rises, the insider can reap risk-free profits by buying shares of stock from the company and immediately selling them in the open market at a higher price. This immediate buying and selling is sometimes referred to as "flipping" the shares.

When an insider does exercise options, he or she sometimes exercises and sells several lots within a small time frame, usually because the insider doesn't have the money to exercise them all at once. If an insider's shares are trading in the open market for $25, and the insider has options to buy 10,000 shares of stock from the company for $10, he or she has an enviable $150,000 risk-free capital gain coming but must still pony up $100,000 to the company to get that profit ($10 × 10,000 = $100,000). That's a fair amount of money to have on hand. The insider may choose to exercise only 1,000 options at first (which requires only $10,000 up front), then use the $25,000 from the sale to exercise

---

2. *Source:* Vickers Stock Research, Huntington, N.Y.

more options and continue doing that until all the options have been cashed in.

Exercising options piecemeal like this can make for a pretty messy insider history for a stock. It also takes time and increases the overall transaction costs of the insider who is exercising the options. In response to insiders' needs, brokerage firms help insiders exercise their options by lending them the up-front money. Insiders repay the borrowed amount used to exercise options from the proceeds of the sales, and brokerage firms generate fees and commissions from the transactions.

With this kind of help, insiders are now more likely to exercise their options in one big block.

The so-called flipping of stock options was clearly evident at Yahoo! in 1998 and remains so today (as well as at most every other high-flying Internet firms). The transaction dates and share amounts of the option-related buys (indicated with the transaction code B*) often match the sales (transaction code S) by the same insider. But if you had viewed this feeding frenzy at the options trough as a negative indicator of the stock's future prospects, you would have been dead wrong. Yahoo!

FIGURE 3.4 Insider History for Yahoo! (Nasdaq: YHOO)

Insider Name	Title	Trans Type	# of Shares	Trans Date(s)	Trans Price(s)	Total Holdings	D/I Own
Koogle, Timothy	PR	B*	6,535	12/28/98	0.60	NA	—
Moritz, Michael	DIR	S	9,697	11/25/98	206.00	3,388,188	I
Nelson, James J.	VP	B*	4,900	11/2/98	13.25	229,439	—
Nelson, James J.	VP	S	4,900	11/2/98	138.62	44,411	D
Nelson, James J.	VP	B*	14,379	10/29/98–10/13/98	5.67–0.50	234,339	—
Valenzuela, Gary	CFO	B*	10,000	10/26/98	5.67–0.33	621,214	—
Valenzuela, Gary	CFO	S	12,000	10/26/98	126.50–126.37	109,298	D
Valenzuela, Gary	CFO	B*	81,570	8/28/98	5.67–0.33	111,398	—
Valenzuela, Gary	CFO	B*	14,689	5/26/98	11.33–0.67	14,689	—
Koogle, Timothy	PR	B*	30,000	5/14/98	0.13	131,698	—
Koogle, Timothy	PR	S	30,000	5/14/98	122.68	131,698	D
Nazem, Farzad	OFF	S	10,000	5/4/98	120.50	3,166	D
Nazem, Farzad	SR VP	B*	10,000	5/4/98	4.67	NA	—
Place, John	SEC	B*	3,120	4/20/98–4/13/98	12.83	NA	—

Insider Name	Title	Trans Type	# of Shares	Trans Date(s)	Trans Price(s)	Total Holdings	D/I Own
Place, John	SEC	S	3,120	4/20/98– 4/13/98	125.63– 110.50	—	D
Mallett, Jeff	COO	B*	80,000	4/16/98– 4/13/98	0.13	NA	—
Mallett, Jeffrey A.	PR	S	80,000	4/16/98– 4/13/98	127.30– 112.64	1,800	D
Valenzuela, Gary	CFO	S	40,227	4/16/98– 4/13/98	126.56– 111.87	—	D
Valenzuela, Gary	CFO	S	40,227	4/16/98– 4/13/98	126.56– 111.87	—	D
Nelson, James J.	VP	S	6,720	4/14/98– 4/13/98	117.13– 116.25	—	D
Singh, Anil	SR VP	B*	10,628	4/14/98	0.13	—	—
Singh, Anil	SR VP	S	11,092	4/14/98	114.13	3	D
Valenzuela, Gary	CFO	B*	39,690	4/13/98	11.33– 0.67	—	—
Mallett, Jeff	COO	B*	88,300	2/27/98– 2/2/98	0.13	—	—
Singh, Anil	SR VP	S	5,780	2/27/98	71.00	3	D
Nazem, Farzad	SR VP	B*	50,000	2/26/98– 2/23/98	4.67	—	—
Nazem, Farzad	SR VP	S	50,000	2/26/98– 2/23/98	66.69– 63.25	3,166	D
Nelson, James J.	VP	S	4,064	2/26/98	64.00	-	D
Place, John	SEC	B*	1,560	2/26/98	12.83	-	—
Place, John	SEC	S	1,560	2/26/98	65.50	-	D
Koogle, Timothy	PR	B*	30,000	2/25/98	0.13	131,698	—
Koogle, Timothy	PR	S	30,000	2/25/98	61.25	131,698	D
Mallett, Jeffrey A.	PR	S	88,300	2/2/98	72.13– 65.00	1,800	D
Singh, Anil	SR VP	S	42,361	1/29/98– 1/20/98	65.00– 61.00	—	D
Kern, Arthur H.	DIR	B*	25,000	1/26/98– 1/23/98	0.67	—	—
Softbank Holdings Inc.	B/O	S	470,000	1/26/98– 1/21/98	63.25– 59.51	13,452,842	D
Kern, Arthur H.	DIR	S	25,000	1/23/98	61.81– 61.64	—	D
Mallett, Jeff	COO	B*	1,700	1/20/98	0.13	1,800	—
Mallett, Jeffrey A.	PR	S	1,700	1/20/98	65.13	1,800	D
Nelson, James J.	VP	S	21,754	1/20/98	65.25	—	D
Place, John	SEC	B*	18,750	1/20/98	12.83	—	—
Place, John	SEC	S	19,250	1/20/98	64.23	—	D
Valenzuela, Gary	CFO	S	76,729	1/20/98	63.79	537	D

Transaction Type Codes: B=Form 4 Buy, S=Form 4 Sale, B*=Option-Related Form 4 Buy.
Ownership Codes: D=direct, I=Indirect. For all other codes, see the full Key in Figure 3.2 on page 47.

soared 265 percent in 1999 despite its insiders' rush to divest their stakes in the company the year before. While the sky-high valuations of this deified Internet stock may yet cause Yahoo! to come back to Earth, insider activity did not help you make money in this case.

Yahoo!'s case is not an aberration. It is very common to see tremendous amounts of option-related insider selling of a high-flying stock and also common for the stock to keep rising. We don't use this illustration to show how wrong insiders can be (they certainly can be, but we'll get to that later). What is wrong in these cases is for investors to assign great significance to option-related sales.

To see why it is wrong, try to put yourself in the insiders' shoes (an exercise you should always do when assessing insider trading.) Insiders with large in-the-money stock options I have spoken with have described an air of giddiness around the office when the company's stock begins to soar—as if people had just found money on the street. In these situations you can almost hear the option-holding employees collectively saying: "Wow, my options are really in the money. Our stock has never been this high before. I know business is great, but who the heck understands how the market prices shares. I'm cashing in some options, paying off my mortgage, and taking my family on a well-deserved holiday."

In other words, insiders cashing out options aren't generally undertaking a fundamental analysis of their company's shares to determine if they should sell. Most of the time they aren't even cashing out to rebalance their net assets into a properly balanced portfolio. They just want their free money—wouldn't you!

The bad news is that following insider data would not have led you into Internet-related investments. These stocks have rocketed so fast out of the gate after going public that option-related selling is all you'll see in their insider histories. In any case, insiders at these firms often have so many incentive options that they don't need to buy any more shares in the open market even if they did think their stock was a good value.

The good news is that insiders have been excellent at indicating when more established high-tech firms are ready to pop again. There are also plenty of examples of insiders buying shares after their stock has run up in price (see Figure 6.4 on page 81). Relating to this, my favorite screen for finding such momentum investments is explained on page 109. The other good news about the lack of significance of option-related selling is that you don't have to panic if you see insiders at a company you're invested in flipping their options for a risk-free profit. The selling should usually be considered as noise and disregarded.

Some exceptions. Usually is not always, of course, and as with other non-open-market types of insider transactions, you can sometimes get some interesting insights from option-related sales. (The first two exceptions I describe below hold true for analyzing open-market sales as well.) For instance, scan the column that indicates the total holdings of insiders in a Form 4 history that has a lot of option-related selling. You may want to make a mental note if most insiders seem to hold no shares at all after they exercise their options. Even though these insiders likely have many other options vesting in the future, a virtual lack of real share ownership should be considered a negative.

Even more important, look at the trend in option-related selling and the stock's price chart. If a past high-flying stock has recently started to fall back to Earth, the selling should dry up if insiders feel that the stock will recover. It is a positive signal if the selling does lessen. Selling that continues or increases as shares fall is a big negative. The further a stock falls from its highs, the more negative the indication of heavy selling.

Another aspect of analyzing option-related insider trades is that most options granted to insiders by their employers have expiration dates. These dates are on the Form 4, although such data is not distributed by most services. If insiders' options are getting ready to expire, the insiders might exercise them but not sell the stock immediately—a valid positive signal.

The fact that insiders didn't have to put as much capital at risk via this exercise than if they had purchased in the open market does mitigate the strength of the positive signal. That they could still make money on the trade even if the stock declines a little lessens the strength as well. But insiders who keep their risk-free profits open to market risk are betting that there is yet more upside in the stock. That they are letting the profits ride, so to speak, is even more impressive when you consider that insiders are often immediately liable for taxes on the risk-free profits the options have generated. See Figure 3.5 for an illustration of insiders exercising options and not selling them immediately.

In December 1997, two Corecomm insiders exercised a total of 105,151 options that were about to expire and purchased shares for between $0.08 and $1.11 each. They held onto them even though they could have flipped the stock immediately for $10 a share. A good call as it turned out. Corecomm's stock rose steadily for a more than 700 percent gain over the next two years. At the turn of the millennium, the stock was priced at over $40 after splitting two for one during its run-up. (As is explained on page 40, historic insider data is not usually split-adjusted, so the insiders' transaction prices in Figure 3.5 should be halved to calculate their phenomenal gains.)

FIGURE 3.5 Insider History for Corecomm (Nasdaq: COMM)

Insider Name	Title	Trans Type	# of Shares	Trans Date(s)	Trans Price(s)	Total Holdings	D/I Own
Blumenthal, George S.	CB	B	4,000	7/2/98	25.88	133,000	D
Patricof, Alan J.	DIR	B	6,000	6/3/98	21.25	7,622	I
Blumenthal, George S.	CB	B	5,000	04/30/98– 04/01/98	17.00– 17.13	129,000	I
Blumenthal, George S.	CB	B	4,000	03/27/98– 03/31/98	16.88– 17.13	131,449	I
Blumenthal, George S.	CB	B*	103,276	12/30/97	0.08– 0.88	127,449	
Mintz, Del	DIR	B	50,000	12/23/97– 12/03/97	10.25– 12.38	282,286	D
Williams, Stanton	CFO	B*	1,875	12/22/97	1.11– 1.11	1,916	

Transaction Type Codes: B=Form 4 Buy, S=Form 4 Sale, B*=Option-Related Form 4 Buy.
Ownership Codes: D=direct, I=Indirect. For all other codes, see the full Key in Figure 3.2 on page 27.

Investors seeing these option-related Form 4s after they were filed at the SEC in January 1998, along with Del Mintz's large open-market trade, had plenty of time to call the company to investigate whether the option-related purchases were sold. Finding that they weren't, the transactions of all three insiders could be viewed as an impressive cluster of buys that gave a strong positive signal that COMM was worth investing in.

Knowing the expiration date of options can also help you find stocks to avoid or sell short. If an insider exercises options long before they are due to expire and immediately sells the shares even though the exercise price of the options is not much lower than the market price, this is clearly a bad sign. In the course of reviewing option-related trades, you will often see insiders flipping their options at one-half or one-third the market price for the stock. In our Yahoo! example, some insiders had options that allowed them to buy shares from the company for as little as $.0125, and they turned around and sold the shares in the open market for a whopping $122.675.

But an insider exercising options with a strike price of, say, $10, and selling them in the open market at the going rate of $12 would *not* be a good sign. The profit on this trade is fairly small when you consider the transaction costs involved. If the options were about to expire, then the trade is understandable. If the options were good for another six months or more, however, a trade like this is surely a sign of pessimism by the insider. The place to find out if options were about to expire is on the Form 4 itself or the specific company's investor relations department. The company's latest proxy statement may also be able to tell you.

So option-related data is hardly worthless, but if you are using insider data from a source that does not include option-related trades, don't be too upset. Most option-related trades are just noise, and not seeing them may actually help you focus on the much more significant open-market transactions. When option-related trades do impart useful information, there is often similar positive or negative sentiment indicated by the open-market trades anyway.

DON'T GET CONFUSED BY "FUNNY DATA"

While sticking with open-market transactions that are not option related removes most of the noise from insider data, the static caused by "funny data" still remains to be dealt with. By funny data we refer to trades in which some aspect of the data don't appear to make sense. Transaction prices may be below the stock's trading range for the day and sometimes even for the year. Perhaps the number of shares traded by insiders is more than was recorded in the open market on the day. The price of the transaction may also not mesh with the price range you see on a historical chart. The transaction may also be of an odd lot of shares and at a strange fractional price that just doesn't occur in the course of normal trading. In all these cases, something about the data seems funny.

Welcome to the world of insider data. Collecting the forms filed at the SEC and manually typing them into a database is a very labor-intensive process that can sometimes fall prey to human error. No provider of insider data would be foolish enough to boast that its information is completely correct. An accuracy rate of 95 percent would be doing well.

However, many (if not most) errors in an insider database are created by the insiders themselves or by the people who fill out the SEC forms for them. Relatively few of the errors you will inevitably find are introduced in the data input process of the data providers. Even lawyers who are paid well to do this paperwork for busy executives sometimes make mistakes. Form 144s, which are generally filled out by an insider's stockbroker, are even more prone to error.

The most common mistakes made on the forms that can result in funny data are the following:

- Submitting a form twice to the SEC
- Filling in the transaction price incorrectly
- Submitting a form with an incorrect transaction code
- Submitting an option-related trade as an open-market one

But human nature being what it is, any of the numerous fields on the SEC's forms can be filled in incorrectly.

The firms that type the SEC forms into an electronic database for resale to institutional buyers sometimes try to correct obvious mistakes by contacting an insider and inquiring about some inconsistent information. Usually, however, they just type in the data on the forms as submitted, which has the odd effect of making some of the insider data they present incorrect, yet accurate. Accurate from the point of view that what is reported on the SEC form was input correctly. Incorrect from the point of view that what was written on the form was inaccurate.

It is unreasonable to expect data providers to clean up after insiders. Besides the legal issue of changing a government form, double-checking every figure the insiders write would add a gruesome burden to the process of collecting the data. And the added cost of cleaning up the data is not justified by any increase in value that would result. Interpreting the forms also leaves open the chance of adding incorrect data to the database. Better to pass along the forms as they are submitted to the SEC and leave any investigation of funny data to people interested in the transactions.

Not all funny data result from mistakes, however. Private transactions, a hot initial public offering (IPO), or even a simple stock split can make insider data appear incorrect at first glance.

Annoyingly, since 1991 open-market and private transactions are lumped together. A private transaction is simply a trade between two parties who have agreed on the terms of the exchange. The trade may be done in the open market and may even be done by brokers. The big difference is that the buying and selling parties know each other. Again, there is nothing illegal or innately sneaky about private transactions, and they may even provide an interesting insight if they are consummated at market prices. But traits of many private transactions mitigate their importance as indicators of sentiment. Fortunately, private transactions are only a small percentage of all the P and S transactions recorded at the SEC, and if they result in funny data, it is usually easily discovered when you look at a company's price chart.

The detailed history for Miami Computer Supply (Figure 3.6) shows seven open-market purchases made on June 29, 1998, all with a trans-

FIGURE 3.6 Insider History for Miami Computer Supply (Nasdaq: MCSC)

Insider Name	Title	Trans Type	# of Shares	Trans Date(s)	Trans Price(s)	Total Holdings	D/I Own
Peppel, Michael E.	PR	B	2,000	8/3/98	17.25	303,906	D
Peppel, Michael E.	PR	B	2,100	7/27/98	18.25	301,906	D
Radcliffe, Harry F.	DIR	B	42,000	7/2/98	16.00	302,595	D
Value Partners Ltd.	B/O	B	40,000	6/30/98	16.00	1,265,691	D
Hecht, Robert G.	DIR	B	46,596	6/29/98	15.16	275,941	D
Huffman, John C. III	VP	B	1,000	6/29/98	15.16	31,937	D
Liberati, Anthony W	DIR	B	40,000	6/29/98	15.16	269,345	D
Peppel, Michael E.	PR	B	40,000	6/29/98	15.16	299,806	D
Radcliffe, Harry F.	DIR	B	38,000	6/29/98	15.16	260,595	D
Stanley, Ira H.	VP	B	750	6/29/98	15.16	1,500	D
Winstel, Thomas C.	DIR	B	5,000	6/29/98	15.16	300,590	D
Winstel, Thomas C.	DIR	B	3,000	03/19/98–03/12/98	22.25–24.25	197,060	D
Peppel, Michael E.	PR	B	150	3/12/98	21.63	173,204	D
Peppel, Michael E.	PR	B	6,300	3/10/98	21.50	126,884	D
Value Partners Ltd.	B/O	B	50,000	1/14/98	13.25	817,127	D
Value Partners Ltd.	B/O	B	36,000	11/24/97	13.50	NA	D
Value Partners Ltd.	B/O	B	39,000	10/1/97	13.50	731,127	D
Value Partners Ltd.	B/O	B	80,000	7/2/97	11.88	692,127	D
Value Partners Ltd.	B/O	B	53,000	05/29/97–05/13/97	9.63	612,127	D
Value Partners Ltd.	B/O	B	69,500	04/30/97–04/07/97	9.13–9.50	559,127	D

Transaction Type Codes: B=Form 4 Buy, S=Form 4 Sale, B*=Option-Related Form 4 Buy.
Ownership Codes: D=direct, I=Indirect. For all other codes, see the full Key in Figure 3.2 on page 27.

action price of $15.16. Something is definitely funny here. The odds that these insiders separately bought shares on the same day at the same price are low enough, but the fact that $15.16 is a strange transaction price should also raise your eyebrows. To boot, the recorded low for MCSC on that day was only $16.25, and the volume of the insiders' trades is nearly four times greater (although the trading volume on June 30 seems to be related to the buys). Also, one of the insiders purchased 46,596 shares—an odd lot. What all this adds up to is that these were not truly open-market trades.

In fact, the Form 4 activity resulted from insiders buying into a secondary offering. The $15.16 transaction price was a perk for insiders and equaled the market price of the secondary offering minus invest-ment banking fees. When investigating this activity, I was told that in-siders were not lent money to participate in the secondary offering. So even though they got a slight price break, insiders still had invested an-other $2.6 million in their company. The fact that MCSC had nearly doubled in price in the previous 12 months meant that this investment was a significant averaging up for most of these insiders as well—a real vote of confidence that there was more appreciation to come.

I looked into the fundamentals of the company, determined that it indeed had good earnings growth potential, and invested in MCSC along with the insiders. This was one time when I judged insiders' activity to be significant even though the data was funny in several ways. Many times, however, funny data ends up being noise that can be overlooked.

Insiders who buy into their firm's hot IPO at the original offering price can easily file a Form 4 with a transaction price below the stock's 52-week trading range. This funny data is simply the result of their stock's shares immediately opening higher than the offering price.

Adjusting past insider data for stock splits is considered too onerous a task to attempt, and most data sources don't do it. This results in an insider history that can be confusing if an investor is not familiar with the company's stock history.

The open-market sales of Microsoft's stock by its billionaire-chairman Bill Gates are a good illustration of the mental arithmetic investors need to perform, because it does not reflect stock splits. Notice that Gates's total ownership of Microsoft more or less doubles from a mere 476 mil-lion shares to nearly 930 million between his January 1999 and April 1999 sales. Also notice that his sale price in April is significantly below that of his January trades.

This data looks very funny, but a little research uncovers the fact that there was yet another stock split at Microsoft between these two sales by Gates. In this case, it was a 2-for-1 split effective March 1999.

It is similarly obvious by the funny data in his history that a split of some sort also occurred in early 1998 (a 3-for-2 split went effective February 1998). With a well-known and much publicized company like Microsoft, you may be aware that a split has occurred in the recent past. With lesser-known firms, don't get bogged down by the type of funny data illustrated in Figure 3.7. Check out the stock's history of splits.

MGM's Form 4 history is a good example of duplicate filings. The large purchases by both Kirk Kerkorian and his investment vehicle, Tracinda Corporation, turned out to be half as interesting as they appeared.

FIGURE 3.7 Bill Gates's Form 4 Trades at Microsoft (Nasdaq: MSFT)

Insider Name	Title	Trans Type	# of Shares	Trans Date(s)	Trans Price(s)	Total Holdings	D/I Own
Gates, William H.	CB	S	10,000,000	7/27/99–7/23/99	91.00–87.63	919,555,600	D
Gates, William H.III	CB	S	10,000,000	4/28/99–4/23/99	88.88–83.25	929,555,600	D
Gates, William H.	CB	S	5,000,000	1/26/99–1/22/99	169.50–156.25	476,277,800	D
Gates, William H.	CB	S	5,000,000	10/28/98–10/23/98	109.25–104.88	—	D
Gates, William H.	CB	S	4,355,742	8/20/98–8/3/98	111.63–105.00	515,222,222	D/I
Gates, William H.	CB	S	645,000	7/31/98	112.88–111.88	520,133,542	D
Gates, William H.	CB	S	130,000	5/1/98	90.25–90.00	523,077,800	D
Gates, William H.	CB	S	4,410,000	4/30/98–4/27/98	91.88–90.00	524,707,800	D
Gates, William H.III	CB	S	2,000,000	10/31/97–10/23/97	133.81–128.25	268,773,900	D
Gates, William H.III	CB	S	1,701,519	8/19/97–8/1/97	143.93–135.50	270,797,000	D
Gates, William H.III	CB	S	300,000	7/31/97–7/30/97	141.94–140.75	272,498,519	D
Gates, William H.III	CB	S	2,540,000	5/21/97–5/2/97	122.63–115.00	272,797,000	D
Gates, William H.III	CB	S	2,004,194	2/20/97–2/14/97	99.75–95.25	276,214,000	D
Gates, William H.III	CB	S	800,000	11/14/96–11/1/96	148.44–137.50	139,109,097	D
Gates, William H.III	CB	S	200,000	10/30/96	136.75–135.00	139,909,197	D

Transaction Type Codes: B=Form 4 Buy, S=Form 4 Sale, B*=Option-Related Form 4 Buy.
Ownership Codes: D=direct, I=Indirect. For all other codes, see the full Key in Figure 3.2 on page 27.

Kerkorian's compliance department at Tracinda obviously wanted to keep itself busy and filed two Form 4s for the same trade. The actual investment was made by Tracinda, which is indicated as being the direct holder of the shares by the D in the D/I Own column. Because Kerkorian controls Tracinda, another Form 4 indicating his indirect owner-

FIGURE 3.8 Insider History for Metro-Goldwyn-Mayer (NYSE: MGM)

Insider Name	Title	Trans Type	# of Shares	Trans Date(s)	Trans Price(s)	Total Holdings	D/I Own
Tracinda Corporation	B/O	B	238,663	12/3/97– 12/1/97	21.19– 21.38	42,700,000	D
Kerkorian, Kirk	DIR	B	238,663	12/3/97– 12/1/97	21.19– 21.38	42,700,000	I
Tracinda Corporation	B/O	B	2,190,600	11/26/97– 11/13/97	19.88– 22.06	42,461,337	D
Kerkorian, Kirk	DIR	B	2,190,600	11/26/97– 11/13/97	19.88– 22.06	42,461,337	I
Mancuso, Frank G.	CB	B	67,454	11/18/97– 11/17/97	24.00	205,205	D
Gleason, Michael R.	DIR	B	500	11/13/97	20.00	500	D
Pisano, A. Robert	VCB	B	4,080	11/12/97	20.00	19,080	I
Aljian, James D.	DIR	B	5,000	11/12/97	20.00	5,000	D
Yemenidjian, Alejandro	DIR	B	5,000	11/12/97	20.00	5,000	D
Corrigan, Michael G.	CFO	B	1,000	11/12/97	20.00	NA	D
Mancuso, Frank G.	CB	B	5,000	11/12/97	20.00	NA	I

Transaction Type Codes: B=Form 4 Buy, S=Form 4 Sale, B*=Option-Related Form 4 Buy.
Ownership Codes: D=direct, I=Indirect. For all other codes, see the full Key in Figure 3.2 on page 27.

ship of these shares was also filed. Only the trades by Tracinda were real, however; the Kerkorian filings were redundant.

The SEC doesn't discourage such duplicate filing by investment companies and their principals under the belief that more disclosure is better. But it *can* make the consumption of the information a bit more difficult. Fortunately, the duplication in this example is easy to spot.

As annoying as it is to filter out funny data from open-market transactions, concentration of funny data increases markedly when looking at other transaction types. This increase is a consequence of what those other codes really mean. If an insider acquires shares via a gift (indicated by a G on the form), for instance, it's pretty obvious that the transaction price will be below the stock's market price on the day of the transaction. The insider may even have paid nothing at all. And if you see an insider giving away shares as a gift, it's not because the insider thinks that's what they're worth. The insider may be transferring shares into family trusts as part of his or her estate planning.

Focusing on open-market transactions will reduce your confusion about funny data tremendously. Even so, you're bound to run into some funny data as you review insider histories. Don't be put off. Just move on to the numerous other, more straightforward insider signals instead of trying to figure out how an insider bought below the going market price. More often than not, funny data is not worth your time to investigate further—especially if you are looking for new investments.

But if you simply must get to the bottom of any strange data, the definitive place to get answers is from the company's investor relations department—not your data provider.

Chapter 3 AT A GLANCE

1. Insider data must be analyzed for importance. It is not a technical indicator.

2. Open-market Form 4 transactions supply the most useful insider data for investors.

3. Option-related Form 4 transactions are less useful, but some points to analyze include:
   • The difference between the option exercise price and the market price of the shares
   • The expiration date of exercised options
   • How many shares insider holds after exercising options

4. Insider data is not 100 percent accurate as a result of errors by insiders and data input services.

5. Correct data may appear inaccurate as the result of:
   • Duplicate filings
   • Stock splits
   • IPOs
   • Secondary offerings
   • Private transactions

4

Analyzing
Form 4 Transactions:
Judging Relative
Importance

PURCHASES ARE EASIER TO INTERPRET
THAN SALES

It is more difficult to divine useful information from insider selling than insider buying for the simple reason that there are just too many legitimate reasons for insiders to sell. They may need money to buy a new car or house, or to send a kid to college. For some founding executives, the stock holdings in the company they helped build may represent the vast majority of their net worth. In such cases it's just prudent for them to diversify assets. The prevalence of legitimate reasons to sell is reflected in the fact that, in any given week, there are usually more open-market Form 4 sales filed with the SEC than open-market Form 4 purchases.

In contrast, there is usually just one reason executives buy shares in their company in the open market: They think the price will rise. It is common to see massive insider selling (especially options-related selling, as pointed out in the last chapter) in a stock that is soaring, and just as common to see that stock continue rising.

Unfortunately, a lot of the stories in the popular media spotlighting insider transactions focus on Form 4 sales rather than buys. A typical story reports how insider selling occurred at a company shortly before something happened that caused its stock to fall. This may be interesting to investigative reporters looking for a conspiracy or class-action lawyers looking for business, but investors require foresight to make money, not hindsight. And the lesson that such articles imply—that insider selling is a reliable harbinger of bad things—is misleading.

To be fair, newspapers are interested in news stories and tend not to be outlets for research. Individuals need information they can act on, however, so don't make the same mistake as most reporters do.

The good news for investors is that when you see lots of insiders selling the same shares you've placed in your retirement fund, it doesn't mean you have made a huge mistake. It's always better to see insiders buying, but it doesn't mean imminent catastrophe for your nest egg if there is selling.

Look again at all the insider selling at Yahoo! (Figure 3.4 on page 32) and Bill Gates's sales at Microsoft (Figure 3.7 on page 41). Gates's selling at Microsoft is hardly isolated, either. Week after week, insider after insider sells huge dollar amounts of shares. Scary? No. Understandable? Yes. Who can blame Bill Gates and the other mere millionaires at Yahoo! and Microsoft for diversifying their assets? A huge percentage of their total net worth is wrapped up in the firm's stock.

At Microsoft, the reasons for most of the selling are acceptable enough that one should probably dismiss all of the selling as noise, and view any open-market buying at all as a positive. In fact, if investors had used Jeffrey Raikes's May 1998 open-market purchase of a whopping $848,800 worth of MSFT as an entry signal, they would have done very well.

If there is bad news for the lesser significance of insider selling versus buying, it applies primarily to short sellers. Unfortunately, insider selling is not that one magical indicator that will help short sellers profit in a raging bull market. Although many stocks that tank do show that insiders were selling before the fall, there are just too many companies with sales to use the data as a sole indicator. Better to tie in the data with other factors, such as high valuation of the stock, declining profit margins, and so on.

The one major flag for identifying stocks to avoid and possibly sell short is insiders selling after their company's shares have already declined markedly. This is not at all normal. More on using this screen and other approaches for using insider data to identify short-sale candidates is in Chapter 10.

SIZE MATTERS

Common sense will tell you that the more money insiders are trading, the more significant the transaction. If you're looking for new investments, it's a good idea to start your research with the larger transaction values first. When a company catches your attention, look at the detailed history and start putting other rules of thumb of this book into practice.

Figure 4.1 provides an illustration of a useful tool for practicing this rule. It is a summary of all the open-market Form 4 purchases during a certain week as displayed on InsiderTrader.com (see Chapter 15 for a fuller review of this Web site). The transaction value of all the Form 4 purchases filed for a company during the period is aggregated, and the table is sorted by the aggregate transaction value with the greatest dollar value first. The number of shares traded and the number of insiders

---

FIGURE 4.1 A Portion of the Insider Summary for the Week Ending November 5, 1999

Company	Ticker	$ Value of Purchases	# Shares Bought	# Insiders Buying Rel to Company	Trans Date(s)	Ave Trans Price
Telewest Communications PLC-ADR	TWSTY	148,721,773	42,130,814	1–B	10/4/99– 10/4/99	3.53
M/A/R/C Inc	MARC	98,826,880	4,941,344	1–B	11/2/99– 11/2/99	20.00
CNA Financial Corp	CNA	39,031,904	1,145,000	1–B	10/13/99– 10/1/99	34.09
Boulder Total Return Fund Inc	BTF	31,633,830	3,476,245	3–B,B,B	10/25/99– 9/28/99	9.10
RJ Reynolds Tobacco Holdings	RJR	25,870,330	952,000	2–B,D	10/27/99– 10/5/99	27.17
Immunex Corp	IMNX	17,102,710	301,810	1–B	10/29/99– 10/27/99	56.67
Amylin Pharmaceuticals Inc	AMLN	12,000,000	2,400,000	1–B	10/6/99– 10/6/99	5.00
Networks Electronics Corp	NWRK	5,898,668	786,489	1–B	10/15/99– 10/15/99	7.50
Mutual Risk Management Ltd	MM	5,375,000	500,000	1–C	10/12/99– 10/12/99	10.75
Nucentrix Broadband Networks	NCNX	4,117,850	197,400	1–B	10/26/99– 10/21/99	20.86
United Dominion Realty Trust	UDR	4,024,254	365,509	15–D,V,V,D, D,D,D,D,V, E,D,D,D,V,V	10/1/99– 10/1/99	11.01

Company	Ticker	$ Value of Purchases	# Shares Bought	# Insiders Buying Rel to Company	Trans Date(s)	Ave Trans Price
Prime Hospitality Corp	PDQ	2,750,471	358,300	1–C	10/22/99–10/15/99	7.68
Autozone Inc	AZO	2,607,984	97,045	10–C,V,V,V,V,V,F,V,D,P	10/26/99–10/1/99	26.87
Egain Communications Corp	EGAN	2,415,840	201,320	5–F,V,V,C,P	9/23/99–9/23/99	12.00
Mail-Well Inc	MWL	1,320,660	198,000	1–C	10/14/99–10/14/99	6.67
Globalstar Telecommunications Ltd	GSTRF	1,010,500	50,000	1–C	10/27/99–10/27/99	20.21
Dynatech Corp	DYNA	999,999	307,692	4–D,D,D,D	10/1/99–10/1/99	3.25
ESC Medical Systems Ltd	ESCM	999,999	151,515	1–D	10/19/99–10/19/99	6.60
Lifeway Foods Inc	LWAY	975,000	97,500	1–B	10/30/99–10/21/99	10.00
Policy Management Systems Cp	PMS	955,839	50,000	1–C	11/2/99–11/2/99	19.12
PSS World Medical Inc	PSSI	943,110	118,000	4–E,D,F,D	10/29/99–10/28/99	7.99
Aeroflex Inc	ARX	926,980	154,000	6–OT,C,OD,D,V,P	10/29/99–10/25/99	6.02
Newcor Inc	NER	883,262	592,600	2–B,B	10/27/99–10/20/99	1.49
Goodrich (B.F.) Co	GR	864,458	37,600	4–F,D,OD,D	11/1/99–10/6/99	22.99
Doral Financial Corp	DORL	848,750	65,800	3–S,E,D	10/25/99–10/15/99	12.90
Indian Village Bancorp Inc	IDVB	761,050	75,930	8–D,OD,F,D,D,E,D,D	9/9/99–7/1/99	10.02
Perfumania Inc	PRFM	756,000	108,000	1–C	10/6/99–10/6/99	7.00
Mattel Inc	MAT	652,286	50,000	1–D	10/25/99–10/25/99	13.05
BRT Realty Trust	BRT	575,265	69,900	1–B	10/20/99–10/14/99	8.23
Alliance Capital Mgmt Holding	AC	490,500	18,000	1–D	8/23/99–8/23/99	27.25
Fischer Watt Gold Co Inc	FWGOE	485,230	3,281,000	1–D	9/2/99–2/9/99	0.15
Polaroid Corp	PRD	484,570	23,000	5–F,C,V,D,D	10/26/99–10/22/99	21.07
Financial Inds Corp	FNIN	422,568	42,700	1–H	10/7/99–10/1/99	9.90

(continued)

FIGURE 4.1 *(Continued)*

Company	Ticker	$ Value of Purchases	# Shares Bought	# Insiders Buying Rel to Company	Trans Date(s)	Ave Trans Price
Dial Corp	DL	402,998	18,000	3–V,C,V	10/21/99–10/21/99	22.39
MFC Bancorp Ltd	MXBIF	385,876	46,300	1–B	10/29/99–9 10/7/9	8.33
Rochester Medical Corporation	ROCM	376,818	43,100	2–P,D	10/22/99–10/6/99	8.74
Gatefield Corp	GATE	332,963	51,225	1–B	10/14/99–10/14/99	6.50
Burns Intl Services	BOR	289,400	25,000	2–E,D	11/1/99–10/15/99	11.58
Intervoice-Brite Inc	INTV	272,180	28,000	2–F,C	10/20/99–10/20/99	9.72
Sturm Ruger & Co Inc	RGR	270,000	30,000	1–D	10/29/99–10/29/99	9.00
Citizens Banking Corp/Michigan	CBCF	266,000	10,000	1–B	9/2/99–9/2/99	26.60
Community West Bancshares	CWBC	263,778	47,352	3–D,D,D	11/1/99–9/1/99	5.57
Express Scripts Inc -Cl A	ESRX	249,340	4,700	6–V,V,V,O,F,E	11/1/99–10/29/99	53.05
Genesco Inc	GCO	241,228	88,363	1–V	10/8/99–10/8/99	2.73
Homestead Village Inc	HSD	232,308	88,000	1–D	9/20/99–9/15/99	2.64
HCC Insurance Holdings Inc	HCC	231,900	25,000	2–D,D	10/27/99–10/27/99	9.28
Meridian Insurance Group Inc	MIGI	225,273	13,500	1–B	10/29/99–10/5/99	16.69
Echelon Intl Corp	EIN	222,309	9,300	1–B	10/25/99–10/22/99	23.90
Silver Diner Inc	SLVR	215,040	384,000	1–D	10/1/99–10/1/99	0.56
Trans World Entertainment Corp	TWMC	198,190	17,000	1–P	9/29/99–9/29/99	11.66

Insider Relationship Codes: **A**=Affiliated person. **B**=Beneficial owner of 10% or more of a company's shares. **C**=Chairman. **CP**=Controller. **D**=Director. **E**=Chief executive officer. **F**=Chief financial officer and/or treasurer. **G**=General partner. **H**=An Officer, Director, and Beneficial owner of 10% or more of a company's shares. **IA**=Investment advisor. **L**=Limited partner. **N**=None. This code is only found on Form 144 filings, and relates to the fact that not all owners of unregistered shares are insiders. **M**=Member of a policy-making committee. **O**=Officer. **OD**=Officer and Director. **OS**=Officer of a subsidiary. **OT**=Officer and Treasurer. **OX**=Officer of a division. **P**=President and/or chief executive officer. **S**=Shareholder of 10% or more of a class of stock. **T**=Trustee. **TT**=Treasurer. **U**=Unknown. Usually the result of a form that was not filled in properly. **V**=Vice President.

trading is also aggregated in the figure, and the average transaction price of the trades is also listed.

One of the companies from the weekly summary excerpt in Figure 4.2 that caught the attention of InsiderTrader.com's senior analyst, Glenn Curtis, was Aeroflex. The combined dollar value of the four Form 4s filed during the week was an impressive $926,980. (Other factors that made Aeroflex stand out were the fact that there were a cluster of six buyers, and that five of these buyers had titles that indicate they have hands-on duties at the company. The importance of these factors will be discussed shortly.)

As Aeroflex's insider history indicates, there were actually seven insiders who bought at the end of October 1999 and the beginning of November 1999. The other Form 4s were filed at the SEC in different weeks. Remember that filing a Form 4 is the responsibility of insiders themselves, and executives trading on the same day don't necessarily file the forms on the same day.

The dollar values of several of these insiders' purchases were large by most people's measures. Chairman Harvey Blau, for instance, invested over $600,000. Director Milton Brenner put more than $140,000 in the stock, and President Michael Gorin ponyed up more than $120,000.

Another aspect of the Size Matters rule is that the magnitude of an insider's purchase or sale relative to his or her total holdings should also be noted. Generally speaking, the larger the percentage change in total holdings the transaction represents, the more important it can be considered. The purchases at Aeroflex also looked favorable from this point of view. Blau's 100,000 share purchase nearly doubled his holdings to 214,709. Brenner's buys boosted his exposure to his firm's shares by nearly 25 percent, and Gorin owned 17.5 percent more of his company than he did before his buy.

The other smaller insider purchases start to look a little more important as well when viewed by how much they increased the exposure of the buyers to Aeroflex's fortunes. Director Donald Jones may have *only* invested $7,228 via his trade on October 29, 1999, but it increased his total holdings by 130 percent. Charles Badlato's investment of $30,000 nearly doubled his holdings.

Aeroflex was put on InsiderTrader.com's Buy List in November 1999 when its stock was trading for $8.75. The shares rose to as high as $71.50 within four months.

The importance of the relative size of an insider's purchase should not be downplayed in favor of the actual dollar value of the trade. Most insiders are not chairmen with multi-million-dollar bonuses and a stock picture on hand in the *Wall Street Journal*'s art department. The aver-

FIGURE 4.2 Insider History for Aeroflex (NYSE: ARX)

Insider Name	Title	Trans Type	# of Shares	Trans Date(s)	Trans Price(s)	Total Holdings	D/I Own
Jones, Donald S.	DIR	B	1,100	11/5/99	6.46–6.45	3,400	D
Brenner, Milton	DIR	B	1,200	11/2/99	5.38	116,866	D
Patton, John S.	DIR	B*	1,000	11/2/99	4.70	59,000	—
Borow, Leonard	EX VP	B	10,000	10/29/99	5.69	444,405	D
Caruso, Carl	VP	B	5,000	10/29/99	5.69	66,501	D
Jones, Donald S.	DIR	B	1,300	10/29/99	5.56	2,300	D
Gorin, Michael	PR	B	20,000	10/28/99–10/25/99	6.20–5.81	134,204	D
Blau, Harvey R.	CB	B	100,000	10/27/99–10/25/99	6.25–5.88	214,709	I
Badlato, Charles	TR	B	5,000	10/25/99	6.01	10,965	D
Brenner, Milton	DIR	B	3,000	10/25/99	6.06	3,000	I
Brenner, Milton	DIR	B	20,000	10/25/99	6.13	112,666	D
Novikoff, Eugene	DIR	S	20,000	9/14/99	18.03–18.00	1,183	D
Novikoff, Eugene B	DIR	B*	20,000	9/14/99	4.18–4.70	40,000	—
Blau, Harvey R.	CB	JS	5,102	6/1/99	—	107,436	D
Badlato, Charles	TR	S	8,184	5/20/99–5/12/99	15.39–14.01	5,965	D
Blau, Harvey R.	CB	S	69,996	5/20/99–5/12/99	15.39–14.01	—	D
Borow, Leonard	EX VP	S	52,194	5/20/99–5/12/99	15.39–14.01	434,405	D
Caruso, Carl	VP	S	8,665	5/20/99–5/12/99	15.39–14.01	61,501	D
Gorin, Michael	PR	S	52,194	5/20/99–5/12/99	15.39–14.01	114,204	D
Badlato, Charles	TR	B*	12,184	5/7/99–4/28/99	3.88	—	—
Blau, Harvey R.	CB	B*	103,996	5/7/99–4/28/99	3.88	—	—
Borow, Leonard	EX VP	B*	78,194	5/7/99–4/28/99	3.88	—	—
Caruso, Carl	OFF	B*	13,665	5/7/99–4/28/99	3.88	—	—
Badlato, Charles	TR	S	4,000	4/28/99	15.63	14,149	D
Blau, Harvey R.	CB	S	34,000	4/28/99	15.61	182,534	D
Borow, Leonard	EX VP	S	26,000	4/28/99	15.60	486,599	D
Caruso, Carl	VP	S	5,000	4/28/99	15.65	70,166	D
Gorin, Michael	PR	S	26,000	4/28/99	15.60	166,398	D
Gorin, Michael	PR	B*	78,194	4/28/99	3.88	—	—
Blau, Harvey R.	CB	B*	22,775	3/4/99	3.88	—	—
Blau, Harvey R.	CB	S	22,775	3/4/99	13.84	112,538	D
Borow, Leonard	EX VP	B*	22,775	3/4/99	3.88	—	—
Borow, Leonard	EX VP	S	22,775	3/4/99	13.84	434,405	D

Insider Name	Title	Trans Type	# of Shares	Trans Date(s)	Trans Price(s)	Total Holdings	D/I Own
Gorin, Michael	PR	B*	22,775	3/4/99	3.88	—	—
Gorin, Michael	PR	S	22,775	3/4/99	13.84	114,204	D
Blau, Harvey R.	CB	S	27,600	11/2/98	11.50–11.38	112,538	D
Blau, Harvey R.	CB	B*	27,692	11/2/98	3.50	—	—
Borow, Leonard	EX VP	S	27,600	11/2/98	11.50–11.38	434,405	D
Borow, Leonard	EX VP	B*	27,692	11/2/98	3.50	—	—
Gorin, Michael	PR	S	27,600	11/2/98	11.50—11.38	114,204	D
Gorin, Michael	PR	B*	27,692	11/2/98	3.50	—	—
Blau, Harvey R.	CB	JB	36,142	9/1/98	—	114,709	I
Blau, Harvey R.	CB	JS	36,142	9/1/98	—	112,446	D
Blau, Harvey R.	CB	JB	39,261	8/31/98	—	148,588	D
Blau, Harvey R.	CB	B*	36,142	8/14/98	2.38	148,588	—
Borow, Leonard	EX VP	B*	24,095	8/14/98	2.38	434,313	—
Gorin, Michael	PR	B*	24,095	8/14/98	2.38	114,112	—
Abecassis, Paul	DIR	3	—	8/13/98	—	18,000	D
Badlato, Charles	TR	B*	11,501	3/24/98	4.63–3.25	—	—
Badlato, Charles	TR	S	11,501	3/24/98	13.00	5,965	D
Blau, Harvey R.	CB	S	43,125	3/24/98	13.00	73,185	D
Borow, Leonard	EX VP	S	43,125	3/24/98	13.00	410,218	D
Brenner, Milton	DIR	S	23,000	3/24/98	13.00	92,666	D
Caruso, Carl	OFF	B*	17,250	3/24/98	3.88	61,501	—
Caruso, Carl	VP	S	17,250	3/24/98	13.00	61,501	D
Gorin, Michael	PR	S	34,500	3/24/98	13.00	90,017	D
Blau, Harvey R.	CB	B*	61,482	2/9/98–2/6/98	2.00	—	—
Borow, Leonard	EX VP	S	19,000	2/9/98–2/6/98	11.75–11.38	453,343	D
Gorin, Michael	PR	S	19,000	2/9/98–2/6/98	11.75–11.38	124,517	D
Gorin, Michael	PR	B*	41,017	2/9/98–2/6/98	2.00	324,517	—
Blau, Harvey R.	CB	S	28,500	2/6/98	11.75–11.38	55,922	D
Borow, Leonard	EX VP	B*	41,017	2/6/98	2.00	453,343	—
Blau, Harvey R.	CB	JB	994	2/5/98	11.81	142,576	I
Blau, Harvey R.	CB	JB	73,886	9/12/97	—	141,582	I
Blau, Harvey R.	CB	JS	73,886	9/12/97	—	22,940	D
Borow, Leonard	EX VP	JS	4,000	7/14/97	4.44	431,326	D
Caruso, Carl	VP	3	-	2/5/97	—	34,356	D
Blau, Harvey R.	CB	B*	65,515	2/4/97	2.25	96,826	—
Borow, Leonard	EX VP	B*	16,134	2/4/97	2.25	439,326	—
Caruso, Carl	OFF	B*	9,356	2/4/97	2.25	61,501	—
Gorin, Michael	PR	B*	16,134	2/4/97	2.25	102,500	—
Blau, Harvey R.	CB	JS	29,581	8/20/96	5.38	—	D
Blau, Harvey R.	CB	B*	200,000	8/20/96	1.50	—	—

Transaction Type Codes: B=Form 4 Buy, S=Form 4 Sale, B*=Option-Related Form 4 Buy, JB=Non-Open-Market Form 4 Buy, JS=Non-Open-Market Form 4 Sale, 3=Form 3.
Ownership Codes: D=direct, I=Indirect. For all other codes, see the full Key in Figure 3.2 on page 27.

age vice president and chief financial officer at a company may make a comfortable living, but for many a $10,000 trade, or even a $5,000 one, is serious money. The transaction value may look puny beside all the others you see on a given day, but it doesn't mean it's not significant.

I would actually put as much meaning in the 5,000-share purchase of a vice president if it doubles his total holdings as a 50,000 purchase by a rock star chairman who has a million shares as a result of the trade. The vice president's investment may very well represent a larger share of his net worth than his boss's big-bucks buy.

TRANSACTIONS BY HANDS-ON INSIDERS ARE MORE IMPORTANT THAN TRANSACTIONS BY OTHER INSIDERS

Just as some transaction codes are more useful to look at than others, there is also a hierarchy of usefulness involving who is doing the transacting.

Figure 4.3 lists the numerous SEC codes insiders can now use on Forms 3, 4, 5, and 144 to record their relationships to their respective companies. Services that redistribute the data may use slightly different codes when presenting the trades, but they won't be too different from these.

As with transaction codes, the number of relationship codes insiders can use on the forms has changed since they were first used in 1935. There were first six codes insiders could use, but that was quickly simplified to three. The list has only expanded since 1937, however, as the SEC had to account for the reality that the securities markets have gotten more complicated.

Generally speaking, it is better to focus your time on transactions by insiders with a hands-on role in the company. Trades by a chairman, president or chief executive officer, vice president, chief financial officer, or even just an officer should all be given credence. Though directors generally lack day-to-day responsibilities, their transactions are also useful to analyze because of their access to information about the company's financial condition and strategy.

Academic studies have determined that the insider activity of CEOs, vice presidents, and directors is more profitable to follow than that of beneficial owners (see the Bibliography for a list of academic studies), but common sense brings you to a similar conclusion. Keep on applying common sense when judging the relative importance of other codes on the list. A director who is also an officer (or DO on a Form 4) is

---

FIGURE 4.3 Relationship Codes Used on SEC Forms 3, 4, and 5

AF — Affiliated person
AI — Affiliate of Investment advisor
B — Beneficial owner of more than 10% of a class of the company's equity securities
BC — Beneficial owner as custodian
BT — Beneficial owner as trustee
CB — Chairman of the Board
CEO — Chief executive officer
CFO — Chief financial officer
CP — Controlling person
D — Director
DO — Director and Beneficial owner of more than 10% of a class of the company's equity securities
DS — Indirect shareholder
GP — General partner
H — Officer, Director, and Beneficial owner of more than 10% of a class of the company's equity securities
IA — Investment advisor
LP — Limited partner
MC — Member of committee or advisory board
O — Officer
OB — Officer and Beneficial owner of more than 10% of a class of the company's equity securities
OD — Officer and Director
OP — Officer of parent company
OS — Officer of subsidiary company
OT — Officer and Treasurer
OX — Divisional officer
P — President
SH — Shareholder
T — Trustee
UT — Unknown
VP — Vice President
VT — Voting trustee

---

probably in a better position to judge his company's prospects than a plain outside director (D). An H is probably better positioned than all of them, being a director, an officer, and a beneficial owner of more than 10 percent of a class of the company's equity securities. Not only is that guy well positioned to judge both the strategy and operations of his company, he also has enough riding on the stock's performance to really pay attention to both.

Transactions by affiliated persons, trustees, large shareholders, and passive beneficial owners, on the other hand, tend to be less important to analyze, the major reason being that these insiders are often other companies, investment partnerships, or other such entities—not individuals. These trades may be more related to corporate finance needs or policy decisions than to a fundamental analysis of the shares or knowledge of future developments at the company.

Venture capital firms sometimes remain large shareholders or beneficial owners of stock after the companies they seeded go public. But the bylaws of their fund may mandate that they cash out their ownership within a certain time frame so the money can be reinvested in other start-ups. An investment partnership that holds enough shares to make it an insider by the SEC's definition may even have a limited life. When the partnership dissolves, profits must be distributed, and that means selling investments and divvying up the cash.

INITIAL PURCHASES BY NEW INSIDERS ARE LESS IMPORTANT THAN PURCHASES BY LONG-TIME INSIDERS

This rule applies particularly to new directors. Many directors feel obligated (or are required) to take a token stake in the companies on whose boards they serve, and it generally happens soon after they "join the club," so to speak. Companies may even give new directors a below-market-rate loan to pick up their token shares. New employees may feel similar pressure (or be given a similar incentive) to pick up a stake in the company they just joined. I generally discount initial purchases by new insiders completely.

If an insider has been around for a while and is just buying, however, that's a different story. A grizzled veteran who finally "shows the faith" is something I give credence to. How do you find out if an initial purchase is by a new or old insider? Get hold of an insider history that has at least a few years of data and try to find the Form 3 the insider had to file when becoming an insider. You can also ask the company's investor relations department. A useful, though less reliable, method is to look at the total holdings of the insider after the trade. If a recent purchase accounts for all the insider's holdings, it may be the insider's maiden transaction. (It could also be another purchase after the insider previously sold all his or her shares, however, so look through some past history for a previous trade by the insider.)

TRANSACTIONS OF DIRECT HOLDINGS ARE MORE IMPORTANT THAN TRANSACTIONS OF INDIRECT HOLDINGS

Most insider data vendors have a column on their detailed histories with either a D or an I in it to indicate direct or indirect ownership, respectively, of the shares that were traded.

Direct/indirect ownership is a straightforward concept. Direct ownership means that the shares are actually registered under the insider's name. But it is very easy for an insider to tell a spouse or relative about a major event that will soon move the company's shares. An insider could even give his relative the money to trade with, or make the trade himself in an account under the name of a relative. This is one of the oldest tricks in the book, and the SEC is not blind to this abuse.

Legally, insiders must report all such indirect ownership and the trades involved in it. To clarify things, the SEC lists several circumstances in which an insider is automatically assumed to have indirect ownership of shares. These are spelled out in the SEC's Rule 16-1(a)(2)(ii) of the *Code of Federal Regulations,* which is part of Appendix B of this book.

Simply put, an insider is deemed to have indirect ownership of "securities held by members of a person's immediate family that share the same household." The SEC further assumes insiders have indirect ownership of shares owned by a partnership or corporation insiders are a part of, and of trusts they are involved in.

Rule 16-1 goes on to define *immediate family* as "any child, stepchild, grandchild, parent, stepparent, grandparent, spouse, sibling, mother-in-law, father-in-law, son-in-law, daughter-in-law, brother-in-law, or sister-in-law, and shall include adoptive relationships." Oddly, aunts, uncles, nieces, and nephews aren't included in the definition of immediate family, which seems to open up a loophole for slimy insiders inclined to look for one. But the definition obviously had to stop somewhere. The SEC also allows insiders to rebut the presumption of ownership of shares owned by immediate family.

Even if insiders abuse or stretch the definition of indirect ownership to not declare it, however, their actions are still limited by a solid body of case law. Passing along material, nonpublic information is illegal no matter who the insider leaks it to. And any insiders dead set on breaking the law aren't likely to worry about filling out a Form 4 properly. They just won't fill out anything at all.

Generally speaking, insider trades of direct holdings are more significant than indirect ones. This is simply a nod to the common sense that individuals are more likely to practice more discretion when the results hit them directly in the pocketbook. By contrast, when an indirect trade involves a partnership or corporate entity, the stock's rise or fall affects the insider's financial position much less. Looking at Metro-Goldwyn-Mayer's insider history again (see Figure 3.8 on page 42), the trades by Kerkorian of his indirect holdings were not only less significant but were actually noise that needed to be filtered out.

There are enough exceptions to this rule, however, that I actually start out giving indirect trades the same credence as direct ones. If the indirect ownership is via the insider's spouse or a child's trust fund, for instance, it's difficult to argue that the insider would practice less discretion than if it were his own account. A call to the firm's investor relations department for more details on the relationship usually makes it very clear whether we should view it as significant.

An example of indirect trades that I did deem significant are those in Saul Centers. This real estate investment trust (REIT) came into my sights by showing up on a screen of stocks with high yields and insider buying (a screen discussed more in Chapter 10). The 8.7 percent indicated yield of this REIT looked like a good candidate for the income portion of InsiderTrader.com's Buy List. The fact that insiders were buying when the yield was high gave me confidence that the indicated yield was attainable and not just the result of the REIT's price falling before some imminent bad news that would affect its funds from operations.

But when I looked at the detailed Form 4 history, I saw that most of the recent buying was by Chairman Francis Saul for accounts he had only indirect ownership of (see Figure 4.4). Instead of discounting the trades, I investigated them.

As it turned out, Saul Centers is a closely held company, with Chairman Francis Saul controlling over 25 percent of the 12.3 million shares outstanding. Many of his holdings are through various entities in which he is listed as an indirect owner, but he definitely has control over the shares and a beneficiary interest in most of them. His various limited partnerships, trusts, and the like (which include Chevy Chase Bank) are actually referred to as the Saul Organization. Many of the trusts he controls are for his family as well, which certainly motivates him to act prudently.

So we deemed Francis Saul's indirect holdings and purchases as significant enough to include BFS on our list of companies to research. After determining that the REIT had a decent, sustainable yield, it was added to the conservative portion of InsiderTrader.com's Buy List.

FIGURE 4.4 Insider History for Saul Centers (NYSE: BFS)

Insider Name	Title	Trans Type	# of Shares	Trans Date(s)	Trans Price(s)	Total Holdings	D/I Own
Saul, B. Francis Ii	CB	B	101,000	1/28/98–1/9/98	18.38–17.50	3,245,740	I
Jackson, Philip C. Jr.	DIR	B	6,000	11/7/97	17.38	23,000	D
Saul, B. Francis II	CB	B	6,700	10/13/97–10/10/97	19.19–18.75	3,084,136	I
Saul, B. Francis II	CB	B	3,000	9/3/97	18.75–17.50	3,077,436	D
Schneider, Scott V.	VP	B	125	4/30/97	15.63	354	I
Saul, B. Francis II	CB	B	91,000	3/31/97–3/3/97	17.38–16.38	2,946,179	I
Saul, B. Francis II	CB	B	9,000	2/28/97–2/27/97	17.25–16.75	2,855,179	I
Saul, B. Francis II	CB	B	51,600	1/14/97–1/2/97	17.50–15.75	—	I
Jackson, Philip C. Jr.	DIR	B	2,000	12/6/96	15.25	16,000	D
Noonan, Patrick F.	DIR	B	500	10/16/96	14.25	2,500	D
Noonan, Patrick F.	DIR	B	500	10/16/96	14.25	2,500	I

Transaction Type Codes: B=Form 4 Buy.
Ownership Codes: D=direct, I=Indirect. For all other codes, see the full Key in Figure 3.2 on page 27.

Chapter 4   AT A GLANCE

1. Form 4 purchases are easier to interpret than are sales.

2. The size of a Form 4 transaction should be analyzed both in terms of the dollar amount and in relation to the number of shares the insider owns. The larger, the better.

3. Transactions by insiders with duties at the company are more significant than transactions by insiders with no duties.

4. Initial purchases by new insiders are less important than purchases by long-term insiders.

5. Transactions of direct holdings are usually more significant than transactions of indirect holdings.

5

Analyzing
Form 4 Transactions:
Pattern Recognition

LOOK FOR CLUSTERS OF ACTIVITY

It is always more significant to see a group of insiders trading within a short period. Insiders are only human and, as such, can be wrong. So activity that indicates there is a consensus among a few insiders about their company's prospects is a strong signal. After all, the odds of two, three, four, or more insiders being wrong are much less than the odds with just a single insider.

You might think it unlikely that four or five insiders would call their stockbrokers in the same week, but you'd be surprised. It is actually a pretty common phenomenon. Corporate governance also acts to cluster insiders' transactions. To prevent lawsuits by shareholders, most companies have adopted trading policies that make the SEC's oversight look downright slack. To avoid any appearance of improperly trading on nonpublic information, the compliance procedures of many companies allow insiders to trade only during certain windows. These time windows generally follow the release of such important news as quarterly earnings, new contracts, merger and acquisition activity, and the like. These compliance procedures tend to get more onerous the larger a corporation becomes. Deeper corporate pockets, it seems, attract more attention from class-action lawyers.

Looking back, Figure 4.1 (on page 46) illustrates how common clusters of activity are. The figure shows numerous companies with anywhere from 2 to 15 insiders filing Form 4s at the SEC in the same week for purchases they recently made. And this figure shows only a portion of the Form 4s filed for the week of November 5, 1999.

Do you call up your broker and immediately buy shares in all the companies with clusters of buying activity? No, but it is a good way to start narrowing the field of companies on which to focus your fundamental research. And even before you start delving into the minutia in a 10-K, you can apply several more of my rules of thumb for analyzing insider activity (summarized in Figure 3.1 on page 26) to further narrow the companies to which you need to apply fundamental analysis.

Analyzing Figure 4.1 from the top down, the Boulder Total Return Fund and RJ Reynolds Tobacco are the first clusters you come across, and the transaction values of the purchases are utterly enormous. But wait. Looking at the relation of the buyers to the company you see that they are mainly beneficial holders (as denoted with a B in that column). Don't get your hopes up. Usually one glance at the details of transactions by numerous beneficial owners quickly shows that they seem to be part of some kind of corporate action instead of a hard-nosed analysis of the stock's prospects.

The rule of thumb that hands-on insiders are more important than those without day-to-day duties (expounded in Chapter 4) turns out to hold true in these cases. The supposed large purchase of the Boulder Fund turns out to be composed mainly of a private transaction that is offset by a similar sale. And although there is a director involved with part of the RJ Reynolds purchase, it is a small part. An entity known as Ross Financial Corp. is responsible for all but 2,000 shares of the immense purchase. And if you were tempted to investigate further into this entity's relationship to RJ Reynolds, that urge would disappear when you realize that Ross purchased the stock days before its price gapped down markedly. This is not an investing style I like to follow.

The first buying by a cluster of hands-on insiders when taking a top-down approach to Figure 4.1 is a whopper: 15 insiders filed Form 4s indicating purchases of this real estate investment trust in one week! But hold down your enthusiasm again. Fifteen insiders is quite a cluster, too big to expect that there wasn't some sort of orchestration to the buying. A look at the details confirms this. The purchases were made of odd lots of shares that were bought at transaction prices that don't conform to market trades. The large indicated yield of more than 10 percent may still get you to investigate this investment if yield is what you need, but the insider cluster is definitely tainted by the details of the trades. I'll talk more of these "bad clusters" later this chapter.

My firm and I investigated several companies that came to our attention from the insider filings made during the week of November 5, 1999, and as I described in Chapter 4, Aeroflex was the company that made it on our Buy List. Aeroflex didn't have the largest number of buyers in its cluster, or the largest dollar amount of purchases made by a cluster of buyers. I have found that the clusters of purchases that tend to pass through enough rules of thumb to deserve in-depth fundamental analysis—and then look attractive enough after analysis to invest in—aren't necessarily the biggest clusters in terms of either aggregate transaction value or number of insiders.

THROW OUT BAD CLUSTERS

All that glitters is not gold, of course, and some clusters of activity that appear too good to be true are just that.

If you look at an insider history and see that numerous insiders bought the same number of shares on the same day at the same price, the purchases were probably not open market. It is highly unlikely that all these officers called their brokers and ended with the same exact trades. I call these "bad clusters," not because insiders did anything wrong or illegal, but because this type of activity is usually just time-wasting noise.

Sometimes clusters of transactions are obviously "bad" and show that all the insiders bought odd lots of shares, sometimes at prices outside of the stock's trading range for the day or even year. The number of shares insiders traded may also be more than the total trading volume of the shares on the day. Bad clusters often include these types of funny data, which were discussed in Chapter 3.

If you come across bad clusters when looking for new investments, just move on to the next company with interesting insider activity. If this activity occurs in a company you own, you should probably give investor relations a call for a quick explanation. The trades are likely some sort of corporate buying on insiders' behalf and will probably happen again, so you might as well familiarize yourself with this corporate buying.

The explanation you will probably get is that the transactions were part of a deferred compensation program by which insiders are granted new shares issued by the company in lieu of salary.

NorthWestern's very funny insider history (shown in Figure 5.1) is the result of it having both an employee stock purchase program and a

FIGURE 5.1 Insider History for NorthWestern Corporation (NYSE: NOR)

Insider Name	Title	Trans Type	# of Shares	Trans Date(s)	Trans Price(s)	Total Holdings	D/I Own
Lewis, Merle D.	CB	JB	1,313	1/31/00–1/12/00	22.25–21.31	78,523	D
Thaden, Rogene A.	VP	JB	59	1/31/00–1/12/00	22.25–21.31	11,518	D
Bradley, Walter A. III	VP	JB	67	1/26/00–1/12/00	22.25–21.31	5,731	D
Dietrich, Alan D.	SEC	JB	36	1/26/00 –1/12/00	22.25–21.31	10,693	D
Hylland, Richard R.	PR	JB	98	1/26/00 –1/12/00	22.25–21.31	28,429	D
Lavallee, Michelle M.	VP	JB	61	1/26/00–1/12/00	22.25–21.31	931	D
Leyendecker, Rodney F.	OFF	JB	84	1/26/00–1/12/00	22.25–21.31	16,474	D
Monaghan, David A.	TR	JB	30	1/26/00–1/12/00	22.25–21.31	1,839	D
Newell, Daniel K.	CFO	JB	179	1/26/00–1/12/00	22.25–21.31	14,571	D
Bradley, Walter A. III	VP	B	62	1/20/00–1/3/00	22.95–22.13	—	D
Dietrich, Alan D.	SEC	B	55	1/20/00–1/3/00	22.95–22.13	—	D
Hylland, Richard R.	PR	B	13	1/20/00–1/5/00	22.95–22.62	—	D
Leyendecker, Rodney F.	OFF	B	3	1/20/00–1/5/00	22.95–22.62	—	D
Monaghan, David A.	TR	B	20	1/20/00–1/3/00	22.45–22.13	—	D
Thaden, Rogene A.	VP	B	201	1/20/00–1/3/00	22.62–22.13	—	D
Lewis, Merle D.	CB	JS	105	1/11/00	—	—	D
Childers, Michael L.	VP	B	5	1/3/00	22.13	8	D
Lavallee, Michelle M.	VP	B	45	1/3/00	22.13	—	D
Lewis, Merle D.	CB	B	382	1/3/00	22.62 - 22.13	—	D
Lotsberg, Warren K.	VP	B	5	1/3/00	22.13	2,033	D
Newell, Daniel K.	CFO	B	23	1/3/00	22.13	—	D
Gulbranson, Thomas A.	OFF	B	235	12/31/99–12/9/99	22.00–21.88	11,568	D
Lavallee, Michelle M.	OFF	JB	60	12/31/99–12/9/99	22.00–21.88	826	D
Lewis, Merle D.	CB	JB	1,549	12/31/99–12/9/99	22.00–21.88	77,802	D
Thaden, Rogene A.	VP	JB	155	12/31/99–12/9/99	22.00–21.88	11,113	D
Lewis, Merle D.	CB	JS	1,300	12/29/99	—	—	D
Bradley, Walter A. III	VP	JB	153	12/27/99–12/9/99	21.94–21.88	5,557	D
Dietrich, Alan D.	SEC	JB	112	12/27/99 –12/9/99	21.94–21.88	10,610	D
Hanson, Michael J.	OFF	B	118	12/27/99–12/9/99	21.94–21.88	500	D
Hylland, Richard R.	PR	JB	877	12/27/99–12/9/99	21.94–21.88	28,265	D
Leyendecker, Rodney F.	OFF	JB	147	12/27/99–12/9/99	21.94–21.88	16,408	D
Monaghan, David A.	TR	JB	69	12/27/99–12/9/99	21.94–21.88	1,789	D
Newell, Daniel K.	CFO	JB	488	12/27/99–12/9/99	21.94–21.88	14,365	D
Bradley, Walter A. III	VP	B	70	12/20/99–12/1/99	22.55–22.04	—	D
Dietrich, Alan D.	SEC	B	102	12/20/99–12/1/99	22.56–22.04	—	D
Hylland, Richard R.	PR	B	79	12/20/99–12/6/99	22.56–22.16	—	D
Leyendecker, Rodney F.	OFF	B	3	12/20/99–12/6/99	22.55–22.15	—	D
Monaghan, David A.	TR	B	20	12/20/99–12/1/99	22.56–22.04	—	D

Transaction Type Codes: B=Form 4 Buy, S=Form 4 Sale, B*=Option-Related Form 4 Buy, JB=Non–Open-Market Form 4 Buy, JS=Non–Open-Market Form 4 Sale.
Ownership Codes: D=direct, I=Indirect. For all other codes, see the full Key in Figure 3.2 on page 27.

dividend reinvestment plan. Both are generating bad clusters of insider buying data. NorthWestern's insider activity would likely register as pretty significant if you simply looked at the number of purchases and their aggregate dollar amounts (as some technical insider ratings systems do). But NorthWestern's insider history is the "poster child" for why I don't believe insider analysis lends itself to being computerized.

A quick glance at the details of the history show it to be meaningless: odd lots of purchases by clusters of insiders on the same days and for odd transaction prices. While it's not so surprising to see the odd transaction amounts and prices for the non-open-market JB trades (which generate a lot of funny data as explained in Chapter 3), notice that even the open-market trades (denoted by transaction type B) have the funny numbers.

This is because NorthWestern's plans give it the option of issuing new shares to its employees or buying them in regular lots in the open market to distribute piecemeal to its employees. When the company uses this latter method, the transaction is technically an open-market one. Don't think that bad clusters are only generated by non-open-market trades—and don't waste your time looking into insider histories like NorthWestern's when you come across them.

CHECK CREDENTIALS

As I have pointed out before, insiders are only human and, as such, can be wrong. But if an insider has traded well in the past, it gives more credence to any recent actions. Check out the insider history of a company's Form 4 transactions to see if the insider you're looking at has been right in the past. Past performance may not be a guarantee of future results, but it's certainly a valuable piece of information to consider.

An insider's credibility as an indicator is low if he or she has purchased frequently in the past only to have the stock price fall after the trades. But if the insider has shown a knack for buying well (i.e., the stock rises in price after the purchases), his or her importance as an indicator is enhanced. More important still is the insider who has shown that he or she has both bought and sold well in the past. Knowing when to sell a stock is more difficult for most people than knowing when to buy; and the same applies to insiders.

Looking back once more at the insider history of Aeroflex (see Figure 4.2 on page 50), six of the seven recent purchasers of the stock had sold it for much higher prices at least once in the past. Five of these smart sellers had done so just over six months at more than double the price at which they recently bought the shares back. The prescient selling done so recently was a huge booster of our confidence that their recent buying was a hugely bullish signal.

Particularly interesting is Harvey Blau's insider history (see Figure 5.2). He not only seems to have traded Aeroflex's shares well for at least four years, but also appears to have done reasonably well trading another company indicated on his history: Griffon Corp. Intriguingly, Blau has started purchasing Griffon's shares again as they trade at five-year lows. Given his past acumen, this company also seems to deserve to be further analyzed. By checking out an insider's credentials, you may often find yourself introduced to another prospective investment. And once you find an insider who trades particularly well, make a point of looking up their specific insider histories every so often.

Checking the credentials of Aeroflex's insiders turned out to be particularly productive; however, it's not common for insiders to illustrate such prescient out-and-in trading within a year's time. Remember that insiders are limited by the short-swing rule (see Chapter 2) and cannot buy and sell—or sell and buy—their companies' shares in the open market within a six-month period. It is therefore important to access as long a history of transactions as possible to thoroughly check the credentials of an insider. I think a three-year history is the least that is needed for this task.

Unfortunately, much of the free data available to individual investors on the Internet consist of one-year histories only (see Chapter 15 for a

---

FIGURE 5.2 Insider History for Harvey Blau

Title	Company	Ticker	Trans Type	Shares Traded	Trans Date(s)	Trans Price(s)	D/I Own	Total Hldgs	% Owned
CB	Griffon Corp Com	GFF	B	80,000	2/28/00– 2/7/00	8.44– 7.75	I	260,266	—
CB	Griffon Corp Com	GFF	B	20,000	12/20/99– 12/16/99	6.88– 6.81	I	180,266	—
CB	Griffon Corp Com	GFF	B	10,000	11/16/99	7.56	I	160,266	—
CB	Aeroflex Inc	ARX	B	100,000	10/27/99– 10/25/99	6.25– 5.88	I	214,709	—

(continued)

FIGURE 5.2 *(Continued)*

Title	Company	Ticker	Trans Type	Shares Traded	Trans Date(s)	Trans Price(s)	D/I Own	Total Hldgs	% Owned
CB	Aeroflex Inc	ARX	JS	5,102	6/1/99	—	D	107,436	—
CB	Aeroflex Inc	ARX	S	69,996	5/20/99–5/12/99	15.39–14.01	D	—	—
CB	Aeroflex Inc	ARX	B*	103,996	5/7/99–4/28/99	3.88	—	—	—
CB	Aeroflex Inc	ARX	S	34,000	4/28/99	15.61	D	182,534	—
DIR	Aeroflex Inc	ARX	144	156,000	4/27/99	—	—	—	—
DIR	Aeroflex Inc	ARX	144	60,000	—	—	—	—	—
CB	Aeroflex Inc	ARX	B*	22,775	3/4/99	3.88	—	—	—
CB	Aeroflex Inc	ARX	S	22,775	3/4/99	13.84	D	112,538	—
CB	Aeroflex Inc	ARX	S	27,600	11/2/98	11.50–11.38	D	112,538	—
CB	Aeroflex Inc	ARX	B*	27,692	11/2/98	3.50	—	—	—
DIR	Aeroflex Inc	ARX	144	27,600	11/2/98	—	—	—	—
CB	Aeroflex Inc	ARX	JB	36,142	9/1/98	—	I	114,709	—
CB	Aeroflex Inc	ARX	JS	36,142	9/1/98	—	D	112,446	—
CB	Griffon Corp Com	GFF	JB	111,360	9/1/98	—	I	150,266	—
CB	Griffon Corp Com	GFF	JS	111,360	9/1/98	—	D	307,297	—
CB	Aeroflex Inc C	ARX	JB	39,261	8/31/98	—	D	148,588	—
CB	Aeroflex Inc	ARX	B*	36,142	8/14/98	2.38	—	148,588	—
CB	Griffon Corp Com	GFF	JS	65,783	5/1/98	13.44	D	418,657	—
CB	Griffon Corp Com	GFF	B*	150,000	5/1/98	1.50	—	418,657	—
CB	Aeroflex Inc	ARX	S	43,125	3/24/98	13.00	D	73,185	—
CB	Aeroflex Inc	ARX	B*	61,482	2/9/98–2/6/98	2.00	—	—	—
CB	Aeroflex Inc	ARX	S	28,500	2/6/98	11.75–11.38	D	55,922	—
CB	Aeroflex Inc	ARX	JB	994	2/5/98	11.81	I	142,576	—
CB	Aeroflex Inc	ARX	JB	73,886	9/12/97	—	I	141,582	—
CB	Aeroflex Inc	ARX	JS	73,886	9/12/97	—	D	22,940	—
CB	Griffon Corp Com	GFF	JB	9,300	2/20/97	—	I	45,265	—
—	Griffon Corp Com	GFF	13D	—	2/8/97	—	—	1,724,440	5.4
CB	Aeroflex Inc	ARX	B*	65,515	2/4/97	2.25	—	96,826	—
CB	Aeroflex Inc	ARX	JS	29,581	8/20/96	5.38	D	—	—
CB	Aeroflex Inc	ARX	B*	200,000	8/20/96	1.50	—	—	—

Transaction Type Codes: B=Form 4 Buy, S=Form 4 Sale, B*=Option-Related Form 4 Buy, JB=Non–Open-Market Form 4 Buy, JS=Non–Open-Market Form 4 Sale, 13D=Schedule 13D, 13G=Schedule 13G, 3=Form 3. Ownership Codes: D=direct, I=Indirect. For all other codes, see the full Key in Figure 3.2 on page 27.

review of the Web sites). There is a reason that providers of the data have cut off the freebies at that time frame: they realize that serious users of the data need more history and will pay for it. The trend is definitely toward more free data on Internet sites, however, and it won't be long until longer histories are given away.

Some insiders' credibility almost goes without saying, however. Who wouldn't want to know, for example, what an investor like George Soros is buying and selling? But when following well-known investors, you often have to know the names of their investment vehicles. Soros, for instance, has several different ones: Soros Capital LP, Soros Fund Management LLC, and Soros Fund Management. Besides reviewing the trades he's made under his own name, which are shown in Figure 5.3, all of his vehicles should be monitored to get a feeling for what Soros likes.

The trades made under Soros's own name are enough to supply some interesting information by themselves, however. Soros was a steady buyer of Ortec International in 1998 and a seller of practically everything else for which he had to file an insider form. He obviously had a change of heart in 1999, as he started selling Ortec in November of that year. At the same time, his buying tastes leaned toward Internet-related investments like Bluefly and Interworld and the biotech firm Viropharma. Soros also purchased more of a decidedly old-economy company: Apex Silver Mines.

Notice how it's important to look at all the different insider form types for an investor like Soros. His Ortec and Apex Silver trades may have been done on Form 4s, but Schedule 13Ds are used for his Bluefly and Viropharma investments. His Interworld stake was announced on a Form 3.

Don't think Figure 5.3 is Soros's entire personal portfolio, however. Remember, he only has to file a Form 4 for equity trades made in companies in which he is considered an insider. He most assuredly has investments in numerous other companies as well but not enough to give him the 10 percent ownership at which he is considered a beneficial owner.

Other smart money forms, such as Schedule 13D, must be filed when a person or entity acquires a 5 percent stake and should be used in concert with Form 4s for large investors like Soros. But even all this data will not give you a picture of Soros's total portfolio. Many large investors actually make it a practice to stay under the threshold of ownership that requires them to disclose what they are buying and selling. It simply makes it more difficult to get in and out of positions if everybody knows what they own. (More on the smart money forms and how

FIGURE 5.3 Insider History for George Soros

Title	Company	Ticker	Trans Type	Shares Traded	Trans Date(s)	Trans Price(s)	D/I Own	Total Hldgs	% Owned
—	Integra Lifesciences Hldgs	IART	13D	—	3/29/00	—	—	3,757,800	18.72
—	Bluefly Inc Com	BFLY	13D	—	3/28/00	—	—	876,190	15.10
—	IRSA Inversiones Y GDR	IRS	13D	—	2/11/00	—	—	10,363,630	4.89
B/O	Apex Silver Mines	SIL	B	566,210	2/4/00	100.00	I	4,992,800	—
B/O	Ortec Intl Com	ORTC	S	41,300	11/23/99–11/4/99	7.38–6.34	I	1,249,900	—
P	Earthlink Network Inc	ELNK	144	65,527	9/29/99	—	—	—	—
P	Earthlink Network Inc	ELNK	144	23,000	9/27/99	—	—	—	—
—	Bluefly Inc Com	BFLY	13D	—	8/26/99	—	—	876,190	15.16
B/O	Interworld Corp	INTW	3	—	8/9/99	—	D	2,338,265	—
B/O	Globalstar Telecommun Ltd	GSTRF	S	120,000	8/4/99–8/2/99	25.98–23.42	I	8,060,000	—
B/O	Globalstar Telecommun Ltd	GSTRF	S	220,000	7/30/99–7/26/99	30.88–27.19	I	8,180,000	—
B/O	Bluefly Inc Com	BFLY	3	—	7/27/99	—	D	—	—
—	IRSA Inversiones Y GDR	IRS	13D	—	7/21/99	—	—	25,058,348	13.13
—	Viropharma Inc	VPHM	13D	—	5/5/99	—	—	2,895,000	20.00
—	Viropharma Inc	VPHM	3	—	5/5/99	—	D	—	—
—	Cresud S.A.C.I.F. YA Spon Adr	CRESY	13D	—	4/16/99	—	—	14,138,323	11.38
B/O	Primus Telecommun Grp	PRTL	S	45,000	3/31/99	10.01	I	2,205,051	—
B/O	Integra Lifesciences Corp Co	IART	3	—	3/29/99	—	D	—	—
—	Integra Lifesciences Hldgs	IART	13D	—	3/29/99	—	—	2,857,800	15.37
—	Viatel Inc	VYTL	13G	—	1/27/99	—	—	938,270	4.05
—	R & B Falcon Corp Com	FLC	13D	—	12/31/98	—	—	14,817,639	7.62
B/O	Globalstar Telecommun Ltd	GSTRF	S	130,000	12/21/98	18.49	I	8,400,000	—
—	Earthlink Network Inc	ELNK	13D	—	12/9/98–12/4/98	—	—	1,110,167	3.89
—	Indigo N V Ord	INDG	13D	—	12/3/98	—	—	23,861,770	29.59
—	Earthlink Network Inc	ELNK	13D	—	10/27/98–10/15/98	—	—	1,898,767	6.66
—	Earthlink Network Inc	ELNK	144	145,704	10/15/98	—	—	—	—
—	IRSA Inversiones Y GDR	IRS	13D	—	10/1/98–8/3/98	—	—	30,305,655	15.88
B/O	Ortec Intl Com	ORTC	B	15,300	9/15/98–9/1/98	10.47–7.11	I	1,291,200	—
B/O	Ortec Intl Com	ORTC	B	12,600	8/28/98–8/4/98	13.75–9.22	I	1,275,900	—
B/O	Global Telesystems Group Inc	GTS	S	84,000	8/10/98	54.56–54.13	I	4,765,714	—

Title	Company	Ticker	Trans Type	Shares Traded	Trans Date(s)	Trans Price(s)	D/I Own	Total Hldgs	% Owned
—	Protein Design Labs	PDLI	13G	—	8/6/98	—	—	881,700	4.76
B/O	Apex Silver Mines	SIL	JS	1	8/3/98	—	I	4,426,591	—
B/O	Apex Silver Mines	SIL	JB	######	8/3/98	—	I	—	—
B/O	Ortec Intl Com	ORTC	B	14,300	7/31/98–7/7/98	16.88–13.50	I	1,263,300	—
B/O	Global Telesystems Group Inc	GTS	S	793,634	7/22/98–7/2/98	43.34	I	4,849,714	—
B/O	Global Telesystems Group Inc	GSTRF	3	—	7/6/98	—	D	130,000	—
B/O	Ortec Intl Com	ORTC	B	68,800	6/30/98–6/2/98	20.13–18.00	I	1,249,000	—
—	Earthlink Network Inc	ELNK	13D	—	6/23/98	—	—	1,095,555	9.06
B/O	Earthlink Network Inc	ELNK	PS	52,480	6/23/98	57.00	D	126,489	—
B/O	Earthlink Network Inc	ELNK	PS	336,200	6/23/98	57.00	I	878,766	—
—	Ortec Intl Com	ORTC	13D	—	6/23/98–5/29/98	—	—	1,233,200	21.03
—	Digital Impact Inc Del Com	DIGI	13G	—	6/10/98	—	—	4,963,300	4.18
B/O	Earthlink Network Inc	ELNK	S	35,576	6/5/98	45.00	D	—	—
B/O	Earthlink Network Inc	ELNK	S	241,514	6/5/98	45.00	I	—	—
—	Earthlink Network Inc	ELNK	13D	—	6/5/98	—	—	1,484,235	12.28
B/O	Ortec Intl Com	ORTC	B	117,500	5/29/98–5/4/98	22.00–18.75	I	1,180,200	—
—	Ortec Intl Com	ORTC	13D	—	5/28/98–5/8/98	—	—	1,172,800	20
—	IRSA Inversiones Y GDR	IRS	13D	—	5/8/98–3/20/98	—	—	36,456,776	19.1
—	Ortec Intl Com	ORTC	13D	—	5/7/98–4/9/98	—	—	1,082,100	18.76
B/O	Ortec Intl Com	ORTC	B	77,100	4/30/98–4/2/98	20.50–18.25	I	1,062,700	—
—	US Satellite Broadcstng Inc	USSB	13D	—	4/30/98–4/7/98	—	—	362,100	1.55
—	Earthlink Network Inc	ELNK	13D	—	4/9/98–3/25/98	—	—	1,761,325	15.27
—	Ortec Intl Com	ORTC	13D	—	4/8/98–3/19/98	—	—	999,600	17.33
—	US Satellite Broadcstng Inc	USSB	13D	—	4/6/98–3/20/98	—	—	6,540,050	47.56
B/O	Ortec Intl Com	ORTC	B	161,800	3/31/98–3/2/98	19.69–13.75	I	985,600	—
—	US Satellite Broadcstng Inc	USSB	13D	—	3/19/98–3/3/98	—	—	6,887,650	29.57
—	Ortec Intl Com	ORTC	13D	—	3/18/98–1/30/98	—	—	930,300	16.13

(continued)

FIGURE 5.3 *(Continued)*

Title	Company	Ticker	Trans Type	Shares Traded	Trans Date(s)	Trans Price(s)	D/I Own	Total Hldgs	% Owned
—	Extended Stay Amer Inc	ESA	13D	—	3/6/98	—	—	4,200,100	4.39
—	Inhale Therapeutic Sys	INHL	13D	—	3/6/98	—	—	750,000	4.91
—	Pharmacyclics Inc	PCYC	13D	—	3/6/98	—	—	600,000	4.9
—	Indigo N V Ord	INDG	13D	—	3/3/98	—	—	23,392,820	30.36
—	IRSA Inversiones Y GDR	IRS	13D	—	2/18/98–12/24/97	—	—	40,039,856	20.98
—	Seven Seas Pete Inc	SEV	13D	—	2/18/98–2/13/98	—	—	3,058,000	8.76
—	Earthlink Network Inc	ELNK	13D	—	2/10/98	—	—	1,940,602	16.9
—	Hain Food Group Inc	HAIN	13D	—	2/3/98–1/22/98	—	—	2,146,000	18.75
—	Nine West Group Inc	NIN	13D	—	2/3/98–1/28/97	—	—	—	—
—	Homeland Hldg Corp New	HMLD	13D	—	1/30/98–12/31/97	—	—	630,815	13.1
—	Igen Intl Com	IGEN	13D	—	1/29/98–1/12/98	—	—	1,346,349	8.7
—	Ortec Intl Com	ORTC	13D	—	1/27/98–1/6/98	—	—	817,800	14.2
—	Authentic Specialty Foods In	ASFD	13D	—	1/16/98–12/22/97	—	—	404,500	5.19
—	Ortec Intl Com	ORTC	13D	—	1/5/98–12/19/97	—	—	742,800	12.9

Transaction Type Codes: B=Form 4 Buy, S=Form 4 Sale, B*=Option-Related Form 4 Buy, JB=Non–Open-Market Form 4 Buy, JS=Non–Open-Market Form 4 Sale, 13D=Schedule 13D, 13G=Schedule 13G, 3=Form 3. Ownership Codes: D=direct, I=Indirect. For all other codes, see the full Key in Figure 3.2 on page 47.

they can be used to check the trading of investors like Warren Buffett, is given in Chapter 8.)

But it's not only well-known investors like Soros who are insiders in numerous entities. There are plenty of lesser-known professional investors with numerous large stakes in smaller companies (as Figure 5.2 showed) or professional board members with director positions in several companies. When checking the credentials of an insider, don't just look at the insider history of the company behind the stock you are researching to see if the insider you are analyzing has traded previously. There are sources (see Chapter 15) that allow you to find all the trades a person has undertaken at all the companies in which they are considered insiders.

Although an insider's trades at the particular company you are researching are the most important for assessing how well the insider has traded that stock previously, the insider's track record at other companies is certainly useful in determining the person's investing acumen. As shown in Figure 5.3, you can even see an insider selling one holding about the same time of buying another. This gives a good sense of how the insider feels about the relative value of his or her holdings. It also takes away the validity of the typical excuses insiders use when asked why they are selling. These excuses center around their needing to raise money for any number of reasons—sending a child to college, buying a house, and so on. If insiders buy one company's shares in the same time frame they sell another company's shares, they obviously didn't need to raise money for personal reasons.

NOTHING CAN MEAN SOMETHING

It can be disappointing to view the detailed Form 4 history of a company and see hardly any activity. But a lack of activity actually tells you something in most every instance.

If a stock has tanked and you think it has finally bottomed out, a lack of insider buying may be telling you there is still some downside. This would be particularly true if there had been some active buyers in the past. For these active buyers to have stepped up to the plate then but not now says a lot. Check with investor relations at the company to see if the old buyers are still with the company.

If a stock you own has doubled in price and you're wondering if you should start taking some profits, find out if insiders are selling. If not, maybe you should let at least some of your winning position ride. Take another look at the proxy, or call up the company and find out what amount of stock options insiders have and if they have vested. It would be an extremely rare and bullish sign if insiders weren't even exercising options after the stock rose so much.

A lack of activity can also help you confirm whether a merger or other major event is in the works. Most companies have internal compliance measures that keep their insiders from either buying or selling shares if a major corporate action—such as a merger—is being considered. As mentioned previously, there are generally more insiders selling than buying in any given company. Sometimes the selling is extremely constant as insiders exercise their options that vest little by little. If this steady selling suddenly dries up, the silence can speak volumes.

DON'T WASTE TIME WITH CONFLICTING DATA

When looking at the insider history of Form 4 transactions for a prospective investment, one often sees buys and sales occurring around the same time. As a general rule you should stop putting time into investigating a company in which buys and sales are occurring almost simultaneously and move on to the next one. Too many clear signals are out there to waste time trying to figure out the relative importance of each trade. The fact is that most companies don't have a strong positive or negative signal from insiders.

About the only time I will continue researching a company with conflicting trades is when the selling is an obvious exception to a significant pattern of buying.

When looking at the insider history of a stock you already own, don't be disappointed to see both buys and sales. Although this non-signal of sorts may not seem like useful information, at least know that insiders aren't running for the exits.

Chapter 5   AT A GLANCE

1. Clusters of trading activity are more significant than a single insider's activity.

2. Research the track record of the insiders who are trading.

3. A lack of insider trades can impart useful information.

4. Don't waste time with conflicting data.

6

Analyzing
Form 4 Transactions:
Other Considerations

INSIDERS TEND TO BE EARLY

Both academic and anecdotal evidence indicates that insiders are generally good at seeing the value in their respective companies but aren't particularly good market timers. In general, they tend to trade early. So it sometimes behooves investors to hold off and bide their time until the fundamentals of the company start indicating proof that the insiders' optimism was well placed. There's no sense holding "dead money" if you don't have to.

It can be particularly useful to wait after a "crash-and-buy" scenario in which a company's stock halves in price in one day because of some awful news, and the Form 4 data indicates that insiders bought in the midst of the tumult. Although the buys may seem prescient a year or two later, a beaten-down stock often moves sideways for months afterwards.

To assess whether a sell-off is overdone takes good ol'-fashioned fundamental analysis. If the stock crashed because of disappointing earnings, why did the company miss the target? Did it lose a contract or was there an internal manufacturing problem? Was the problem something management could have foreseen, and does this disappointment change your opinion of the people running the company? Most important, what are the prospects for getting earnings back on track, and what is the valuation of the down-and-out stock relative to the reduced expectations? The answers to these and other questions will

71

decide whether you think the stock is oversold or deservedly taken behind the barn and shot.

An excellent example of a crash-and-buy situation is shown in Figure 6.1. Callaway Golf traded for around $30 at the beginning of 1998, but by August, declining revenue growth and lower profit margins had caused the company to lose two-thirds of its market capitalization. Insiders were heavy buyers after shares gapped from the high to the low teens in July, and they bought still more when shares slumped to below $10 shortly thereafter.

If you had followed these insiders as soon as you saw the major buying clusters, you would have had the chance to cash out for a 50 percent or so profit within the first year. The insiders did call the bottom for their stock very well. But for most of that year, you would have held dead money. Callaway's stock went sideways more or less for a good eight months before finally making a serious upward move.

I was intrigued by the heavy buying at Callaway and did expect to take a position at some point. My analysis concluded that I should wait,

---

FIGURE 6.1 Insider History for Callaway Golf (NYSE: ELY)

Insider Name	Title	Trans Type	# of Shares	Trans Date(s)	Trans Price(s)	Total Holdings	D/I Own
Port, Frederick R.	DIR	B	8,700	11/13/98–11/14/98	11.30–11.31	30,300	D
Callaway, Ely	CB	B	100,000	11/12/98	11.14	857,746	I
Port, Frederick R.	DIR	B	2,000	9/4/98	9.63	2,000	I
Callaway, Ely	CB	B	100,000	9/1/98	9.94	757,631	I
Callaway, Ely	CB	JB	200,000	8/31/98	9.93	657,631	I
Kobayashi, Yotaro	DIR	B	2,700	8/17/98	12.62	2,700	I
Helmstetter, R. C.	SREXVP	B	100,000	8/3/98	12.25–12.13	366,500	I
Parker, Bruce A.	SREXVP	B	10,000	7/28/98	13.25	22,050	D
Rane, David	EX VP	B	1,400	7/27/98	13.69	9,928	D
Callaway, Ely	CB	B	100,000	7/24/98	13.25	457,631	I
Dye, Donald H.	PR	B	20,000	7/24/98	13.00	351,150	D
Port, Frederick R.	DIR	B	7,000	7/24/98	13.75	21,600	D
Schreyer, William A.	DIR	B	10,000	7/24/98	13.25	20,000	D
Yash, Charles J.	EX VP	B	1,000	7/24/98	13.13	13,873	D
Dye, Donald H.	PR	B	10,000	6/12/98	18.19	331,150	D

Transaction Type Codes: B=Form 4 Buy; S=Form 4 Sale; JB=Non-Open-Market Form 4 Buy.
Ownership Codes: D=Direct; I=Indirect. For all other codes, see the full key in Figure 3.2 on page 27.

however. I didn't see the stock going higher until the company had completed more of its restructuring and cost controls. Announcements at the time alluded to large write-offs expected in the fourth quarter—something that rarely makes investors jump for joy. Also, demand from Callaway's important Asian customers seemed unlikely to increase for the rest of 1998 as that region was still in the midst of a general recession.

I finally recommended Callaway at the end of February 1999, when I assessed that the worst was likely over for the company. This was a good seven months after it had come to my attention because of its insider buying. The stock started a serious ascent a month later.

Callaway is another illustration that stock prices don't go up or down because insiders buy or sell shares. They go up and down for more fundamental reasons. Insider buying is a valuable screen to determine which stocks to analyze further, but it should not necessarily be used to time your movements in and out of stocks. Insiders do tend to be good indicators of a likely stock-moving development, but they tend to be early with their actions.

DON'T PAY MUCH MORE THAN INSIDERS DID

One of the reasons insiders may tend to be early is their fear of liability. It would not do for insiders to buy shares just before they shoot upward or sell just before they tank. Shareholders, not to mention the SEC, might get the impression that the insiders knew about the material, nonpublic piece of information that caused the sharp movement of the stock.

This certainly does happen, however. Nearly every week you can see an instance when insiders seem to have uncannily good timing. In these cases, even the most timely insider data that money can buy may arrive too late. Sometimes a stock moves just days or weeks after insiders place their bets and before the Form 4 is filed at the SEC.

Activity like that shown in Figure 6.2 seems as though insiders could be accused of stretching the gray area between appropriately using their insiders' privilege and trading on material, nonpublic information. Apria Healthcare's shares had done nothing but sink for three years leading up to fall 1998. Some minor buying was done by insiders during that time, but much more selling was done—a very negative response in a weak stock that normally indicates the price hasn't hit bottom. At the end of October 1998 and through November, however, insiders started buying huge amounts of Apria stock, even as the company's debt rating

FIGURE 6.2 Insider History for Apria Healthcare (NYSE: AHG)

Insider Name	Title	Trans Type	# of Shares	Trans Date(s)	Trans Price(s)	Total Holdings	D/I Own	Date Entered
Higby, Lawrence M.	PR	B	2,000	12/1/98	6.50	10,000	D	1/12/99
Maney, John C.	EX VP	B	2,000	12/1/98	6.63	5,000	D	1/12/99
Maney, John C.	EX VP	B	2,000	11/30/98	6.94	3,000	D	1/12/99
Higby, Lawrence M.	PR	B	6,000	11/25/98–11/12/98	6.75–4.00	8,000	D	1/12/99
Holcombe, Robert S.	SR VP	B	100	11/20/98	6.00	200	I	4/23/99
Holcombe, Robert S.	SR VP	B	5,000	11/20/98	6.00	15,000	D	4/23/99
Batchelder, David H.	DIR	B	1,628,100	11/19/98–11/16/98	5.56–4.10	6,797,100	I	12/16/98
Koppes, Richard H.	DIR	B	500	11/19/98	5.88	1,500	D	5/5/99
Maney, John C.	EX VP	3	—	11/19/98	—	1,000	D	9/18/99
Whitworth, Ralph V.	DIR	B	1,628,100	11/19/98–11/16/98	5.56–4.10	6,797,100	I	12/16/98
Suda, George J.	SR VP	B	1,000	11/17/98	3.88	2,600	D	11/30/98
Batchelder, David H.	DIR	B	75,000	11/12/98–11/11/98	4.28–4.40	75,000	D	12/16/98
Batchelder, David H.	DIR	B	27,100	10/26/98	3.91	5,169,000	I	12/16/98
Carter, Philip L.	CEO	B	15,000	10/26/98	3.77	25,000	D	10/29/98
Higby, Lawrence M.	PR	B	1,000	10/26/98	3.44	2,000	D	1/12/99
Holcombe, Robert S.	SR VP	B	5,000	10/26/98	3.63–3.50	10,000	D	4/23/99
Whitworth, Ralph V.	DIR	B	27,100	10/26/98	3.91	5,169,000	I	12/16/98

Transaction Type Codes: B=Form 4 Buy; 3=Form 3.
Ownership Codes: D=Direct; I=Indirect. For all other codes, see the full key in Figure 3.2 on page 27.

Source: BigCharts.com

was lowered by Standard and Poor's and the federal government was probing its pricing practices.

This large cluster of insider buying turned out to be a great signal amid indications that the company's turnaround efforts might bear fruit. The problem was that by the time we saw much of this purchasing, Apria's shares were 50 to 100 percent above the price at which the insiders had bought in. Shortly after insiders bought the shares, but before they filed their Form 4s at the SEC, several large Wall Street brokerage firms had issued extremely positive research reports on Apria. These positive reports, after years of largely negative financial developments, were a major cause of the spike in this microcap stock's price.

The positive reports might also explain why insiders were so ravenous to buy shares when they did. Most, if not all, of the high-ranking officials must have known that the large Wall Street houses were about to issue reports, given that many of them were certainly interviewed by the analysts themselves. They also would have had a reasonable idea of what the reports would say on the basis of the analysts' lines of questioning and subsequent comments. Finally, they certainly must have understood what positive reports would do to Apria's relatively tiny valuation.

Any knowledge of these imminent, positive research reports should have been considered material, nonpublic information as a result of Apria's market capitalization and troubled past. It should have prevented insiders from buying shares even if the company's trading window was open. Insiders could have plausibly denied that they knew the reports would be positive, but could they have denied knowing the positive prospects touted in the reports? I doubt it. Insiders certainly seemed to be taking advantage of the gray area between legal and illegal insider trading in this case.

At the same time, though, seeing stocks like Apria's get away is oddly refreshing. Insiders benefiting from their unfair advantage reminds us why we should look at Form 4 data in the first place. On some level, most insiders have information in their heads that is nonpublic. The big difference is the degree to which they act on it.

Some insiders seem to find a loophole that allows them to act mere days before their stock's price begins a quick ascent, while others trade well before a stock-moving event happens. Instead of eating my heart out about the stocks that got away, however, I focus on the ones that may pop next week, next month, or next year. Plenty of good investment ideas are usually generated each week by the insider filings that have appreciated less than 20 percent from where insiders bought in. That's the rule-of-thumb cutoff point I use, but I have made exceptions when fundamental analysis indicated there was likely much more gain to come.

It can also benefit you to keep an eye on some of the stocks that get away. It was easy to think you missed getting into Apria Healthcare in mid-December 1998 after its stock price doubled in a matter of weeks to $8 a share—and even more so as it continued rising to $12 a month later. But as often happens with soaring stocks, Apria's shares finally weakened in a bout of profit taking. They drifted down to below $8 again in both February and March—the same price level that you probably deemed too high last December because it was double what insiders had paid according to the Form 4s filed up to that time.

Having kept your eye on this company, however, you noticed that Form 4s filed in January indicated that insiders had continued buying during the recent run-up of the stock price. Some insiders purchased as high as $6.75 and $6.94 per share. Now the $8 price was well below 20 percent from where insiders had bought in—so much for Apria having gotten away. Keeping your eye on Apria's insiders should have prompted a purchase in February 1999 at around $8. The stock traded up to $20 a share just three months later.

Sometimes the mysterious price increase just after insiders purchase shares happens with no apparent news to justify it. Sometimes the insider purchases themselves are the news that sends a stock spiking skyward. This happens enough that some insiders appear to buy shares just to create a stir in their stock for public relations purposes.

If no fundamental change in a company's prospects occurred to justify a sudden stock price increase after insider buying, the price may very well decline again after the people who traded on rumors move on to speculate on another stock. Does the stock coming back to Earth mean that insiders were wrong? No. They were likely getting in early, as they tend to do. Do your fundamental research, and be patient. Perhaps the company's long-term prospects do justify how much its price had risen, but the shares just got ahead of themselves. You may get another chance to buy the stock around the same price insiders did, and you can ride the stock back up as it appreciates in a more orderly fashion back to where your fundamental analysis indicates it should.

PRICE ACTION AFFECTS INSIDER ANALYSIS

As you apply the rules of this book to reach your conclusions on how significant a company's insider history is, also incorporate the movement of the stock's price into your calculus. Was the stock's price rising or falling when insiders traded? Was the stock's price near its yearly highs or lows when insiders bought or sold? Both these aspects of the stock's price action affect how you interpret insider activity.

We all know how we can feel when stocks we own rise or fall dramatically. Insiders are not immune to such emotions. Look at the stock's price chart and note where insiders traded. Now, imagine how you would have to feel about the stock to trade like insiders did when they traded.

The most typical combinations of price action and insider activity you will see are

- insiders buying when their stock's price is trading near its 52-week lows, and
- insiders selling when their stock's price is trading near its 52-week highs.

Academic studies have determined that insiders tend to be value investors, so these patterns are as we would expect. Any deviation from these typical scenarios can speak volumes, however. What would induce insiders to buy their company's shares after they had already doubled in price over the past year? They must feel pretty confident that their company's stock has more upside potential. On the flip side, insiders selling shares that have fallen dramatically is an awful sign. These insiders are not showing much faith that their out-of-favor shares are going to recover soon.

I often note a stock's present price and 52-week range before delving into the insider history. I know that if the stock is hitting new 52-week highs and is up tremendously from its lows, I should be prepared to see insiders cashing in stock options and generally taking profits. If I don't see insiders taking profits, I interpret this as a positive signal—even though there is no actual buying. The fact that insiders aren't doing what you expect them (or any other normal investor) to do relays important information. This is a case where no insider activity actually sends potentially important investment information. If I own this stock and have a nice profit, I'm much more likely not to take profits if I also see insiders holding on to their positions.

Even better, of course, is if you see insiders buying after their stock has already climbed markedly (see Figure 6.4 for an example). Such activity tells me that insiders remain especially enthusiastic about their company's prospects. If I don't own this stock, I'll certainly investigate it further. If I own the stock already, I would consider averaging up and buying more.

If I see a stock scraping its yearly lows, I expect to see insiders buying if they think their stock has been oversold. If there are no insiders buying the beaten-down stock, I'll skip analyzing its turnaround prospects. There are enough laggards with insider buying, and my time is more likely to be better spent analyzing them. And if insiders are selling after a sharp price decline, watch out! In my experience these stocks should be avoided and could even be assessed as short-selling candidates.

This is not to say that any small amount of insider activity combined with certain price action is significant. You still have to assess the strength of the insider signal using my rules of thumb outlined previously. Screening for significant levels of insider activity combined with specific price-action criteria is a powerful tool, however, and an important aspect of the special screens outlined in Chapter 10.

THERE'S MORE BUYING AT SMALLER COMPANIES

My experience suggests that insider buying is more prevalent at mid-to-smaller capitalization companies than at large capitalization ones. I can't help but notice that after analyzing a day's or week's insider purchases to determine which companies to analyze further, there are more lesser-known, smaller-cap companies on the list than large cap, household names. There are several possible explanations for this. The first is that large caps make up only a small percentage of all the publicly traded firms in the United States.

As of the beginning of 2000, 72 percent of the 8,275 stocks followed by Market Guide, Inc., a Long Island, New York, financial data firm, had a market capitalization of $1 billion or less (a common definition of a small cap company). A whopping 64 percent of the companies in the database were even microcaps, with less than $250 million in total market value. So all things being equal, there should be fewer large caps with interesting insider trading activity.

Another explanation of why larger companies seem to have less open-market purchases by insiders is that stock option grants to insiders at larger companies tend to be worth more than those made at smaller firms. While option grants at a smaller firm may represent a larger percentage of the company's shares outstanding, the potential dollar value of the grants depends on the absolute movement of the company's share price. And because larger companies generally have higher share prices, their insiders have less need to buy shares in the open market even if they believe they are undervalued. They already have a huge windfall coming when their stock rises because of their option grants.

To illustrate, compare the incentives of two imaginary vice presidents during 1999: one at General Electric (NYSE: GE), whose stock rose 52 percent that year to $154.75 per share, and one at SonoSite (Nasdaq: SONO), whose stock rose 205 percent to $31.625 per share. Both executives have the same base salary, and both were issued options to purchase 40,000 shares of their firm's stock on January 1. Let's say that the total grant vests over four years, so each can exercise 10,000 options on January 1, 2000. Typically, the option exercise price is the market price of the stock on the day of the grant.

Even though SonoSite's shares far outperformed General Electric's, the GE vice president made significantly more money. He was able to buy 10,000 shares of GE from the company at $102.00 per share and sell them in the open market at the beginning of January 2000 for $154.75 per share: a profit of $527,500. The SonoSite executive was able to purchase 10,000 shares of SONO for $10.375 each and sell them for $31.625 each: a $212,500 profit.

Even if SonoSite's shares double to over $63 in the next three years (when the 40,000 options can all be exercised), the total award would be worth only $2.1 million. Hardly chump change, but only a fraction of what the General Electric vice president can expect. In fact, the GE executive can pull down that same $2.1 million even if the stock moves sideways for the next three years. And for every $25 each GE share rises over the vesting period (which is only a 16 percent increase from the $154.75 where each share ended 1999), it's another $1 million of risk-free profits in that vice president's pockets, assuming he doesn't exercise any of the 40,000 options until the end of the four years.

So when it comes to stock options, it is much more lucrative to have them in a good-performing company with a triple-digit share price than a fantastic-performing company with a single-digit share price. It is the incremental dollar increases in a share's price that are important to option holders, and it is much easier for a $100 stock to gain $10 than it is for a $2 stock to gain $10 (assuming both companies are equally well run with equally good prospects, of course). This reality isn't lost on insiders at firms with lower stock prices, who have a lot more incentive to actually pony up some money and buy shares in the open market if they think their company is undervalued.

These opinions are reflected in the insider histories of General Electric (Figure 6.3) and SonoSite (Figure 6.4). Even though GE is one of

FIGURE 6.3 Insider History for General Electric (NYSE: GE)

Insider Name	Title	Trans Type	# Of Shares	Trans Date(S)	Trans Price(s)	Total Holdings	D/I Own
Fresco, Paolo	DIR	S	273,928	11/19/98–11/6/98	92.50–88.00	20,000	D
Fresco, Paolo	DIR	S	113,072	10/31/98–6/23/98	93.97–87.47	293,928	D
Nardelli, Robert L.	SR VP	S	36,000	10/30/98	87.61	—	D
Nardelli, Robert L.	SR VP	B*	36,000	10/30/98	24.16	—	—
Nelson, Robert W.	VP	S	35,000	10/26/98–10/14/98	87.12–76.56	675	D
Nelson, Robert W.	VP	B*	35,000	10/26/98–10/14/98	31.94–24.16	—	—
Reiner, Gary M.	SR VP	S	47,000	10/26/98	85.88	19,188	D
Reiner, Gary M.	SR VP	S	47,000	10/26/98	85.88	19,188	D
McNerney, Walter J. JR	SR VP	B*	40,000	10/23/98	24.16	116,000	—
McNerney, Walter J. JR	SR VP	S	40,000	10/23/98	86.51	38,938	D
Rice, John G.	VP	S	20,000	10/23/98	85.75	6,577	D
Rice, John G.	VP	B*	20,000	10/23/98	15.94–13.84	—	—
Bunt, James R.	VP	S	25,000	10/21/98–10/14/98	83.70–74.31	10,000	D
Bunt, James R.	VP	B*	35,000	10/21/98–10/14/98	31.94–24.16	—	—
Fresco, Paolo	DIR	S	98,396	10/21/98–10/16/98	84.67–83.25	—	D
Dammerman, Dennis D.	VCB	S	97,500	10/14/98	87.28	96,779	D
Dammerman, Dennis D.	DIR	B*	97,500	10/14/98	25.50–23.13	1,825,000	—
Trotter, Lloyd G.	SR VP	S	30,000	7/17/98	96.14	18,205	D
Trotter, Lloyd G.	SR VP	B*	30,000	7/17/98	25.50	—	—
Immelt, Jeffrey R.	SR VP	B*	8,000	7/15/98	13.84	42,152	—
Michelson, Gertrude G.	DIR	S	6,000	7/15/98	93.74	—	D
Michelson, Gertrude G.	DIR	B*	6,000	7/15/98	15.56	—	—
Rice, John G.	VP	S	1,500	7/14/98	94.63	6,577	D
Dammerman, Dennis D.	VCB	S	20,000	6/24/98	89.63	96,779	D
Fresco, Paolo	DIR	S	50,000	4/30/98	85.19–85.13	170,396	D
Fresco, Paolo	VCB	B*	50,000	4/30/98	25.50	170,396	—
Calloway, D. Wayne	DIR	B*	18,000	4/13/98	21.53–18.81	22,000	—
Immelt, Jeffrey R.	SR VP	B*	5,000	4/12/98	13.84	34,200	—
Nardelli, Robert L.	SR VP	S	35,000	2/10/98	78.50	19,632	D
Nardelli, Robert L.	SR VP	B*	35,000	2/10/98	25.50	—	—
Immelt, Jeffrey R.	SR VP	B*	11,000	2/9/98	14.88–13.84	34,200	—
Rhodes, Frank H.T.	DIR	S	6,000	2/9/98	77.00	800	D
Rhodes, Frank H.T.	DIR	B*	6,000	2/9/98	12.16	—	—
Sigler, Andrew C.	DIR	S	18,000	2/4/98	77.25	8,000	D
Michelson, Gertrude G.	DIR	S	6,000	2/2/98	77.69	—	D
Michelson, Gertrude G.	DIR	B*	6,000	2/2/98	12.16	—	—

Insider Name	Title	Trans Type	# Of Shares	Trans Date(S)	Trans Price(s)	Total Holdings	D/I Own
Bunt, James R.	VP	S	15,000	1/27/98	76.69	—	D
Bunt, James R.	VP	B*	15,000	1/27/98	25.50	—	—
Nelson, Robert W.	VP	S	15,000	1/27/98	75.94	675	D
Nelson, Robert W.	VP	B*	15,000	1/27/98	25.50	—	—

Transaction Type Codes: B=Form 4 Buy; S=Form 4 Sale; B*=Option-Related Form 4 Buy.
For all other codes, see the key in Figure 3.2 on page 27.

FIGURE 6.4 Insider History for SonoSite (Nasdaq: SONO)

Insider Name	Title	Trans Type	# of Shares	Trans Date(s)	Trans Price(s)	Total Holdings	D/I Own
Sarti, Dennis A.	DIR	B	3,000	9/3/99	25.75	3,000	I
Goodwin, Kevin M.	CEO	B	2,000	8/12/99	19.13	14,000	D
Gusdorf, David	VP	B	1,500	8/10/99	17.75–17.56	1,500	I
Cramer, Kirby L.	DIR	B*	2,832	6/18/99	9.41–2.82	—	—
Parzybok, William G.Jr	DIR	B	4,000	6/1/99	18.25	7,000	D
Seaton, Donald F.	CFO	B	500	5/28/99	17.88	4,500	D
Sarti, Dennis A.	DIR	B	2,000	5/19/99	19.69	22,000	D
Sarti, Dennis A.	DIR	B	2,000	5/19/99	19.69	22,000	I
Quistgaard, Jens U.	VP	B	1,000	5/11/99	16.66	1,000	I
Cramer, Kirby L.	DIR	B	10,000	5/7/99	15.38	39,000	D
Guisinger, Allen	OFF	B	1,400	4/30/99	14.81	1,400	I
Pfeffer, Jeffrey	DIR	B	700	11/13/98–11/4/98	6.50	5,800	D
Parzybok, William G. Jr	DIR	B	3,000	11/10/98	7.19	3,000	D
Sarti, Dennis A.	DIR	B	20,000	11/2/98–8/31/98	6.88–5.75	20,000	I
Pfeffer, Jeffrey	DIR	B	100	10/20/98	5.88	5,100	D
Goodwin, Kevin M.	CEO	B	2,000	9/24/98–9/4/98	5.88–4.75	12,000	D
Seaton, Donald F.	CFO	B	1,000	9/11/98	5.52	4,000	D
Seaton, Donald F.	CFO	B	2,000	8/13/98	6.88	3,000	D
Fritzky, Edward V.	DIR	B	1,000	7/28/98	6.73	1,000	D
Pfeffer, Jeffrey	DIR	B	2,000	7/28/98–7/9/98	7.25–7.00	5,000	D
Pfeffer, Jeffrey	DIR	B	2,000	5/5/98	8.00	3,000	D
Pfeffer, Jeffrey	DIR	B	1,000	4/28/98	8.13	1,000	D
Goodwin, Kevin M.	CEO	B	10,000	4/13/98	9.13	10,000	D

Transaction Type Codes: B=Form 4 Buy; S=Form 4 Sale; B*=Option-Related Form 4 Buy.
For all other codes, see the key in Figure 3.2 on page 27.

the largest publicly traded U.S. companies with 293,000 employees all over the world, not one insider purchased shares in the open market during 1998 (only one did in 1999). It's hard to fathom that none of the insiders at this massive firm had an inkling about the prospects for GE's stock in 1999. The more likely explanation for the lack of buying is, as I've explained, that many insiders no doubt felt good about the prospects but felt they had enough options to participate on the upside.

This isn't to say that no employees at GE bought shares. Out of the hundreds of thousands of people working at GE, there may indeed have been hundreds of employees who did buy shares in the company. They just weren't classified as insiders by the SEC's definition and didn't have to file a Form 4. By contrast, tiny SonoSite, with a market capitalization of only $50 million at the beginning of 1999, had plenty of insiders buying and no insiders selling during both 1998 and 1999. Interesting, considering that the company's stock price tripled during 1999 to over $30 a share. It seems that the $20 dollar increase in the firm's price wasn't enough to allow the insiders here to simply reap the risk-free profits of their options over the next few years and retire wealthy. During 1999, these insiders were actually buying more shares at higher prices than those they had previously purchased.

This type of averaging up by insiders is an excellent indication that whatever prospects have propelled a stock in the past may continue. But because of the way stock options at well-run firms with high share prices dampen the tendency of insiders there to purchase in the open market, we rarely see this very positive insider pattern in larger companies.

INSIDER ACTIVITY IS NOT A TECHNICAL INDICATOR

This major point I have stated before, but it is worth repeating: Insider activity should not be considered a technical indicator. You should not blindly buy a stock only because insiders do, and you certainly shouldn't bail out only because you see a lot of insiders selling.

I have received extremely misleading direct mail pieces marketing one of the insider-oriented newsletters available that touts insider data as the closest thing to a perfect indicator around. It's absolute rubbish. I feel strongly that insider trading data should be used as a first screen for picking stocks and a flag for further investigation in stocks that you already own—not a technical indicator.

The reason for this stance is obvious: *Insiders can be wrong!* Figure 6.5 shows just one glaring example. The buying cluster at Sun Healthcare during August 1998 was significant enough for me to investigate its stock further. Four insiders had purchased nearly $1.2 million worth of the shares at higher prices than the stock was presently trading. Furthermore, Tweedy Brown & Co., a well-respected money management firm, had also been adding to its position.

Sun Healthcare Group is a provider of long-term care services, including nursing, subacute care, and therapy. This whole industry was under a cloud because of changing government regulation of how much Medicare would pay for certain services, and Sun had added to its own misery by making a bad acquisition in 1997. Still, the firm appeared well placed in an industry that could be expected to grow as the baby boomers were beginning to hit retirement age. The downside risk of investing also appeared to be limited. Trading for $5.56 per share in November 1998, the company was valued at 0.5 times book value, 0.1 times sales, 6.9 times fiscal 1998 earnings-per-share estimates, and 5.2 times fiscal 1999 estimates. Even so, we limited our downside by setting a stop loss at $4.25.

Both the insiders and I were extremely wrong. Six months after insiders had bought in so confidently and two months after we had recommended the stock, the stock fell through the conservative stop loss

---

FIGURE 6.5 Insider History for Sun Healthcare (NYSE: SHG)

Insider Name	Title	Trans Type	# of Shares	Trans Date(s)	Trans Price(s)	Total Holdings	D/I Own
Noonan, Kenneth	SR VP	S	880	4/16/99	0.69	—	D
Woltil, Robert D.	CFO	S	15,677	11/20/98	5.75	44,600	D
Tolbert, James R. III	DIR	B	3,000	9/9/98	9.31	7,564	D
Turner, Andrew L.	CEO	B	25,000	8/31/98	9.00–8.88	327,267	I
Bingaman, John E.	DIR	B	3,500	8/28/98	8.88	149,027	D
Karkomi, Zev	DIR	B	100,000	8/28/98	8.98	146,546	D
McInteer, Warren H.	VP	B	318	8/28/98	9.13	318	I
McInteer, Warren H.	VP	B	3,875	8/28/98	9.13–8.94	3,875	D
Silverman, Lois E.	DIR	B	1,000	3/4/98	19.38	3,704	D
Schelling, Warren C.	DIR	B	2,000	3/4/97	14.13	2,000	D

Transaction Type Codes: B=Form 4 Buy; S=Form 4 Sale; B*=Option-Related Form 4 Buy.
For all other codes, see the key in Figure 3.2 on page 27.

we had set. Government regulation of the industry hurt more than anyone expected, and Sun (along with other peers) had to take massive write-offs. Sun was particularly hard hit. It declared bankruptcy in October 1999, and its shares were last seen trading for a few pennies each.

The fact that insiders can be wrong is one of the reasons I also shy away from turning the various trades of a company into a single quantitative measure. There are a few services that have an insider index or ranking, whereby a clever programmer has downloaded years' worth of transactions into a database and crunched them together with recent trades. The result: a neat little number that rates a company's stock as attractive or not based on its insiders' activity.

I view these quantitative systems as too clever by half. As I have explained previously, screening out the noise in the data and doing some additional investigation is necessary to come to a decent determination of whether activity is significant. A computer can certainly screen out option-related and other non-open-market trades because they are obviously indicated in the electronic record of an insider's trade. Determining if there were bad clusters of activity is a bit more involved, however, and checking the credentials of individual insiders requires even more subjective reasoning over objective calculation.

And what of the problem of insiders often acting early? To assess whether a stock is dead money for the next six months takes good ol'-fashioned fundamental analysis and scrutiny of its recent trading patterns. This isn't to say that I believe in efficient markets and that technical indicators don't work. Too often I have seen that it doesn't pay to fight the tape, and I do use technical analysis of a stock's price chart to try and enter and exit the shares better. But while this type of technical analysis merely gives a nod to the influence of the supply and demand of a company's stock on its short-term price movements, insider data doesn't have such a direct effect.

The fact is, stock prices don't go up or down because insiders buy or sell shares; they go up and down because of revenue trends, changes in profit margins, manufacturing efficiencies, distribution issues, and any other factor that affects the company's cash flow, earnings, and financial condition. Insider data is an excellent signal that the people who should know think one or more of these stock-moving events will happen, but it is just a flag for further investigation, not a technical indicator.

The quantitative analysts establishing various insider-ranking systems have undoubtedly back-tested their block boxes and have proof that their system works. But the problem with the rating systems in practice is the same as that of trying to use the large body of academic research that shows insider data is a valuable tool: Rating systems work on generalities, whereas most individual investors need specifics.

Academic research may show that stocks with Form 4 purchases by several executives tend to outperform stocks with purchases by only one insider. But while this helps narrow your group of potential new investments, you still may end up with 100 or more stocks to choose from in any given month.

The same problem arises with the ranking systems. Back-testing may very well show that all the stocks with a system's insider ranking of 1 outperform the market. But if there are presently 100 stocks with that ranking, you still need to figure out which specific stocks to invest in. As a group, these 100 stocks may outperform, but they won't all outperform.

Institutional investors may be able to make use of such ranking systems because they can afford to put money into all 100 stocks, but individuals usually need to narrow their choices to a specific handful. Fundamental analysis will have to be the final winnowing tool whether you gather your population of potential investments via some computer-ranking system or via the hands-on process I've laid out.

With the amount of value-added insider data available via the Internet (see Chapter 15), it is already easy enough to find a quality group of potential investments without using a block box. You shouldn't feel that some rating system is going to beat you in determining that a stock is worth investing in. For while the techie with the block box is making sure all his data is accurate for using to perform calculations, you could already be doing what's really important: reading the company's financial statements and talking to management.

Chapter **6**   *AT A GLANCE*

1. Insiders tend to be early.

2. Don't pay much more than insiders did.

3. Price action affects insider analysis.

4. There's more buying at smaller companies.

5. Insider activity is not a technical indicator.

7

Analyzing Form 144 Transactions

I've already explained in Chapter 4 that Form 4 buying is easier to interpret than Form 4 selling. Form 144s, indicating intent to sell, are far weaker than even Form 4 sales in terms of revealing investors' feelings about their firm's shares. This data stream is still worth tracking, however, for the same reason following Form 4 sales is. You certainly get a sense from the data of how interested people who should know the firm are in taking their money out of its stock. Even though there are plenty of good reasons for those in the know to sell (also explained in Chapter 4), you may sometimes be able to identify alarming patterns that raise a red flag.

LIMITATIONS

The limitations of Form 144 data as harbingers of future sales are numerous, however, and I cringe every time I see the data presented as "planned sales" as they are on several mass-market Internet sites. It's much too simplistic a description that generates more confusion than enlightenment.

First of all, a Form 144 does not commit the filer to sell the shares indicated. Technically, it is only a notice of the filer's intent to sell restricted shares. If the shares are not sold within a three-month period, another Form 144 must be filed to amend the previous one. To people who think of 144s only as planned sales, this regulation can lead to the misconception that the same person is selling the same amount of shares every quarter, when actually no sales occurred.

How can you know if the shares indicated on Form 144 were sold? If the person filing the 144 is an insider by the SEC's definition, you'll see a Form 4 filed that documents the sale. But not all holders of restricted stock are insiders. The only way you'll know if noninsiders really sold the shares indicated on their 144 is if you don't see an amendment within a few months, and by then the information will basically be useless.

Another basic of 144s worth repeating is that only shareholders with *unregistered shares* have to file the form. The number of unregistered shares issued by a firm is a small number compared with total shares outstanding. Unregistered shares are also usually held by venture capitalists, a company's founders, or individuals who received the stock as part of a buyout by the company. Often, and particularly in the case of venture capitalists, this restricted stock was obtained at prices well below the present market price, and the decision to sell it is based on a venture fund's bylaws instead of on an in-depth analysis of the equity's future prospects.

I don't mean to discourage investors from viewing 144s—far from it. But it is important to understand the potential limitations of the data. The good news is that, practically speaking, most shares indicated on a Form 144 *are* sold soon after the filing. Often the 144 is even filed at the same time the shares are sold. After all, it doesn't make much sense for a person (or, as usually happens with Form 144s, the person's stockbroker) to undertake this annoying paperwork if the shares aren't going to be sold. Still, the fact that most shares indicated on a Form 144 are already sold by the time you see the form negates the data as a useful harbinger of future selling volume. Instead of terming them *planned sales* by the mass-market Web sites, it would actually be more accurate to term Form 144s *unrestricted shares already sold.* But better still is to just call the transaction a Form 144 and explain it a bit as I have done here.

Looking at the insider history for Progressive Software in Figure 7.1, it's easy to match the share amounts of most of the 144s and Form 4 sales. The date the filings were entered into our database is also indicated in the Date Entered column, which clearly shows that the sales occurred before the public saw the 144.

FIGURE 7.1 Insider History for Progress Software (Nasdaq: PRGS)

Insider Name	Title	Trans Type	# of Shares	Trans Date(s)	Trans Price(s)	Total Holdings	D/I Own
Alsop, Joseph W.	PR	S	3,500	1/24/00	26.00	811,390	D
Alsop, Joseph W.	OFF	144	3,500	1/24/00	—	—	—
Bergantino, Jennifer J	VP	S	10,416	1/14/00	50.54	3,074	D
Bergantino, Jennifer J	OFF	144	10,416	1/14/00	—	—	—
Benton, David H. JR	VP	S	2,000	12/28/99	55.00	1,058	D
Robertson, Norman R.	CFO	S	4,000	12/28/99– 12/22/99	59.00–50.69	10,255	D
Robertson, Norman R.	OFF	144	1,000	12/22/99	—	—	—
Alsop, Joseph W.	PR	S	70,000	12/20/99	56.66–53.53	407,445	D
Alsop, Joseph W.	OFF	144	70,000	12/20/99	—	—	—
Reidy, Richard D.	VP	S	20,000	11/19/99	39.88	539	D
Reidy, Richard D.	OFF	144	20,000	11/19/99	—	—	—
Robertson, Norman R.	CFO	S	20,000	11/15/99– 11/1/99	39.00–33.50	10,255	D
Robertson, Norman R.	OFF	144	5,000	11/15/99	—	—	—
Alsop, Joseph W.	DIR	S	91,500	11/12/99– 11/4/99	37.50–36.54	477,445	D
Alsop, Joseph W.	OFF	144	40,000	11/12/99	—	—	—
Alsop, Joseph W.	OFF	144	18,000	11/5/99	—	—	—
Robertson, Norman R.	OFF	144	5,000	11/5/99	—	—	—
Alsop, Joseph W.	OFF	144	33,500	11/4/99	—	—	—
Ireland, David G.	VP	S	10,000	11/4/99– 11/3/99	36.00–34.00	1,699	D
Robertson, Norman R.	OFF	144	5,000	11/1/99	—	—	—
Alsop, Joseph W.	DIR	S	30,000	10/26/99	33.25	571,945	D
Alsop, Joseph W.	OFF	144	30,000	10/26/99	—	—	—

Transaction Type Codes: B=Form 4 Buy; S=Form 4 Sale; B*=Option-Related Form 4 Buy.
For all other codes, see the key in Figure 3.2 on page 27.

You may be confused about the transaction date for the 144 filings. How can there be a transaction date when the 144, by definition, is a form indicating that a sale may occur in the future? The answer is that on Form 144, the filer is requested to state the date on which the sale is likely to occur, and most electronic services simply put the date in the Transaction Date column used by the Form 4s. Yes, this is technically incorrect, but it shouldn't throw you off now that you know.

Interestingly, the transaction dates and the dates entered in Figure 7.1 also point to the fact that Form 144s appear to have been filed on the same day the stock was sold. This is indicated by the fact that the transaction dates for most of the Form 144s are the same dates as those of the corresponding sales.

So the Form 144s in Figure 7.1 weren't real harbingers of future selling given that the shares were already sold by the time the 144 reached the public. But at least it was easy to see that the 144 stock registered was actually sold, which is not always the case.

In the various codes the SEC uses for filers to indicate their relation to the company there is a U, which stands for unknown, and an N, which means none. Filers using these codes on their Form 144 can certainly fill out a Form 4 to record the sale if they want. The SEC doesn't mind if people fill out more forms than they legally must (I also mentioned that unnecessary form filing in Chapter 3 produces duplicate records). But why would filers do the paperwork if they don't have to?

Corporate Express's insider history (see Figure 7.2) shows numerous Form 144s that were not followed by Form 4 sales. Looking at the titles of the Form 144 filers makes it obvious why: Most of the filers have no active title and are not insiders by the SEC's definition and therefore don't have to file a Form 4 when they sell the restricted shares. Corporate Express, in fact, had been on an acquisition binge over the past few years, and the filers were people who had accepted restricted shares as part of their company's buyouts.

PRIMARY CONSIDERATIONS

Lest I have deflated your opinion of Form 144s altogether, know that I do look at them. Although factors mitigate the use of Form 144s as specific harbingers of future selling pressure and future Form 4 filings, they are still useful to look at. They indicate that somebody has sold, or is expected to sell, shares. That's useful information to at least keep in the back of your mind when researching a new investment idea or following a stock you own.

I use Form 144s as an adjunct to my analysis of Form 4 sales. After identifying a particularly onerous pattern of insider selling, I'll look at the Form 144s for an indication that the selling pressure might continue. When looking at the 144s, I keep in mind an abbreviated list of the four rules of thumb used to analyze Form 4s:

1. Transactions by hands-on insiders are more important than transactions by other insiders.

FIGURE 7.2 Insider History for Corporate Express (Nasdaq: CEXP)

Insider Name	Title	Trans Type	# of Shares	Trans Date(s)	Trans Price(s)	Total Holdings	D/I Own
Argyropoulos, James P	DIR	S	79,750	12/31/98–11/30/98	6.30–4.90	1,111,267	I
Argyropoulos, J. (TR 8/91)	DIR	144	78,750	12/31/98	—	—	—
McDowell, Marietta J.	—	144	500	12/30/98	—	—	—
Hoffman, Mark	PR	B	28,500	12/11/98	5.94	38,925	D
McDowell, Marietta J.	—	144	2,000	12/2/98	—	—	—
MacDonald, Ida B.	—	144	1,684	12/1/98	—	—	—
Duncan, Russell L.	—	144	54,400	11/13/98	—	—	—
Mastracchio, Nicholas	—	144	2,000	10/5/98	—	—	—
Duffy, Alicia D.	—	144	705	9/29/98	—	—	—
Toma, Michael T.	—	144	1,187	9/22/98	—	—	—
Glasheen, Ronald S.	—	144	1,207	9/1/98	—	—	—
Stewart, Jeffrey M.	—	144	2,234	—	—	—	—
Duncan, Russell L.	—	144	54,400	8/7/98	—	—	—
Andreas, Barbara	—	144	584	8/4/98	—	—	—
Bates, Warren E.	—	144	3,570	8/4/98	—	—	—
Kelley, Frederick Jr	—	144	2,422	8/4/98	—	—	—
Ashabranner, Jack D. II	P	144	35,000	7/28/98	—	—	—
Hallenbeck, Frank F.	—	144	3,496	—	—	—	—
Wood, Charles L.	—	144	735	7/21/98	—	—	—
Hersh, David	—	144	16,257	6/18/98	—	—	—
Brown, Clarence E. Sr	—	144	2,097	6/16/98	—	—	—
Dolke, Robert	—	144	4,859	6/16/98	—	—	—
Cea, Francis M.	—	144	569	6/9/98	—	—	—
Ives, Michael S.	—	144	724	6/9/98	—	—	—
Levy, Lewis E.	—	144	17,420	—	—	—	—
Cybulski, Judith A.	—	144	1,305	6/2/98	—	—	—
Kraham, Michael R.	—	144	3,282	6/2/98	—	—	—
Gottung, Carol Ann	—	144	3,095	5/19/98	—	—	—
Greenquist, Roy A.	P	144	7,112	5/18/98	—	—	—
Cole, John R.	—	144	3,479	5/12/98	—	—	—
Rafferty, Brian J.	—	144	1,336	5/12/98	—	—	—

Transaction Type Codes: B=Form 4 Buy; S=Form 4 Sale; B*=Option-Related Form 4 Buy.
For all other codes, see the key in Figure 3.2 on page 47.

2. Size matters.
3. Check credentials.
4. Look for clusters of activity.

(Please see the discussions in Chapters 4 through 6 for how these rules are put into practice.)

Chapter 7   AT A GLANCE

1. Form 144s are not perfect harbingers of future sales.
   - Filers do not have to sell but usually already have.
   - Not all filers are insiders.

2. Primary considerations are the following:
   - Transactions by hands-on insiders are more important than transactions by other insiders.
   - Size matters.
   - Check credentials.
   - Look for clusters of activity.

8

Analyzing
Smart Money Filings

I term the SEC's Schedule 13D, Form 13F, and Schedule 13G *smart money* filings because they are filed by wealthier individuals and larger institutions that can reasonably be assumed to have access to better investment information regarding the company by virtue of their monetary resources. Schedule 13Ds are filed by holders of 5 percent or more of any class of a company's shares. Anyone filing a Form 13F is an investment manager with at least $100 million under management. Schedule 13Gs are filed by such entities as banks, broker/dealers, insurance companies, and other passive shareholders with 5 percent or more of a company's shares.

The key to using these forms for making investment decisions is to determine how smart the filers have been in the past. Just because they can afford more research resources than individual investors doesn't necessarily mean that they use them well. Relating this back to the rules of thumb for analyzing Form 4 data, the section of checking insiders' credentials (in Chapter 5) is what you should use to organize your assessment of how well these filers have performed in the past.

Past performance is not a guarantee of future results, as the well-worn disclaimer of mutual fund companies warns, but it's all we have to judge by. As it turns out, according to numerous studies, statistics show that investment managers who have done well in the past year tend to outperform in the next as well.

Because checking the credentials of the persons or organizations filing the smart money forms is so important, we can be thankful that they tend to have a long history to analyze. Money managers and other large shareholders most always own numerous—sometimes hundreds—of positions at a time. Combine this fact with the number of years the filer has been trading, and the number of present and past positions to use in assessing the investor's savvy can become overwhelming.

As it is with an insider with numerous Form 4 positions, it is the track record of the smart money filer in the specific stock you are interested in that is most important. If the filing is an initial position by the filer in the stock you're investigating, find out if the filer has a good track record investing in companies in the same industry. Also look at the investment approach the stock you're investigating seems to fit. If it seems to you to be a value play and you see a smart money form filed recently, check to see if the filer has a decent track record with past value stocks.

If you already have a handful of names of big investors whom you respect and may want to mimic, start your research by searching for them directly. They will likely have filed one or more of the three smart money forms besides any Form 4s you might see. Even well-considered money managers sometimes check out what other notables are doing. "We look at everything Warren Buffett buys," says John Spears, a principal at venerable New York money manager Tweedy Brown. "We think it would almost be a conceit not to."

Although Buffett does have Form 4 transactions over the past three years, most of the public domain data on what he owns is via the smart money forms. In fact, he and his investment vehicle have filled out every type of insider form covered in this book over the past three years, making him a good illustration of how the various forms should be used together.

Figure 8.1 lists all of Buffett's related transactions over the past three years and will be referred to at various times throughout this chapter. As you can see, some of the data seem to duplicate themselves across the filing types. But each filing type also adds some fresh information as well. You may also be surprised at how few filings Buffett has made. Not everybody concentrates their investments as much as Buffett does. Even fewer buy and hold as long as he does. Other lesser-known, but highly successful, large investors will have much more data to analyze than Buffett has.

Remember, however, that the information in the public domain does not represent all of Buffett's investments. He must file Form 4s only for

FIGURE 8.1 Insider Transactions by Warren Buffett

Insider Name	Title	Company	Ticker	Trans Type	Trans Date(s)	Trans Price(s)	D/I Own	% Owned
Buffett, Warren E.	B/O	Jones Apparel Group	JNY	B	2/28/00– 2/2/00	25.80– 20.68	I	—
Buffett, Warren E.	B/O	Great Lakes Chem Corp	GLK	B	2/11/00– 2/4/00	33.75– 31.67	I	—
Buffett, Warren E.	—	Bell Inds Inc	BI	13G	12/19/99	—	—	0.05
Buffett, Warren E. et al	—	Midamerican Energy Hldgs New	MEC	13D	10/14/99	—	—	6.2
Buffett, Warren E.	CB	Berkshire Hathaway 'A' Del	BRK.AA	JS	8/30/99	0.00	I	—
Buffett, Warren E.	B/O	MGI Properties	MGI	B	5/26/99– 5/10/99	27.88– 27.56	D	—
Buffett, Warren E.	B/O	MGI Properties	MGI	B	4/21/99– 4/5/99	27.50– 27.00	D	—
Buffett, Warren E.	B/O	MGI Properties	MGI	B	3/31/99	27.66	D	—
Buffett, Warren E.	B/O	MGI Properties	MGI	3	3/30/99	—	D	—
Buffett, Warren E.	CB	Berkshire Hathaway 'A' Del	BRK.AA	JS	12/3/98	0.00	D	—
Buffett, Warren E.	CB	Berkshire Hathaway 'A' Del	BRK.AA	JS	12/3/98	0.00	D	—
Buffett, Warren E.	—	MGI Properties	MGI	13G	10/23/98	—	—	5.08
Buffett, Warren E.	B/O	American Express Co	AXP	B	10/7/98– 10/1/98	72.92– 71.17	I	—
Buffett, Warren E. et al	—	General Re Corp	GRN	13D	6/19/98	—	—	19.6
Buffett, Warren E. et al	—	Berkshire Hathaway 'A' Del	BRK.AA	13D	6/19/98	—	—	43.2
Buffett, Warren E.	—	USAir Airways Group	U	13G	5/11/98	—	—	3.79
Buffett, Warren E.	—	General Dynamics Corp	GD	13G	2/13/98	—	—	6.3
Buffett, Warren E.	—	USAir Airways Group	U	13G	2/13/98	—	—	9.21
Buffett, Warren E.	—	Wells Fargo & Co New Com	WFC	13G	2/13/98	—	—	7.8
Buffett, Warren E.	CB	Berkshire Hathaway 'B' Del	BRK.B	JS	12/2/97	0.00	I	—
Buffett, Warren E.	CB	Berkshire Hathaway 'A' Del	BRK.AA	JS	12/2/97	0.00	I	—
Buffett, Warren E. et al	—	Intl Dairy Queen Inc Cl B	INDQB	13D	10/21/97	—	—	31.2
Buffett, Warren E. et al	—	Salomon Smith Barney Inc	SB	13D	10/17/97	—	—	18.1
Buffett, Warren E. et all	—	Salomon Smith Barney Inc	SB	13D	9/24/97	—	—	17.8
Buffett, Warren E. et al	—	USAir Airways Group	U	13D	8/22/97	—	—	10.34
Buffett, Warren E. et al	—	USAir Airways Group	U	13D	8/15/97	—	—	10.41
Buffett, Warren E.	CB	Berkshire Hathaway 'A' Del	BRK.AA	JS	11/25/96	0.00	I	—
Buffett, Warren E.	CB	Berkshire Hathaway 'B' Del	BRK.B	JS	11/25/96	0.00	I	—

Insider Name	Title	Company	Ticker	Trans Type	Trans Date(s)	Trans Price(s)	D/I Own	% Owned
Buffett, Warren E. — et al		Salomon Smith Barney Inc	SB	13D	11/22/96	—	—	17.8
Buffett, Warren E. — et al		Salomon Smith Barney Inc	SB	13D	10/31/96	—	—	17.8
Buffett, Warren E.	B/O	Salomon Smith Barney Inc	SB	JB	10/29/96	0.00	I	—
Buffett, Warren E. — et al		Salomon Smith Barney Inc	SB	13D	9/12/96	—	—	17.6
Buffett, Warren E. — et al		USAir Airways Group	U	13D	5/6/96	—	—	13.41
Buffett, Warren E. — et al		Berkshire Hathaway 'A' Del	BRK.AA	13D	4/12/96	—	—	43.2
Buffett, Warren E. — et al		USAir Airways Group	U	13D	11/29/95	—	—	13.41
Buffett, Warren E. — et al		Salomon Smith Barney Inc	SB	13D	10/19/95	—	—	17.6
Buffett, Warren E. — et al		Geico Corp	GEC	13D	8/25/95	—	—	50.6

Transaction Type Codes: B=Form 4 Buy, S=Form 4 Sale, B*=Option-Related Form 4 Buy, JB=Non-Open-Market Form 4 Buy, JS=Non-Open-Market Form 4 Sale, 13D=Schedule 13D, 13G=Schedule 13G, 3=Form 3. Ownership Codes: D=direct, I=Indirect. For all other codes, see the full Key in Figure 3.2 on page 27.

owning stocks in companies in which he personally is considered by the SEC's definition to be an insider. His vehicle for filing Schedule 13Ds. "Buffett, Warren E. et al." may also own numerous other stocks— but less than 5 percent of their shares. Still, the information in the public domain is impressive and more than enough to give you, me, and Tweedy Brown's John Spears an eyeful.

SCHEDULE 13D

This SEC document is filed by holders of 5 percent or more of any class of a company's outstanding shares. When a person or entity first reaches the 5 percent ownership level, a 13D must be filed within ten days, and the intention of the acquisition (i.e., a passive investment or the beginning of an attempt to take over the company) must be indicated. Subsequent trades must be promptly stated on an amended 13D as long as the filer continues to own at least 5 percent.

Any investor or investment group that can afford to own 5 percent of a publicly traded company has a fair amount of money at its disposal, which presumably means it can afford better resources than an individual for analyzing a firm's prospects.

Schedule 13Ds were considered so useful in the 1980s that numerous financial and arbitrage firms stationed people in the SEC's public room (where all the insider data forms I discuss are first released to the public) to report 13D filings and amendments as soon as they were released. (See Chapter 13 for more about the SEC's public room.) Finding a 13D with the name Ivan Boesky or Carl Icahn on it before anyone else was like finding gold. The forms were only meant to be photocopied by the people stationed in the public room before passing them along, but many of the choice 13Ds (and Form 4s for that matter) disappeared into the pockets of individuals so that the information could be hoarded. Veterans of the SEC's public room recall fights breaking out over such dirty tricks.

To help reign in the mayhem, the SEC mandated in 1993 that 13Ds be filed electronically on its EDGAR system (see Chapter 13 for more details on EDGAR). Not only can anyone now see this information nearly as soon as the SEC gets it, but anyone can also do so from any computer in the world with an Internet connection. By equalizing access to Schedule 13Ds, EDGAR has also lessened their importance. Acting on 13D information before others was the key for arbitrageurs and other speculators to make money with it. That is now more difficult to do.

Another factor that has reduced the importance of the 13D is the advent of legal defenses put into place by many companies (so-called poison pills) to make them less attractive takeover targets. This has reduced hostile takeover activity as a whole. Also equalizing access to the potentially important corporate actions highlighted by a 13D is today's 24-hour business news on TV and radio. With all the nosey reporters around looking for a big story to break, the first information on corporate takeovers now often appears in the popular media instead of on an SEC filing.

But investors saving for retirement or a child's college tuition shouldn't be speculating on takeovers anyway, so the reduced importance of Schedule 13Ds for those purposes isn't a loss. These forms still provide insights to longer-term investors about how a large cross section of well-moneyed investors are behaving.

Looking at Buffett's Schedule 13D history, we see several important filings. He first went over the 5 percent ownership level (through his entity, Buffett, Warren E. et al.) in Midamerican Energy on 10/14/99, in General RE on 6/19/98, and in Dairy Queen on 10/21/97. You can tell this because the amendment number for these filings is coded 0, meaning they were initial filings. Buffett's vehicle most likely owned shares in all these entities before the initial 13Ds were filed, but there was no way to know that. Initial Schedule 13D filings by large, successful investors are definitely worth keeping your eye out for.

Other important intelligence garnered from his Schedule 13D history is that Buffett's entity picked up nearly 3.7 million more shares of Salomon Smith Barney on 10/17/97, while selling some shares of U.S. Air. In the fall of 1997, it was obvious to anyone looking at these filings which stock Buffett thought had better prospects.

Was Buffet correct? Well, the price of U.S. Air's stock did more than double in the next year after his last 13D filing to more than $80 a share, but at the beginning of the new millennium, it had fallen to nearly $20—below the mid-$30 level where it was in the fall of 1997. Salomon Smith Barney, on the other hand was purchased in November 1998 for more than 80 percent more than the price at which Buffet picked up his last position.

General RE was also acquired less than six months after Buffett's 13D was filed, but he didn't do as well with this position. It actually appears that he had a loss on the investment, even though there was a large spike in General RE's stock price in reaction to Buffett's filing. Buffett did better with his investments in Geico and Dairy Queen, both of which were also acquired.

You get a clear sense of Buffett's investing style. He obviously has an eye for value, considering the large percentage of buyout situations he seems to find. He also tends to buy and hold as well as concentrate his resources on relatively few investments. Also clear is that the mere announcement of Buffett's investing in a stock tends to make the stock jump. The dates of the release of his 13Ds covering his investments in General RE and MidAmerican Energy correspond with both stocks gapping up in price.

At the turn of the millennium, Buffett has taken some heat in the press about his underperforming the market averages recently, mainly because he hasn't invested heavily in companies within the now-hot technology sector. Seemingly unrepentant, his latest purchases of Jones Apparel Group and Great Lakes Chemical appear as value-based as ever. And despite the press questioning his recent performance, the announcement of these stakes also correspond with increases in the trading volume and share prices of both companies' stocks. The lesson: Buffett's actions are still watched and mimicked by many investors.

We've already learned quite a lot from looking at Buffett's Schedule 13Ds, but one of the most important bits of intelligence has yet to be mentioned. Buffett owns a large percentage of a company named Berkshire Hathaway (NYSE: BRK.A). What's more, he apparently has owned a piece of this company for a long time judging by the large number of Schedule 13D amendments he has filed. To most investors, Berkshire Hathaway is immediately recognizable as a Warren Buffett investment vehicle. But if you didn't know it, you would have after a minor amount of research. And once you did know, you would naturally have looked at the filings for Berkshire. We'll look at them ourselves in the next section of this chapter.

FORM 13F

Form 13Fs are quarterly SEC filings made by investment institutions with over $100 million under management. While 13Fs may not be as timely as Schedule 13Ds, they do have the advantage of revealing a complete picture of an institution's portfolio. Whether an institution owns 50 percent or 0.5 percent of a company's shares, you'll see the investment position on the 13F.

All of the big name money management firms have to file 13Fs. Boston-based Fidelity Management files under the institutional name of FMR Corporation. Janus Capital Corporation, Putnam Investment Management, Inc., Vanguard Group Inc., (The), TIAA CREF Investment Management, LLC—all are there. Look up their histories and see details of every position they own and how they traded that position over the past quarter. Some data sources have up to four quarters of data, which really gives you a window into how institutional thinking is changing.

Unfortunately, 13Fs don't break down the holdings of the filing institution by portfolio. So even though you know that the largest of FMR's 3,066 positions as of 12/31/99 is Microsoft and that the institution bought 17.4 million shares of this company in the fourth quarter of 1999, the form won't tell you how many of those shares were held and traded by FMR's flagship Magellan Fund or by any of the more than 150 other funds the institution operates. You therefore can't actually follow the exact trades of a particular portfolio manager using Form 13F data if the manager works for a larger institution. (This data is available separately via the SEC's Form N30D, which is filed semiannually and is based on the fiscal year of each mutual fund. I much prefer following Form 13Fs, however, because they are much more timely and comprehensive.) Even so, not being able to follow your favorite manager at Fidelity isn't such a horrible limitation nor is every institution as huge as Fidelity. There are also plenty of institutions that have only one fund. The 13F is as good as the fund-specific N-30D data in these cases.

The greatest limitation to Form 13Fs as far as I'm concerned is that average transaction prices are not reported on the forms. A stock's price can fluctuate substantially over a quarter's time, but the form doesn't even indicate the trade dates that would allow you to find the average price of the purchases or sales.

These limitations are not lost on the portfolio managers and money management institutions that fill out the 13F. Most investors have heard that some money managers undertake window dressing of their port-folios at a quarter's end so that managers are seen to own many of that quarter's winning stocks and none of the quarter's losers. Well, the Form 13F is one of the windows they dress. They do this by buying good-performing stocks near the quarter's end and selling the quarter's losers. On the 13F they fill out at quarter's end, they merely indicate that the trades occurred and the subsequent position. The manager would like the world to think that these trades were presciently made at the beginning of the quarter. Sometimes they actually may have been, but we don't know. A manager cannot hide bad performance, however, and no amount of window dressing will protect a bad money manager from the truth.

Buffett's previously mentioned investment vehicle, Berkshire Hath-away, is a Form 13F filer (see Figure 8.2), and the investment style of this insurance company already seems familiar now that we've looked at Buffett's Schedule 13Ds and Form 4 transactions. Berkshire tends to concentrate its money in relatively few positions, and it takes a buy-and-hold approach. Definitely no window dressing here.

Berkshire's portfolio could actually use some dressing up, though. With the exception of American Express, the performance of Berkshire's major investments has been less than stellar over the past two years. Like Buffett, Berkshire Hathaway also has not joined in the technology-investing frenzy that has rewarded so many other investment managers, and it has paid a short-term price. Anyone following Berkshire's lead has also no doubt underperformed the market recently. Buffett and his in-vestment vehicle are obviously long-term investors, however, and any-one mimicking them had better have the same patience.

Even Berkshire's patience appears to be lessening, however. Notice how many more transactions its portfolio had in the last quarter of 1999 than in the previous three quarters. Berkshire appears to be diversifying over more investment positions than previously, even if the newer positions continue to be those of a value investor instead of a technology investor.

FIGURE 8.2 Form 13F Filings of Berkshire Hathaway (NYSE: BRK.A)

Company	Ticker	Latest Report	Latest Quarter's Data					Previous Quarter's Data				Date from 2 Quarters Ago				Data from 3 Quarters Ago	
			Current Holdings	% of Port	% Own	Shares Traded	% Change	Previous Holdings	% Own	Shares Traded	% Change	Holdings	% Own	Shares Traded	% Change	Holdings	% Own
American Express Co	AXP	12/31/99	50,536,900	30.08	11.4	—	—	50,536,900	11.4	—	—	50,536,900	11.4	—	—	50,536,900	11.4
Citigroup Inc Com	C	12/31/99	8,062,349	1.93	0.2	3,399,716	72.9	4,662,633	0.1	(2,724,007)	(36.9)	7,386,640	0.2	2,290,256	44.9	5,096,384	0.2
Coca Cola Co	KO	12/31/99	200,000,000	37.51	8.1	—	—	200,000,000	8.1	—	—	200,000,000	8.1	—	—	200,000,000	8.1
Dun & Bradstreet	DNB	12/31/99	12,122,800	1.39	7.5	11,768,300	3,319.7	354,500	0.2	354,500	—	—	—	—	—	—	—
Gatx Corp	GMT	12/31/99	2,634,500	0.40	5.5	2,634,500	100.0	—	—	—	—	—	—	—	—	—	—
Gillette Co	G	12/31/99	96,000,000	14.46	9.1	—	—	96,000,000	9.1	—	—	96,000,000	9.1	—	—	96,000,000	9.1
Great Lakes Chem	GLK	12/31/99	4,258,200	0.58	7.4	258,200	6.5	4,000,000	7.0	—	—	4,000,000	7.0	—	—	4,000,000	7.0
Jones Apparel Group	JNY	12/31/99	12,125,000	1.53	10.3	5,056,100	71.5	7,068,900	6.0	7,068,900	—	—	—	—	—	—	—
M&T Bank	MTB	12/31/99	510,310	0.91	6.6	3,380	0.7	506,930	6.6	—	—	506,930	6.6	—	—	506,930	6.6
Robert Half Intl Inc	RHI	12/31/99	—	—	—	(1,000,000)	(100.0)	1,000,000	1.1	—	—	1,000,000	1.1	—	—	1,000,000	1.1
Suntrust Bks Inc	STI	12/31/99	6,641,400	1.53	2.2	—	—	6,641,400	2.2	—	—	6,641,400	2.2	—	—	6,641,400	2.2
Torchmark Corp	TMK	12/31/99	662,562	0.06	0.5	—	—	662,562	0.5	—	—	662,562	0.5	—	—	662,562	0.5
Waddell & Reed Fin	WDR	12/31/99	—	—	—	(37,699)	(100.0)	37,699	0.1	—	—	37,699	0.1	—	—	37,699	0.1
Washington Post Cl B	WPO	12/31/99	1,727,765	3.74	18.3	—	—	1,727,765	18.3	—	—	1,727,765	18.3	—	—	1,727,765	18.3
Wesco Finl Corp	WSC	12/31/99	5,703,087	5.81	80.1	—	—	5,703,087	80.1	—	—	5,703,087	80.1	—	—	5,703,087	80.1
Zenith Natl Ins Corp	ZNT	12/31/99	816,655	0.07	4.7	—	—	816,655	4.7	—	—	816,655	4.7	—	—	816,655	4.7

SCHEDULE 13G

A Schedule 13G is also a thorough accounting of an institution's holdings, but the entities that fill out 13Gs and 13Fs aren't necessarily the same. (See Chapter 1 for complete definition of both forms.) The fact that Schedule 13Gs have to be filled out only once a year theoretically makes them the least useful of the three smart money forms submitted to the SEC, but you would be foolish not to include them in your analysis if they exist for an entity you're investigating.

The 13G history for Buffett (seen in Figure 8.1) is a good case in point. His 13Gs are the only forms to expose his interests in Wells Fargo, General Dynamics, and Bell Industries. With his Bell Industries filing, Buffett again appears to have moved this stock simply by his association. Interestingly, and quite out of character for him given the other transactions we've seen, Buffett actually sold into the price spike he caused in the stock. He held this position for less than a month! Was this just an anomaly, or can we expect to see more of this opportunistic trading from Buffett? At the very least, this 13G has shown him to be less rigid in his investing style than he seems.

It was also a 13G that would have first alerted you to his interest in MGI Properties. The transaction reflected on the 13G preceded his subsequent Form 4 filings by nearly five months. Anyone not monitoring 13G transactions would have been at a disadvantage. In Buffett's case, however, you probably would have heard about all his transactions in the popular financial press even if you weren't monitoring the filings. But there are plenty of other lesser-known (and better-performing) individuals who aren't in a spotlight. Use the lessons garnered from reviewing Buffett's spectrum of filings and apply them to the bigwig or entity you want to investigate. When doing so, remember to make it a habit of finding out if the particular individual you're investigating owns or controls another entity that files with the SEC.

In Buffett's case, his investment vehicle is itself publicly traded, which made it inevitable that we should find out about its existence by looking at Buffett's own filings. This is more the exception than the rule, however, and finding out if an investment vehicle exists can take some investigating. The investor relations department of the publicly traded company your insider is involved with is a good place to start.

Chapter 8   AT A GLANCE

1. Checking filers' track records is the most important consideration.

2. Although there may be some overlap between the various smart money forms, each has the potential to illuminate a new investment.

3. Reviewing all the forms helps assess a filer's investment style as well as his track record.

9

Corporate Buybacks—
the Company
as an Insider

I have discussed at length information about investing that can be gleaned from knowledge of the trading activity of corporate insiders. But what about the corporation itself? Does our knowledge of the corporation's repurchase of its stock give us the same quality of information that we get when we know that the CEO has purchased stock?

Academic studies say yes. But, as with the insider data we have already discussed, you should not throw money blindly at any firm that announces a buyback program. Companies buy their shares back for different reasons and can execute the buyback in various ways. Understanding these variables can help you find the most promising investments this data stream has to offer.

METHODS USED TO REPURCHASE STOCK

There are three basic means through which a company can repurchase its shares: through open-market repurchases, through fixed-price tender offers, and through Dutch auction tender offers.

Open-Market Repurchases

In an effort to repurchase shares at the lowest possible price, companies will sometimes go into the open market and make purchases anonymously through a broker in the secondary market in which the shares are traded. The anonymity and flexibility inherent in this method help to avoid the need to pay a premium to repurchase the shares, which is often required when repurchases are made through fixed-price and Dutch auction tender offers.

The open-market approach to buybacks is most frequently employed when the number of shares that the board authorizes to be repurchased is relatively small. Because repurchases of this kind avoid premiums, they minimize the transfer of wealth from shareholders who don't sell their shares—a problem of tender offers.

Fixed-Price Tender Offers

Sometimes it just isn't possible to buy back all of the shares authorized for repurchase on the open market. When the repurchase is a relatively large one of, say, 15 percent or more of the outstanding shares, it becomes increasingly difficult to buy back all of them in open-market purchases. The alternative to open-market repurchases is the tender offer, which may be structured as a fixed-price offer or as a Dutch auction.

The fixed-price tender offer often results in a greater premium that must be paid by the company. (Remember, premium is the share purchase price in excess of the current market price.) As a result, there is a transfer of wealth from those shareholders who elect not to sell their shares to those that accept the tender offer. The company announces a fixed price at which it is willing to commit to buy shares.

Because many shareholders will choose not to sell their shares at the current market price (if they would be willing to do that, they would probably already have sold them), the company's tender price is always greater than the current market price. If the tender offer results in more shares than the company has agreed to buy, it can prorate each offer in order to purchase only the authorized number, or it can elect to purchase all of the shares that were offered.

Dutch Auction Tender Offers

In the fixed-price tender offer, the company makes a firm price offer to buy shares at a price it believes will be sufficiently motivating to sellers. It is possible, however, that many shareholders would have been willing to sell their shares at a lower price than the tender offer. Despite that, they will receive the tender offer price. As a result, a company may pay more for the shares that it wants to purchase than is required. The Dutch auction tender offer tends to remedy that excess premium problem.

In the Dutch auction, the company announces both the number of shares that it will buy and the range of prices within which it will consider offers. Shareholders who wish to sell their shares are required to choose a price within this range at which to tender their shares. When the tender offer period expires, the company accumulates the offers to sell in ascending price order from the submitted bids until it has accumulated all of the shares that it intends to purchase. All shareholders who submitted bids at or below the highest accepted bid are paid for their shares at the same price—the highest accepted bid price. All other bids are returned to the shareholders.

These are the three basic methods by which companies repurchase their shares from existing shareholders. More important, perhaps, than *how* companies accomplish these buybacks is *why* they choose to buy shares in their own company. In fact, that reason may be key to determining the importance of a buyback as a signal of stock price movement.

WHY CORPORATIONS BUY BACK THEIR SHARES

It has frequently been indicated that corporations buy their own shares for very much the same reason that traditional insiders buy them—specifically, because the stock is considered undervalued in light of impending corporate developments. If that were the only reason for a corporate buyback, that line of reasoning would be valid. However, that the shares are considered a good buy is only one of the reasons for a corporation's repurchase of its stock. Let's look more closely at that reason and some others.

Shareholder Cash Distributions

To the extent that both a corporate buyback and a dividend result in a distribution, they are similar. Both have the effect of distributing cash to shareholders.[1] However, unlike the cash dividend, which is fully taxable as ordinary income, the share repurchase is only taxable to the shareholder to the extent that the cash received is in excess of the share

---

1. Peter Newman et al. eds., *The New Palgrave Dictionary of Money and Finance* (New York: Stockton Press, 1992), 408.

purchase price—and it is taxable under the generally more favorable capital gains rates. So for the shareholder, a cash distribution via a corporate buyback can be very attractive. For the corporation, the corporate buyback—as a means of distributing cash in lieu of increasing dividends—can be equally attractive.

Managers are reluctant to cut regular dividend levels. Because management (not to mention the stock price) is far more sensitive to dividend changes than it is to dividend levels, there is considerable reluctance to increase dividends unless future earnings are expected to be able to support those higher dividends. Although investors tend to expect that current dividend levels will continue, they view corporate buybacks as sporadic events and clearly do not expect that they will be regularly repeated. So corporate buybacks for the purpose of distributing cash to shareholders has appeal for both the company and its owners. When used for this purpose, however, the corporate buyback would appear to have no information that investors can use to help guide their own stock purchases.

Buybacks to Deter Hostile Takeovers

It is no secret that corporate buybacks can be employed by management to fight hostile takeovers. They can be used to affect the hostile takeover attempt outcome in several ways.

Perhaps the most important way that corporate buybacks help to avert the takeover is by making the corporation less attractive to the corporate raider. Corporations with large cash balances are attractive to many raiders. By reducing the size of the corporate cash balance through a stock repurchase, management removes the feature that may have made the target corporation the takeover target in the first place. By a self-tender offer, the corporate target will also remove those shareholders who would be willing to sell their shares at the lower end of the stock price premium spectrum by purchasing those shares itself. The result is an increase in the price that the corporate raider would be required to pay in order to purchase a controlling block of stock in the target company, thereby making the takeover target less attractive.

Share repurchase agreements are also used to avoid hostile takeovers when the target corporation agrees to buy back the shares *only* from the corporate raider at a substantial premium. This arrangement—often accompanied by a standstill agreement in which the raider agrees not to purchase any of the company's shares during a specified period—is known as *greenmail* to distinguish it from its more criminal cousin, blackmail. Stock price reactions to a greenmail announcement are typically negative—just the opposite of what might be expected following substantial insider buying.

Targeted Share Repurchases

In addition to greenmail, corporations sometimes target their offers to repurchase the shares of smaller stockholdings. The purpose in doing that is to permit the corporation to avoid the servicing costs associated with producing and mailing dividend checks as well as preparing and sending quarterly and annual reports, proxy statements, and other literature.

Stock Options and Stock Purchase Programs

Corporations sometimes repurchase their stock to have it available for their employee stock purchase plans and for their stock options. When corporations purchase their stock for any of the reasons that I've just looked at, our knowledge of that buyback is likely to be meaningless for making investment decisions. However, when the corporation buys back its shares because it considers them to be undervalued, that is information that can be significant.

Shares Considered a Good Buy

Traditional insiders and the corporation itself are generally considered to be value investors. In other words, they buy shares in the corporation when they believe the shares are a good buy. Furthermore, they usually know much more about the corporation than individual investors do. If executive incentive-based compensation—whether through stock options or some other mechanism—provides incentives to managers to maximize share price, then the managers of firms that are undervalued will be motivated to signal their private information to the market. That signal can be given through a corporate buyback.

When companies announce their intention to buy back their shares, the price of their stock often increases. The type of repurchase also seems to play a part as the largest positive stock price movements are associated with fixed-price tender offers, followed by Dutch auction tender offers. Open-market repurchases are associated with the least amount of stock price movement.

So if we can identify those corporate buybacks that indicate management's assessment that the purchase is a good buy—rather than a purchase made for other reasons—we can use this information to help make important investment decisions.

Buyback announcements are usually reported in the financial press or in a company's press releases. But there is one more important point to add about using buyback information to indicate possible value in a company: Just because a company announces a buyback doesn't mean that it is going to actually execute a buyback. A typical announcement will report that a company's board of directors has authorized the repurchase of a specific amount of shares. But this is not the same as actually executing the buyback. Far more valuable are announcements by the firm that it really has repurchased a specific number of shares.

The differentiation of the announcements is important. Announcing authorization for a buyback could just be a public relations ploy. If the company announcing such a buyback has little cash on hand and also has a negative cash flow, the authorization is pretty meaningless. Check a company's financial statements to assess how likely to occur the buyback is and look for announcements in future press releases that it actually followed through on its intentions.

A few sources of comprehensive buyback information and analysis are available. One excellent source for research based on these data at this time is *The Buyback Letter,* authored by David Fried.

A BUYBACK NEWSLETTER

The Buyback Letter
888-buyback
<www.buybackletter.com>
$14.95 Monthly or $149.99 Annually

The Buyback Letter is an online monthly newsletter devoted to finding investment opportunities among companies that repurchase their own stock. The newsletter consists of several sections, some narrative and some statistical.

A main focus of the letter is its combination of stock buyback information with traditional value-investing measurements, such as a low price-to-book ratio. According to academic studies cited on the letter's Web site, taking a value approach when using buyback information in the investing process increases investment returns substantially. Below is a brief examination of the newsletter's main sections.

Buyback tracker. This section lists corporate repurchase announcements made in the previous month that are in excess of $2.5 million. Arranged by announcement date, the listing includes:

- A description of the listed business and its ticker symbol
- The stock's closing price on the day before to the company's repurchase announcement
- The company's book value per share
- The dollar value of the buyback transaction

The buyback portfolio. *The Buyback Strategy,* which publishes *The Buyback Letter,* maintains several portfolios of stocks purchased after they were recommended on the basis of corporate repurchase announcements. A specific dollar amount of each stock is made, and all stocks currently held in the portfolio are listed along with information relevant to the position in the portfolio.

Although the amount of information provided by *The Buyback Letter* may seem somewhat modest when compared with some of the newsletters devoted to traditional insider trading activity, it would be hard to fault its results. According to the *Hulbert Financial Digest,* a publication that tracks newsletters' performances, *The Buyback Letter* returned 32.2 percent on an annualized basis between the beginning of 1997 and May 1999. That compares favorably with a 25.3 percent return for the Wilshire 5000 index over the same period.

Chapter **9**   **AT A GLANCE**

1. Companies that buy back their own shares do tend to outperform the market.

2. It's important to determine why and how a buyback is being undertaken.

3. Not all announced buyback's are actually undertaken.

10

Special Screens for Analyzing Insider Data

Academic studies conclude that insiders tend to be value investors, and I certainly find that value plays are well represented on the short list of stocks I find after scouring the filings. This hardly means following the insiders only dredges up boring, out-of-favor investments, however.

By combining insider data with numerous other valuation and price action criteria, you can generate investment ideas for virtually any investment style you favor. There are obvious screens for momentum, growth, and income investors. Even short sellers can use the data to generate investment ideas.

SCREENS FOR MOMENTUM INVESTORS

Insider Buying at Share Prices Well above 52-Week Lows

This is one of my favorite screens. Insiders are often early with their purchases, and it can take six months or more before the positive developments they expect for their company actually start moving the stock upward. This means that following the insiders too early can leave you with dead money or losses in the short term. But if insiders buy their company's shares at a price well above its 52-week lows, it means the market already discovered this stock, and it has a higher opinion of the stock's prospects than it had a year ago.

Sure, it would have been nice to capture the capital gains from the stock's 52-week lows to where it has risen in the past year, but the insiders aren't eating their hearts out. They are investing even after the increase and obviously think there is more upside.

The term *well above* 52-week lows is, of course, subjective. I tend to define it as 30 percent above a stock's yearly lows, which seems a comfortable number, although others may set their screens differently. I also troll a bit sometimes by lowering the definition. How low I go depends more on how many companies are returned in the results than any academic conclusion of some optimum setting. It takes time to determine which stocks on the list are the best of the lot, and having too many to start with isn't necessarily helpful.

For this reason, we use some of the rules of thumb presented in Figure 3.1 (see page 26) to narrow down the results that this and other screens return. As Figures 10.1, 10.2, and 10.3 show, I have given a nod to the rule to look for clusters of activity by only including companies that had two or more insiders acting similarly. Also, knowing that size matters, I have only included aggregate transactions of $100,000 or more in share value in the results.

You should first look at the insider histories for each company the screen pulls up so you can determine the healthiest buying patterns by the most successful insiders. These are the companies you should then

---

FIGURE 10.1 Insider Buying at Share Prices Well above Their 52-Week Lows

---

Companies with:
Form 4s filed at the SEC as of 2/29/00, and:
Transaction Type: B (Open-market Form 4 buy)
Trans Value > $100,000
# of Insiders Trading > 1
% Above 52-Wk Low > 30

Company	Ticker	# Insiders Buying - Rel to Company	$ Value of Purchases	% Above 52-Wk Low
Leap Wireless Intl.	LWIN	2-V,P	304,443	647
Ameritrade Holding Corp.	AMTD	2-V,E	406,400	628
McMoRan Exploration Co.	MMR	2-B,B	691,970	614
Internet Capital Group	ICGE	2-E,OD	1,717,422	584
Repligen Corporation	RGEN	2-B,B	786,885	282

Company	Ticker	# Insiders Buying - Rel to Company	$ Value of Purchases	% Above 52-Wk Low
Epoch Pharmaceuticals	EPPH	2-C,B	2,282,500	268
Topps Company, Inc.	TOPP	2-D,D	407,752	207
Kushner Locke Co.	KLOC	2-B,B	3,069,311	187
Westcorp	WES	3-B,D,S	2,173,197	168
Pope & Talbot, Inc.	POP	3-D,E,D	166,604	143
Lone Star Technologies	LSS	2-B,B	2,234,425	134
ebix.com Inc.	EBIX	2-B,B	5,999,972	126
SPAR Group, Inc.	SGRP	2-OD,C	140,596	125
Park Place Entertainment	PPE	2-V,D	127,600	114
MGM Grand, Inc.	MGG	3-P,E,E	127,140	104
National Equipment Svcs.	NSV	2-D,E	125,180	102
Vitrix, Inc.	VTTX	3-D,B,D	130,500	100
Honeywell International	HON	2-D,D	599,488	77
Universal American Finan.	UHCO	7-E,OS,D,O,F,OS,D	1,136,162	75
Fritz Companies, Inc.	FRTZ	5-F,V,V,O,V	164,645	68
America West Holdings	AWA	2-D,D	147,980	65
Tyco Int'l. Ltd. (NEW)	TYC	3-D,C,F	8,173,500	63
Aerocentury Corporation	ACY	3-B,D,H	191,138	62
Stocker & Yale, Inc.	STKR	2-C,V	375,192	61
interWAVE Communications	IWAV	3-V,V,P	167,050	53
Astrocom Corporation	ATCC	3-D,D,E	250,000	50
Bluegreen Corporation	BXG	4-B,B,B,B	29,999,985	46
BRT Realty Trust	BRT	4-C,B,P,V	1,353,786	46
Swift Transportation Co.	SWFT	4-B,C,B,D	474,725	45
Flooring America, Inc.	FRA	4-D,E,C,D	935,030	42
W Holding Company, Inc.	WBPR	2-OD,V	159,385	40
Corn Products Intl., Inc.	CPO	8-D,V,D,D,V,V,C,P	577,470	39
Magnum Hunter Resources	MHR	8-D,D,E,O,D,D,D,D	193,280	39
Ivex Packaging Corp.	IXX	2-V,V	109,003	38
First Commonwealth Fncl.	FCF	3-E,OD,OD	147,690	35
Chart House Enterprises	CHT	2-B,C	1,266,453	34
Global TeleSystems Group	GTS	4-P,F,C,V	1,802,540	33
Knape/Vogt Manufacturing	KNAP	2-D,F	349,641	33
Tupperware Corporation	TUP	2-V,V	828,562	33
Sybron International Corp	SYB	3-D,D,D	527,315	32
Covalent Group, Inc.	CVGR	2-F,F	254,717	31

Insider Relationship Codes: **A**=Affiliated person. **B**=Beneficial owner of 10% or more of a company's shares. **C**=Chairman. **CP**=Controller. **D**=Director. **E**=Chief executive officer. **F**=Chief financial officer and/or treasurer. **G**=General partner. **H**=An Officer, Director, and Beneficial owner of 10% or more of a company's shares. **IA**=Investment advisor. **L**=Limited partner. **N**=None. This code is only found on Form 144 filings, and relates to the fact that not all owners of unregistered shares are insiders. **M**=Member of a policy-making committee. **O**=Officer. **OD**=Officer and Director. **OS**=Officer of a subsidiary. **OT**=Officer and Trea-surer. **OX**=Officer of a division. **P**=President and/or chief executive officer. **S**=Shareholder of 10% or more of a class of stock. **T**=Trustee. **TT**=Treasurer. **U**=Unknown. Usually the result of a form that was not filled in properly. **V**=Vice President.

investigate further. And remember to incorporate the present momentum of the stock's price into your analysis of the insider activity (as Chapter 6 explained). When you screen using the relative price action of the stock as one of the criteria, this is particularly applicable.

Did the stock's price rise slowly and steadily over the past year or did it gyrate wildly? Even though the stock price is up from its lows, its price could also be well off its yearly high as well—and still looking weak. All of these price patterns will affect how you interpret the insiders' actions. Just ask yourself: "If I had owned this stock for the past year like these insiders most likely did, what would I probably be feeling about this stock when the insiders traded?"

If insiders watched their shares steadily climb by 30 percent (or by whatever you want to set the screen at) before investing in them, they must feel pretty strongly that whatever caused the shares to rise over the past year—such as great earnings growth, new products, and so on—is likely to continue. This combination of price action and insider buying is the most attractive for momentum investors.

But if the stock is actually on its way down from much higher highs while still being well off its lows, the situation is still intriguing. Even though the short-term momentum of the shares may be negative, insiders are still buying their company's shares at significantly higher prices than ones they could have purchased them for within the past year.

The fact that the stock's value is perceived as being greater now than at some point in the past year means that the market knows about this investment. You're less likely to be holding dead money as a result. The short-term decline of the stock may even be a normal bout of profit taking by investors who made tremendous profits. This may be a good time for momentum players to begin buying the stock in anticipation of another upswing. Checking the technical measures of the stock's price chart is probably as important in this case as investigating the fundamental health and prospects for the company.

Of the insiders who are buying their shares at prices well above the 52-week lows, did any buy at lower prices as well? I view such averaging up as a particularly bullish sign (see Figure 6.4 on page 81 for an example). Not only does it indicate that such insiders acted smartly in the past (giving their present purchase more credibility as a positive indicator), but it also indicates that the insiders aren't satisfied that the profits they gained so far with the past position are all this stock has to offer. More than simply letting this winner ride, the insiders are adding to their bet.

Insider Buying at Companies with Rising Share Prices

Another related price action measure you can combine with insider activity to find momentum-oriented investments is the percentage of price movements of a stock over the past quarter or two. Remember, however, that the lag of insider filings between the trade date and when you see it can easily be over a month. So make sure that the stock's present price isn't too far above the average transaction price of the most recent insider purchases. As Chapter 6 teaches: Don't pay much more than the insiders did.

A Lack of Insider Selling at Companies with Rising Share Prices

Another novel screen for momentum investors is to search for companies whose stocks have appreciated markedly but reveal no insider selling. As I pointed out in Chapter 5, sometimes no insider activity can mean something. Normally, you would expect insiders to cash out their options and generally take profits after their stock soars. But if they don't, it can be interpreted as a positive sign.

It would be better, of course, if insiders were actually buying as the price rises, but some companies' insiders have so many stock options that they don't have to purchase in the open market even if they do feel their stock is undervalued. In these cases, simply not selling is a positive enough sign. This is particularly true of Internet companies. As Internet stocks rocketed up in the late 1990s, insiders were busy flipping their enormous volume of options for a risk-free profit. They didn't care that their shares' prices continued toward the moon after they sold. This was found money to them, and in any case they had many more options to cash out at the higher prices. Yahoo's insider trading history illustrates this pattern (see Figure 3.4 on page 32).

I saw virtually no insider buying in this sector before or during its great run, but perhaps that is expecting too much of these executives. The fact that they might stop cashing in their options to hold out for higher prices may be the most we can expect. It will be very telling when this sector starts cooling off if insiders continue to cash out their options as furiously as they did while their stocks' prices rose parabolically. It will not show much faith that their stocks have a chance of surpassing their previous highs.

SCREENS FOR SHORT SELLERS

Insider Selling at Share Prices Well below 52-Week Highs

As insiders are generally value players, it is very odd to see them selling when the share price is well below its highs—particularly if the stock price is trending down heavily when the selling occurs. Again, the term *well below* is relative, and I tend to define it as being 30 percent below the 52-week highs, although others may choose a different number.

Screens for short sellers are a mirror image of the momentum screens described above, but the reasoning is similar in that the pattern of insider activity in this price-action scenario is just the opposite of what you would expect. (Page 76 in Chapter 6 discusses these expectations.) It also defies common sense to a great degree. Even considering insiders to be like portfolio managers cutting their losses in a losing position doesn't help mitigate the bad signal the selling sends. Insiders should be in a better position to know if they should be cutting their losses or whether the stock is oversold.

Option-related selling of a stock that has declined markedly from its highs is arguably an even worse signal. In this case, insiders don't actually lose more money if the stock declines more, so there is no cutting of losses about the trade. It appears to be insiders rushing to grab as much risk-free profit as possible while they can.

During the period of January 1995 to April 1996, I relied on this screen substantially to generate ideas for *Individual Investor* magazine's Insider's Out column, which focused on identifying stocks to avoid or sell short. Of the 18 stocks featured during that time, one-half of them declined an average of 47 percent. The overall group rose a piddling 0.1 percent. Not bad considering that during the same time the Nasdaq composite index increased 68 percent. This brings up an important point, however. Though academic studies conclude that stocks with substantial insider selling tend to underperform the general market, that doesn't mean these stocks decline in price, which should be a warning to short sellers.

The stock market's secular trend since its inception has been up, so short sellers are swimming against the current by definition. During the raging bull market of the 1990s, short sellers fared particularly poorly. Still, this simple screen of combining significant insider selling with negative price action criteria appears a good method to identify potential short-sale candidates to investigate further.

Insider Selling at Companies with High Valuations and Negative Fundamental Measures

Other screens that short sellers can use to narrow the choice of candidates are the addition of insider selling to any number of negative fundamental and/or valuation criteria, which include companies with

- negative cash flow;
- high debt-to-equity;
- high price-sales ratio;
- declining inventory turnover;
- high or negative price-earnings ratio;
- declining sales or earnings growth; and
- declining profit margins.

In addition, a combination of any of these criteria will produce a short list of short-sale candidates. Just what levels investors consider "high" or "declining" will differ between investors, but the concept is the same.

SCREEN FOR INCOME INVESTORS

Insider Buying at Companies with High Indicated Yields

A stock may have a high indicated yield often because its price has declined in anticipation of a negative event that will hurt the stock's future yield. In other words, the high indicated yield isn't "real." But insiders buying significant amounts of high-yielding shares is a vote of confidence in the sustainability of the high yield.

Figure 10.2 also shows that once again I am enhancing the results of this screen by putting several rules of thumb to work, besides looking for high indicated yields. By only returning companies with more than one insider buying, I ensure that I will have clusters of activity. And by limiting the lower end of the aggregate purchase price to $100,000, I ensure that companies with piddling transactions aren't returned. Both these added criteria should enrich the quality of potential income investments returned by the screen.

FIGURE 10.2 Insider Buying at Companies with High Indicated Yields

Companies with:
Form 4s filed at the SEC as of 2/29/00, and:
Transaction Type: B (Open-market Form 4 buy)
Trans Value > $100,000
# of Insiders Trading > 1
Indicated Yield > 5%

Company	Ticker	# Insiders Buying - Rel to Company	$ Value of Purchases	% Indicated Yield
Equity Inns, Inc	ENN	7-V,F,D,D,V,C,F	267,281	19.3
Crown American Realty	CWN	3-B,C,V	122,281	15.3
Winston Hotels, Inc.	WXH	2-D,D	122,500	14.3
Agree Realty Corporation	ADC	2-D,D	179,753	13.1
Heritage Propane Partners	HPG	2-V,O	106,113	12.6
Lexington Corp. Prop. Tr.	LXP	4-F,P,E,E	2,213,049	11.9
Crescent R.E. Equities Co	CEI	2-E,D	9,616,184	11.8
Commercial Net Lease Rlty	NNN	2-D,C	102,387	11.5
Equity One, Inc.	EQY	2-C,F	2,257,546	10.7
Urstadt Biddle Properties	UBP	2-P,D	216,972	9.7
Keystone Property Trust	KTR	2-D,C	1,032,429	8.9
Banyan Strategic Rlty.	BSRTS	5-V,V,E,V,F	2,698,242	8.6
Apartment Inv. & Mgt. Co.	AIV	4-C,D,D,D	556,670	7.1
Kimco Realty Corp.	KIM	2-C,D	750,161	6.9
Alliant Energy Corp.	LNT	7-D,S,D,D,D,D,S	126,273	6.8
HSB Group, Inc.	HSB	4-V,D,V,V	133,430	6.5
KeySpan Corporation	KSE	3-D,D,F	121,900	6.5
TECO Energy, Inc.	TE	3-D,C,D	103,899	6.5
KeyCorp	KEY	3-D,V,V	196,680	6.2
Wallace Computer Services	WCS	7-E,O,V,V,D,D,C	237,415	5.7
First Commonwealth Fncl.	FCF	3-E,OD,OD	147,690	5.6
AmSouth Bancorporation	ASO	4-D,D,D,D	938,915	5.4
First Union Corporation	FTU	3-D,D,D	2,045,370	5.4
Bank One Corporation	ONE	2-D,D	8,201,257	5.3
Queens County Bancorp	QCSB	2-D,D	680,700	5.3
Tupperware Corporation	TUP	2-V,V	828,562	5.3
BT Financial Corporation	BTFC	13-P,C,O,O,V,V,V,O,O,O,D,V,D	301,395	5.1

Insider Relationship Codes: **A**=Affiliated person. **B**=Beneficial owner of 10% or more of a company's shares. **C**=Chairman. **CP**=Controller. **D**=Director. **E**=Chief executive officer. **F**=Chief financial officer and/or treasurer. **G**=General partner. **H**=An Officer, Director, and Beneficial owner of 10% or more of a company's shares. **IA**=Investment advisor. **L**=Limited partner. **N**=None. This code is only found on Form 144 filings, and relates to the fact that not all owners of unregistered shares are insiders. **M**=Member of a policy-making committee. **O**=Officer. **OD**=Officer and Director. **OS**=Officer of a subsidiary. **OT**=Officer and Trea-surer. **OX**=Officer of a division. **P**=President and/or chief executive officer. **S**=Shareholder of 10% or more of a class of stock. **T**=Trustee. **TT**=Treasurer. **U**=Unknown. Usually the result of a form that was not filled in properly. **V**=Vice President.

SCREENS FOR VALUE INVESTORS

Value investors need fewer special screens when using insider data to identify potential investments. Academic studies have concluded that insiders as a whole tend to be value investors, and any analysis of recent filings will reveal more value-oriented investments than any other types of investments. Nonetheless, some obvious price action, fundamental, and valuation criteria can still help value investors identify potential investments in a more systematic manner.

Insider Buying at Companies with Low Valuations or Positive Fundamental Criteria

Some obvious criteria to combine with insider buying are the following:

- Low price-to-tangible-book-value ratio
- Low price-to-cash level
- Low price-earnings ratio
- Excellent cash flow
- Increasing earnings growth
- Increasing profit margins
- Increasing sales growth
- Increased inventory turnover
- A combination of one or more of the above

The precise definition of "low," "increasing," and "excellent" will differ between investors.

My personal favorites from the above list are the first two. Tangible book value is not a perfect measure of a company's intrinsic worth, but it's a decent proxy. Some stocks may deserve to be beaten down if the company's future looks bleak. But insider buying at a company trading near its tangible book value is an indication that the company's stock may be oversold. It doesn't seem logical for a company's stock to trade so close to the amount of cash the company has according to its latest SEC documents, but mitigating business or accounting circumstances can make a low price-to-cash value an imperfect measure of value. Insider buying at a company trading near cash on hand is another nice confirmation of value.

FIGURE 10.3 Insider Buying at Companies Trading Below Two Times Tanglible Book Value

---

Companies with:
Form 4s filed at the SEC during the Month of 2/29/00, and:
Transaction Type: B (Open-market Form 4 buy)
Trans Value > $100,000
# of Insiders Trading > 1
Price/Tangible Book Value < 2

Company	Ticker	# Insiders Buying - Rel to Company	$ Value of Purchases	Price/ Tan Book Value
Oakwood Homes Corporation	OH	2-C,D	253,440	0.3
Amer. Real Estate Partner	ACP	3-B,B,H	106,831	0.4
Hawthorne Financial Corp.	HTHR	3-D,B,E	143,960	0.5
Keystone Property Trust	KTR	2-D,C	1,032,429	0.6
Bluegreen Corporation	BXG	4-B,B,B,B	29,999,985	0.6
Winston Hotels, Inc.	WXH	2-D,D	122,500	0.6
Equity Inns, Inc	ENN	7-V,F,D,D,V,C,F	267,281	0.7
BRT Realty Trust	BRT	4-C,B,P,V	1,353,786	0.7
Aerocentury Corporation	ACY	3-B,D,H	191,138	0.7
United Trust Group, Inc.	UTGI	3-D,OD,B	190,409	0.8
Republic First Bancorp	FRBK	3-D,D,D	205,545	0.8
Commercial Net Lease Rlty	NNN	2-D,C	102,387	0.8
Pulte Corporation	PHM	5-F,V,D,P,D	495,192	0.9
Florida Banks, Inc.	FLBK	5-D,E,D,D,O	139,009	0.9
Kushner Locke Co.	KLOC	2-B,B	3,069,311	0.9
Urstadt Biddle Properties	UBP	2-P,D	216,972	0.9
Tower Financial Corp.	TOFC	4-D,D,D,D	100,760	0.9
Coachmen Industries	COA	2-D,F	129,910	0.9
First Citizen Bancshr. NC	FCNCA	2-H,P	1,174,449	0.9
Lexington Corp. Prop. Tr.	LXP	4-F,P,E,E	2,213,049	1.0
Republic Bancshares, Inc.	REPB	2-B,OD	345,473	1.0
Westcorp	WES	3-B,D,S	2,173,197	1.0
Alliant Energy Corp.	LNT	7-D,S,D,D,D,D,S	126,273	1.1
Crown American Realty	CWN	3-B,C,V	122,281	1.1
Toys R Us, Inc.	TOY	2-E,D	351,500	1.1
Corn Products Intl., Inc.	CPO	8-D,V,D,D,V,V,C,P	577,470	1.1
Chart House Enterprises	CHT	2-B,C	1,266,453	1.1
Hudson City Bancorp Inc.	HCBK	2-D,D	408,325	1.2
Agree Realty Corporation	ADC	2-D,D	179,753	1.2
Crescent R.E. Equities Co	CEI	2-E,D	9,616,184	1.2
Smart & Final Inc.	SMF	2-B,C	3,504,303	1.2
Banyan Strategic Rlty.	BSRTS	5-V,V,E,V,F	2,698,242	1.2
Flooring America, Inc.	FRA	4-D,E,C,D	935,030	1.2
Security Fin'l Bancorp	SFBI	13-O,D,D,V,D,F,V,V,D,V,OD,D,D	599,570	1.2
Finish Line, Inc.	FINL	2-V,D	109,850	1.2

Company	Ticker	# Insiders Buying - Rel to Company	$ Value of Purchases	Price/ Tan Book Value
Rawlings Sporting Goods	RAWL	5-D,F,V,C,V	259,902	1.2
Equity One, Inc.	EQY	2-C,F	2,257,546	1.3
Southern Union Company	SUG	3-V,D,C	2,376,506	1.3
Granite State Bankshares	GSBI	11-D,S,D,D,D,D,S,D,D,D,D	127,585	1.3
Universal American Finan.	UHCO	7-E,OS,D,O,F,OS,D	1,136,162	1.3
Magnum Hunter Resources	MHR	8-D,D,E,O,D,D,D,D	193,280	1.3
Macatawa Bank Corporation	MCBC	3-D,D,C	191,500	1.4
Oak Hill Financial, Inc.	OAKF	3-F,C,D	418,685	1.4
BT Financial Corporation	BTFC	13-P,C,O,O,V,V,V,O,O,O,D,V,D	301,395	1.4
Pope & Talbot, Inc.	POP	3-D,E,D	166,604	1.4
Kimco Realty Corp.	KIM	2-C,D	750,161	1.4
Sylvan, Inc.	SYLN	2-OS,B	209,638	1.5
KeySpan Corporation	KSE	3-D,D,F	121,900	1.5
Allegiant Bancorp, Inc.	ALLE	2-D,D	310,299	1.5
Univest Corp. of PA	UVSP	4-P,OD,D,C	156,780	1.6
America West Holdings	AWA	2-D,D	147,980	1.6
Fleetwood Enterprises	FLE	7-V,C,V,V,V,P,V	254,570	1.6
Wayne Bancorp, Inc. /OH/	WNNB	4-P,D,D,D	136,516	1.6
Apartment Inv. & Mgt. Co.	AIV	4-C,D,D,D	556,670	1.6
KeyCorp	KEY	3-D,V,V	196,680	1.6
Associates First Capital	AFS	4-D,V,OS,D	339,250	1.7
McMoRan Exploration Co.	MMR	2-B,B	691,970	1.7
Alabama National Bancorp.	ALAB	3-D,D,D	417,440	1.7
Patriot National Bancorp	PNBK	2-E,V	499,013	1.8
First Commonwealth Fncl.	FCF	3-E,OD,OD	147,690	1.8
Analogic Corporation	ALOG	2-OD,V	123,835	1.8
Bank One Corporation	ONE	2-D,D	8,201,257	1.8
BancWest Corporation	BWE	9-D,C,D,D,OD,D,D,P,OD	354,096	1.8
TECO Energy, Inc.	TE	3-D,C,D	103,899	1.8
FPIC Insurance Group, Inc	FPIC	3-D,D,D	103,034	1.9
F & M National Corp.	FMN	8-D,O,V,OD,C,T,F,O	167,080	1.9
Gulf West Banks, Inc.	GWBK	3-C,S,D	144,400	1.9
Webster Financial Corp.	WBST	3-D,D,D	179,640	1.9
SouthTrust Corporation	SOTR	9-D,D,D,D,D,D,C,D,D	735,156	1.9
Washington Mutual Inc.	WM	3-D,V,F	283,719	1.9
FCNB Corp.	FCNB	3-D,D,D	104,150	1.9
BancorpSouth, Inc.	BXS	2-D,D	3,091,194	1.9

Insider Relationship Codes: **A**=Affiliated person. **B**=Beneficial owner of 10% or more of a company's shares. **C**=Chairman. **CP**=Controller. **D**=Director. **E**=Chief executive officer. **F**=Chief financial officer and/or treasurer. **G**=General partner. **H**=An Officer, Director, and Beneficial owner of 10% or more of a company's shares. **IA**=Investment advisor. **L**=Limited partner. **N**=None. This code is only found on Form 144 filings, and relates to the fact that not all owners of unregistered shares are insiders. **M**=Member of a policy-making committee. **O**=Officer. **OD**=Officer and Director. **OS**=Officer of a subsidiary. **OT**=Officer and Trea-surer. **OX**=Officer of a division. **P**=President and/or chief executive officer. **S**=Shareholder of 10% or more of a class of stock. **T**=Trustee. **TT**=Treasurer. **U**=Unknown. Usually the result of a form that was not filled in properly. **V**=Vice President.

Insider Buying When Stock Price Is Near Its 52-Week Low

This is the obvious price action criterion to combine with insider buying to screen for value. Buying near lows is very typical of insiders, and academic studies have shown that insiders tend to be good indicators of value when they purchase their company's shares. Insiders are often early in their purchases, however, so you may want to wait until the technical strength of a stock meeting this criterion improves before jumping in.

I tend to define "near" its 52-week low as not more than 10 percent above it. Others may use a different number. Remember also to pay attention to how much the stock's price is below its yearly high. If a stock has a narrow 52-week price range, screening with any price action criteria is less useful.

Chapter 10 AT A GLANCE

1. Insider data can be used to find new investments for any investing style.

2. The fundamental approach of using insider data in special screens is to combine the data with the appropriate fundamental and price action criteria for your personal investment style.

11

Insider Data as a Market Indicator

Sometimes it doesn't pay to "fight the tape," as the old saying goes; fighting the tape is a little like swimming upstream. Even if you identify a terrific investment opportunity by analyzing the fundamentals of a company that you originally found by reviewing its insider trading activity, the price of the stock you identified may nonetheless go down in price if the market averages are heading south.

It may not seem fair that the underpriced "diamond" you bought declines in price along with other better-known, but pricier, stocks. But it probably will. During a bear market or market correction, most stocks decline in price regardless of their fundamental value.

Once the collective investment psyche perceives a decline in stock prices is probable, further declines can be self-fulfilling. Worried investors can hold off new investments until they believe the decline has run its course. Present investors become more likely to take their profits or cut their losses in the belief they will probably be able to buy the stock cheaper at a later date anyway. With less demand for stocks and a larger supply of stocks for sale, prices continue down.

Although every academic study you read and most professional advice that you get will say that investors are more likely to harm their performance if they try to time the market, people still do it. It's almost human nature—like trying to determine if you should switch lines at the grocery store or lanes during rush hour. It just seems to make sense to at least try to get a bead on the market's trends considering how important they are to your ability to retire, generate enough money for your child's education, or achieve any other investment goal.

And let's face it, some investors do succeed to some extent in timing the market. There are sophisticated technical analysis software packages that attempt to measure the basic supply and demand factors of market indices via their price and trading volume movements. And they sometimes seem to work.

Likewise, according to academic studies and anecdotal evidence, aggregating the insider data filed with the SEC also appears to have some use in predicting the direction of the general market.

LOGICAL CONNECTIONS

In his book titled *Investment Intelligence from Insider Trading,* H. Nejat Seyhun provides compelling academic evidence that analyzing aggregate insider trading activity is a profitable pastime. Seyhun's logical connections, which he backs up with empirical evidence, note that while macroeconomic developments affect the market (which moves up and down in anticipation of the economy), they also affect individual companies. Although insider trading activity has no direct relationship to market movement, both the market and insiders are reacting to the same macroeconomic developments. For that reason, *aggregate* insider trading activity can be seen as analogous to, and a predictor of, future market movement.

If we characterize an insider buy as a sign of bullishness and an insider sell as a sign of bearishness, the important question is whether there is a positive correlation between a predominance of insider buys and greater upward market movement (or a predominance of insider sells and either smaller upward market movement or a market decline). Seyhun tested for a correlation by comparing periods of aggregate insider buying or selling between 1974 and 1994 with three variables that reflect the general state of the economy: the gross national product (GNP), the index of industrial production (IIP), and corporate profits.

The good news for professional market timers everywhere (and the amateur market timer lurking in many average investors) is that Seyhun found that a correlation does indeed exist and that insider trading activity can predict both future stock price movements for individual stocks *and* for the market as a whole. His conclusions about the correlation between aggregate insider trading data and general stock market movement are shown in Figure 11.1.

FIGURE 11.1 Seyhun's Conclusions

- Although the stock market increases following both aggregate insider buys and aggregate insider sells, it increases more following insider buys.
- The longer the aggregation period—that is, the number of months during which companies with net insider buys outnumbered net insider sells (or vice versa)—the stronger the information content; that is to say, the predictability.
- By requiring that a larger proportion of firms—for example, 75 percent rather than 50 percent—have net insider buys before considering it a net buyer month (or have net insider sells before considering it a net seller month), the ability to predict market changes improves.
- Better forecasting of future stock returns can result from an investor's combining information about company-specific insider trading activity with information about aggregate insider trading activity.
- Future economic growth can be predicted up to two years in the future based on aggregate insider-trading activity.

Do these academic conclusions mean that investors should now slavishly move their money in and out of stocks whenever some insider-based market indicator tells us we should? Of course not. It does seem to be worthwhile, however, to include the information from such indicators in the mosaic of one's investing decisions.

Although there are no regularly published insider-based market indicators that are based specifically on the methodology Seyhun used to generate his conclusions, several sources do present their own versions of insider-based markets indicators. There seem to be pros and cons about the different methodologies that produce the various insider-based market indicators, and although a wealth of empirical study backing up the specific approaches is lacking, anecdotal evidence suggests the methodologies have enough validity to warrant monitoring. The sources for insider-based market indicators also provide other aspects of insider data, which are reviewed fully in Chapters 13 through 15.

The Insiders
2200 SW 10th Street
Deerfield Beach, FL 33442

Published Bimonthly
$49—One Year
800-442-9000

The Insiders, a twice-monthly newsletter, provides various insider barometers that are intended to assess the bullishness or bearishness of the market as seen through the eyes of insiders. In addition to actual raw number counts of the number of insider buyers and sellers in companies listed on the New York Stock Exchange (NYSE), the American Stock Exchange (AMEX), and the over-the counter markets for the previous five-week period, these barometers provide a market assessment along three dimensions:

1. Insiders buying and selling in the Insider Indicator
2. Presidents and chairmen buying and selling in the Presidents Index
3. Insider trades of 5,000 or more shares in the Big Money Index

Before looking at each of the indicators, it's important to understand what level of buying and selling represents neither bullishness nor bearishness. In other words, at what level is buying or selling neutral? According to *The Insiders'* market indicators, *neutral* is that level at which insider buys constitute between 35 and 45 percent of total insider transactions. Aggregate insider buys in excess of 45 percent are considered to be indicators of bullishness, while insider buys of less than 35 percent are considered bearish.

Insider Indicator. The Insider Indicator reflects a composite reading—in percentages—of all open-market transactions reported by insiders for the NYSE, the AMEX, and Nasdaq-listed firms as well as the total of all three markets combined for the most recent 30-day period. A small transaction of a relatively minor officer is given as much weight as a huge transaction by a company president.

Presidents Index. The Presidents Index provides exactly the same information as the Insider Indicator, but the data are limited to trades made by company presidents and chairmen. The belief is that these senior people are generally more attuned to what is happening with the company than other insiders.

Big Money Index. The validity of the Big Money Index is based on the belief that some insiders know more than other insiders, just as in the Presidents Index. For this index, however, only transactions involving 5,000 or more shares are considered. By eliminating smaller trades, the Big Money Index excludes all but the most substantial transactions made by insiders.

Insiders' Chronicle
1455 Research Blvd.
Rockville, MD 20850

50 Weekly Issues and 4 Insider Summaries
$315—One Year
800-488-3908

The *Insiders' Chronicle* is a weekly newsletter that provides both an industry indicator and a market indicator that can be of value to the market timer.

Industry rankings. When the insiders in an entire industry are buying or selling, it presumably means that something important is likely to happen in that industry. The industry rankings section of the *Insiders' Chronicle* ranks industries on the basis of the number of insider purchases *minus* the number of insider sales.

An industry in which 50 insiders purchased and 30 sold their shares would have a sector ranking of 20 (50 − 30 = 20). Similarly, if there were 50 sellers and 30 buyers, the sector would receive a ranking of −20. Because sales are generally more prevalent than buys, an industry ranking of −1 to −4 is considered neutral. Any ranking of 0 or above is considered "accumulating," and any ranking of −5 or below is considered "disposing."

The sell-buy ratio. In the way industry rankings attempt to indicate the bullishness or bearishness of insiders toward a particular industry, the sell-buy ratio does the same for the entire market. It gives the number of insider buys and insider sells—in terms of both the number of trades and the number of shares traded—for each of the five preceding weeks and the total for the five-week period. The ratio, however, is based solely on the number of trades completed rather than the number of shares traded.

The *Insiders' Chronicle* considers that there are normally two insider sellers for each insider buyer so that a ratio of 2:1 (sellers to buyers) would be considered neutral. A ratio of more buyers to sellers (for example, 2:1.5) would therefore be considered a sign of bullishness, whereas a ratio of more sellers to buyers (for example, 3:1) would be considered a sign of bearishness.

Vickers Weekly Insider
226 New York Avenue
Huntington, NY 11743

51 Weekly Issues
$176—One Year
800-645-7715

Vickers Weekly Insider (obviously, a weekly newsletter) also gives its subscribers an indication of how insiders are viewing the market by providing sell-buy ratios and then comparing those ratios historically with the Dow Jones Industrial Average.

Sell-buy ratio. The ratio of insider sellers to insider buyers is a measure of the bullishness or bearishness of the entire market. *Vickers Weekly Insider* tracks these transactions and provides a one-week ratio and an eight-week ratio. Reflecting the generally greater number of sellers than buyers, a ratio of sellers to buyers of 2.0 to 2.5 is considered neutral. Any ratio greater than 2.5 is a sign of bearishness, while a ratio less than 2.0 is considered a sign of bullishness.

Eight-week sell-buy ratio versus Dow industrials. *Vickers* also offers a graphic presentation of how insiders felt about the market. The 8-week sell-buy ratio is graphically overlaid on a line graph of the Dow Jones Industrial Average for the previous 13 months to show the correlation between insider activity and the stock market.

InsiderTrader.com
Subscription Services—$49.95 yearly
Premium Services—$17.95 monthly (in addition to $49.95/year)

InsiderTrader.com, an Internet Web site, provides a market indicator that compares the number of companies with insider open-market buying and selling during a particular week and month. The comparison is couched in terms of a percentage of one type of transaction over another.

If there were 1,000 companies with insider buying activity and 500 companies with insider selling activity during a particular period, the value given to that data point would be +100 percent. Conversely, if there were 1,000 companies with insider selling activity and 500 companies with insider buying activity, the value given to that data point would be −100 percent.

InsiderTrader.com takes into account the prevalence of selling over buying by setting neutral for its market indicator at between 0 and −50

FIGURE 11.2 InsiderTrader.com's Market Indicators

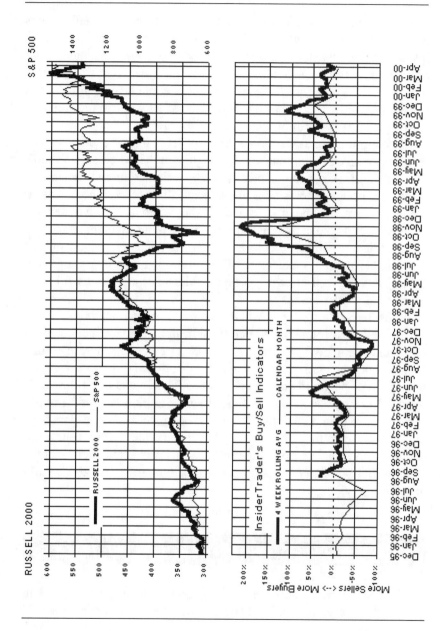

percent. Less than −50 percent is considered bearish, and more than 0 percent is considered bullish. A reading of +50 percent is deemed extremely bullish.

DIFFERING METHODOLOGIES

Under InsiderTrader.com's methodology, each company with insider activity is equally weighted no matter its market cap, the number of insider transactions it had during the period, or the dollar amount of the transactions. A company with six insiders filing Form 4s during a week, indicating sales of $1 million worth of shares, could be counterbalanced if just one insider filed a Form 4 during the same week to indicate that he bought $1,000 worth of the company's shares.

Although this equal weighting does not seem intuitive, consider the problems with other approaches. The argument that Microsoft, Yahoo!, AOL, and other large companies should be weighted more than smaller companies because their stocks' movements affect market indexes more seems intuitive. But the insiders at all of these companies have filed numerous Form 4s indicating sales that total enormous amounts of money, and the prices of all these stocks have risen significantly. Using a market cap, number-of-transactions, or dollar-weight-of-transactions approach exacerbates the well-known fact that insider sales are less useful indicators than insider purchases.

While recognizing logical faults in the varying methodologies, I have nonetheless found the numerous indicators to be useful enough in practice. Case in point: In the fall of 1998, a tremendous debate ensued over whether the market was going through a mere correction, a wholesale crash, or beginning a longer-term bearish move. During this time, InsiderTrader.com's market indicator (see Figure 11.2) consistently showed more than double the number of companies with insiders buying than those selling. In November, a remarkable 200 percent more companies had buyers filing than sellers. This was a tremendous signal from insiders—and a correct one as it turns out—that investors should have been buying.

Chapter 11 AT A GLANCE

1. There is both academic and anecdotal evidence that insider data can be used to predict changes in both the overall market and in individual sectors.

2. There are problems with the methodology of all the existing market indicators, so it is best to look at several.

12

Non–U.S. Insider Trading Data

Illegal insider trading can be found throughout the world. Unfortunately, data on legal insider transactions that you can use in your investment process cannot. Canada, England, and, to a lesser extent, Australia are the only other countries besides the United States to have insider data that can be considered a source of profitable investment information.

When insider trading is mentioned in most capital markets around the globe, there is little thought given to a legal or illegal aspect to it. In many countries, there isn't even a law on the books making *any* type of insider trading illegal. It is almost taken for granted that the business and political bigwigs are trading on material, nonpublic information, and more fool the person who doesn't have access to such knowledge.

Although it's not surprising that countries with emerging economies would fail to have insider trading laws, many countries with more developed capital markets have only recently passed such regulations surprisingly. France banned insider trading in 1967, Britain in 1980 (and toughened insider trading laws in 1994), Switzerland in July 1988, Japan in 1988, Germany in July 1994 (effective January 1, 1995), and Italy only in 1991.

Looking at the evolution of insider trading regulations around the globe, a common thread is that a significant event is often required to motivate lawmakers to acknowledge that some insider trading activity should be considered illegal. In the United States, Congress realized as a result of the 1929 market crash that legislation was necessary to help restore faith in U.S. capital markets. The motivation for several European countries was their desire to enter the European Community (EC). An EC Insider Trading Directive, adopted in 1989, requires all member states to outlaw insider trading in their financial markets. Unfortunately, the EC never quite got around to directing members about how to do this, and this important economic region has disparate levels of regulations that have little hope of unification in the near future. European stock exchanges are presently experiencing a flurry of mergers, however, which can only help speed this process.

Passing laws banning illegal insider trading is the typical first step in generating legal insider data. Enforcing such laws is the next step. In many parts of the world, insider trading has been considered a victimless crime, punishment of which flies in the face of normal business practices. As a result, enforcement of any insider trading regulations is generally lax at first with only small-time players investigated or found guilty. But eventually a high-profile insider trading case spotlights the practice, and the government arm responsible for enforcing the regulations gains more confidence to put teeth in the laws.

Recognition that there is a legal aspect of insider trading and that insiders should disclose their trades seems to be a still further step up the path toward gaining useful insider trading data. But few countries have taken that step. The United States undoubtedly leads other countries in policing the dark side of its securities markets. Kudos also should be given to U.S. congressional leaders of the 1930s for not only differentiating legal from illegal insider trading but for mandating the reporting of trades in the same legislation.

The laws are hardly perfect. Illegal insider trading will always occur in the United States, and some legal insider trading data may not reach the public fast enough to be of much use. But U.S. regulations were extremely progressive for their day and still remain far more stringent than those in most developed countries over half a century later.

KEEPING UP WITH UNCLE SAM

The trend in virtually all countries is toward more regulation of insider trading. Several countries are looking to the U.S. legislative model when developing their own approaches. Within a decade, it is not unrealistic to think that U.S.–style insider data usable by the investing public will evolve in several markets.

A major contributor to the trend of regulating insider trading is the fact that capital markets themselves are in a competitive market. Increasingly, worldly investors know that they can put their money in any number of places, but they logically prefer to invest in an arena they consider more fair. Global companies needing to raise money can also be expected to take into account how large and how fair a capital market is when deciding where to list their shares. This more global outlook by both investors and public companies puts capital markets under the control of clubby and uncompetitive local elites and are not in the best interests of the economies of which they are a part.

Explaining the reasons for Mexico's tightening regulation of its markets, the president of Mexico's National Securities Commission explained in 1993: "We are now convinced that the countries that have the best regulated, the most transparent, fairest markets—where there is the least possibility for manipulation and fraud—will attract the most investment from abroad. What we have done . . . commits the regulators to a path of better regulation."[1] Such a view is likely to be shared by many more in government and finance as financial markets continue their movement toward ever-greater globalization.

Pressure by the United States has also been a force behind stronger insider trading regulations around the world. The SEC has secured memoranda of understanding with regulatory bodies in foreign countries that allows it to gain their assistance when investigating wrongdoing, including that involved with insider trading. The United States has memoranda with Canada, Egypt, France, Germany, Hong Kong, Israel, Italy, Japan, the Netherlands, and Switzerland. As time goes on, it is reasonable to expect more countries will be added to this growing list.

The need for such memoranda arises from the fact that inside information can often be profitably acted on in several stock markets. Not unexpectedly, U.S. pressure on foreign jurisdictions concerning the issue of insider trading regulation has sometimes caused resentment as well as engendered progress.

Besides identifying the legal insider data available in Canada, England, and Australia, I also summarize the state of regulations in such important markets as Japan, France, Hong Kong, and Germany to spotlight areas that may develop useful insider data in the next decade or so.

---

1. *New York Times,* June 7, 1993.

CANADA

Canadian regulations are fundamentally similar to those in the United States, and they offer investors worthwhile data to analyze. It may be improper to talk about a Canadian system as the Canadian provinces have different insider reporting regulations. However, there is a move now underway that will harmonize insider filing procedures (probably by 2001), and it appears that the system of Canada's premier exchange, the Toronto Stock Exchange (TSE), will be adopted.

Under Ontario regulations, which govern the TSE, an insider is

- a director or senior officer of the reporting issuer;
- a director or senior officer of a company that is itself an insider or subsidiary of the reporting issuer;
- a person or company that has direct or indirect beneficial ownership of, or control or direction over, or a combination of direct or indirect beneficial ownership of and of control or direction over, voting securities of a reporting issuer carrying more than 10 percent of the voting rights attached to all the reporting issuer's outstanding voting securities, excluding, for the purpose of the calculation of the percentage held, any securities held by the person as underwriter in the course of a distribution; or
- the reporting issuer itself, where it has purchased, redeemed, or otherwise acquired any securities of its own issue for so long as it continues to hold those securities.

Insiders are required to file a report of a trade by the tenth day of the month following the month in which the trade took place—the same as in the United States. So the reporting period can vary from immediately following the trade to as many as 41 days following it. Insider trades are reported on Ontario's Insider Report, Form 36. The reports may be made by facsimile, by hand, or by mail to the Ontario Securities Commission. Insider reports are processed by Micromedia Solutions, Inc., and are published by Micromedia weekly in the *OSC Bulletin*. Micromedia's phone number is 416-362-5211. The Washington Service (reviewed in Chapter 13) distributes Canadian insider data to institutional clients (phone 202-778-1380).

The impetus for the development of a regulatory and reporting system startlingly similar to the U.S. system appears not to have been the existence of a capital markets scandal occurring in Canada. Rather, it seems to have been the result of the pervasive influence of its cousin directly to the south.

ENGLAND

In the United Kingdom (U.K.), the Financial Services Authority (FSA) is the principal securities regulatory agency, similar to the U.S. Securities and Exchange Commission. Insider dealing regulations are contained within the Criminal Justice Act of 1993, Part V. The Department of Trade and Industry (DTI) is the body that applies the law and policies, and also prosecutes it. In the past, the DTI has had little to do with legal insider trading. That role has been played by the London Stock Exchange (LSE), which establishes the rules by which insiders may trade shares of the corporations in which they are insiders. As part of numerous changes now occurring at the LSE, however, the DTI appears to be taking on the oversight of legal insider trading as well.

U.K. rules prohibit an insider—defined roughly as anyone who has access to price-sensitive information—from trading when he or she is actually in possession of that price-sensitive information, or during the month preceding interim earnings announcements. If these restrictions do not apply, an insider in Britain may trade subject to the following rules:

- Permission of the company's chief executive officer must be obtained prior to trading.
- The individual must notify the market *as soon as possible* following the transaction; "as soon as possible" is interpreted by the LSE to mean "within two days of the trade," according to an LSE spokesman.

The information concerning the insider's trade is available to the public. Notification of insiders' trades is referred to as "directors' notification" and is included as a part of the LSE listing rules that regulate listed companies and to which they agree as a requirement of being listed on the exchange. These listing rules are known as The Yellow Book, a name that derives from the color of its cover.

Reports may be made on Schedule 11 or in a free-text announcement to the exchange. A free-text announcement is, simply, a brief written statement sent to the exchange stating the number of shares traded, their price, and the insider's current holdings.

Trades being made by a quoted U.K. company's directors are reported by the BARRA DIRECTUS SERVICE. BARRA, founded in 1975, provides various analytical services in addition to DIRECTUS. Based in Berkeley, California, BARRA has offices in major financial centers throughout the world. Its global headquarters telephone number in Berkeley is

510-548-5442. The Washington Service also distributes this data to institutional clients. Its phone number is 202-778-1380.

AUSTRALIA

Insider trading is regulated in Australia primarily by the Corporations Law, which was promulgated in 1990. Prior to implementation of the Corporations Law, a state-based system regulated trading activity. Under the law, anyone in possession of nonpublic, price-sensitive information and subsequently trades or encourages someone else to trade has breached Australian law. Although the Corporations Law does not define "nonpublic, price-sensitive information," section 1002G of the law states that insider trading will occur where a person possesses "information that is not generally available but, if the information were generally available, a reasonable person would expect it to have a material effect on the price or value of securities of a body corporate."

The Corporations Law also differentiates between legal and illegal insider trading and has set down reporting requirements. Directors of a listed company must notify the securities exchange of any change in their ownership within 14 days. Shareholders who acquire more than 5 percent of the shares of a company must disclose their holdings within 2 days. These large shareholders must also disclose any subsequent change in their ownership of 1 percent or more within the same time frame.

Information about the trades of these required reporters is publicly available. Forms 603 and 604 must be filed to report the initial substantial shareholder and the change in interests of the substantial shareholder, respectively. This data seems similar to that generated by Schedule 13D in the United States, and knowing what the smart money is doing Down Under is certainly worth reviewing during the investment process.

Unfortunately, officers of a company are not required to file their insider trades (unless, of course, they are also either directors or more-than-5 percent shareholders.) You will recall that in Chapter 4 I discussed the general hierarchy of importance of insiders' trades. Both academic studies and hands-on experience have shown that, while directors' trades did tend to outperform the market, the lion's share of profitable information comes from the trades of a company's officers, ranging from chief executives to vice presidents. So to the extent that executives are not required to report their trades, insider trading activity Down Under doesn't contain as much investment intelligence as U.S. insider trading activity.

While users of insider data wait for the Australian government to plug this hole in its reporting regimen—and there appears to be little current movement in that direction—it seems that investors may want to use the data more for analyzing smaller Australian companies. There is a greater likelihood at smaller firms that officers will also be major shareholders or directors and are therefore required to report their insider trades. For information on how to access Australia's insider data, contact the Australian Stock Exchange at 61-2-9227-0175.

FRANCE

Although the French government has not yet legislated the disclosure of legal trading by insiders, its regulations do seem to be evolving in the right direction. The basic law that governs companies under the French system was passed in July 1966. A year later, Ordinance No 67-833 created the Commission des Operations de Bourse (COB), the French corollary to the U.S. Securities and Exchange Commission. Under the French system, an ordinance is similar to an executive order that has been ratified by the French legislature. The first French law actually dealing with insider trading (No. 70-1203) was passed in December 1970, and subsequent laws have amended and extended it.

No particular scandal prompted the passage of the original 1967 ordinance. Instead, it was in response to the French investors' abandonment of the French stock exchange. Investors were simply not interested in utilizing the French stock exchange to invest their funds. The ordinance was designed to restore the confidence of the French citizens in their financial system following World War II.

French law prohibits an insider from trading in securities about which he or she has information that has not been disclosed to the general public. The time when insider information is deemed to become public is somewhat vague. It is considered public when it is *widely available,* but the term has not been defined and is evaluated on a case-by-case basis. In a 1999 incident, nonpublic information was published in a newsletter to 300 people, one of whom was a newspaper reporter who subsequently reported the information in the newspaper. In that incident, it was only when the reporter reported the information that it was considered public.

An insider, as defined by French law in Article 10.1 of the Ordinance of 1976, includes "[a]ny persons who, in connection with the exercise of their profession or duties, have access to privileged information on the prospects or the position of an issuer whose securities are traded on a regulated market or on the future prospects of a financial instrument listed on a regulated market."

If an insider does not possess nonpublic information, he or she is permitted to trade in the securities of the company in which he or she is an insider. However, the trader is not required to report those trades to any regulatory agency. According to COB officials, reporting is not required for the simple reason that because any insider trades must have been made without the benefit of nonpublic information (otherwise they would be criminal), there is no societal benefit in reporting them!

It is easy to scoff at such reasoning, which seems to imply that French insiders are uniquely capable of policing themselves but not mandating that legal insider trades be reported is more a recognition that there is little political will to police such laws. That there is even a law recognizing that some insider trading is illegal is a giant step for many countries, but the law can take some time to grow teeth.

In France the teeth came in 1988, almost two decades after the first insider trading law was passed. In that year, Alain Boublil, a French official, shared inside information with a friend about the acquisition of U.S. firm Triangle Industries by France's Pechiney. As soon as the purchase was completed, the stock price of a subsidiary of the acquired company—Triangle—soared. So did the wealth of a few French businessmen. Boublil was eventually given a two-year sentence, earning him the unwelcome distinction of being the first person convicted of insider trading in France to go to jail. But the most telling aspect of this case was that one of the beneficiaries of Boublil's information was Roger Patrice Pelat, a close friend of then-president Francois Mitterrand. Those with high connections could no longer count on special treatment when it came to insider trading.

Without laws mandating the reporting of legal insider trades, no data regarding the trading of management is available for investors in French securities at this time. However, there is data worth mentioning that indicates when one publicly traded French company trades the shares of another publicly traded French company.

The Conseil des Marches Financiers (CMF) is a professional body that defines the general principles governing the organization and operation of regulated markets in financial instruments in France, among other important duties. It has mandated the disclosure of trades by one company of another, and it redistributes these *informations et décisions* via its Web site located at <www.cmf-france.org>.

To put this data into perspective, the *informations et décisions* presented by the CMF can be thought of as a type of "smart money" form, as discussed in Chapters 1 and 8. And while not in a database that allows an easy view of historical trades on a company basis, these transactions are presented in straightforward tables.

With French legislation on insider trading further along than in most countries, and initiatives from quasi-governmental organizations like the CMF, France appears as good a candidate as any to develop more useful insider-related data over the next decade.

JAPAN

Japanese insider trading laws are seemingly more advanced than France's given Japan's requirements that insiders record their legal transactions. Unfortunately, the tradition of privacy in this culture makes for a uniquely Japanese reason why the data is not yet useful to investors.

Japan has had insider trading laws almost as long as has the United States. The country's securities legislation was passed during the period of U.S. occupation immediately following World War II and was part of the sweeping political and legal reform initiated at that time. It was not until more than 40 years later, however, that the insider trading laws were enforced.

Japanese authorities were galvanized into action following the securities scandals that occurred in the United States in the late 1980s. Partly as a result of those scandals, Japan created the Japanese Securities and Exchange Surveillance Commission in 1992. The investigation of Nippon Shoji Kaisha in 1994 appears to have been a direct result of the formation of the commission. Insiders at this pharmaceutical firm had unloaded massive numbers of shares of their stock just before the announcement of potentially fatal side effects of a drug developed by the company. Twenty-four company officials were identified in the scheme, some of whom made more than 20 million yen from their illegal trades. No jail sentences were given, and the various fines amounted to only 200,000 yen to 500,000 yen, which translated to a mere $2,000 to $5,000.

Under Article 163 of Japan's Securities and Exchange law, executive officers and owners of more than 10 percent of a company's shares must report their transactions in the company's securities. Furthermore, they must report their trades no later than the 15th day of the month following the month in which the trade took place. Although the reporting requirements would seem to offer opportunities to emulate the trading activity of insiders, the important issue is one of access. Insiders apparently do file forms, but there is no mandate allowing the public to see them!

Public access to information in Japan is startlingly different from what Westerners are accustomed to. It was only after 20 years of struggle by citizen groups that the Japanese parliament passed the first freedom of information law—and information deemed to be private will still not be publicly available when the law takes effect in April 2001 at the earliest.

As if the concerns about public availability of insider trading activity were not enough, there is some evidence that the law requiring insiders to report their trades may not be vigorously enforced. In the first nine years of insider trading regulations, Japan's Securities and Exchange Surveillance Commission filed only four cases against insiders. A joke about Japanese insider trading law in the early 1990s likened it to an ancient samurai sword owned by a family: It is taken out of the closet every now and then but never actually used.

The fourth case (brought in 1997) did give hope for more progress, however, as it was the first time that insider trading charges were lodged against an executive of a well-known company. In that case, Katsurao Suzui, the former president of Suzutan Co., sold shares worth $12.7 million ahead of an announcement that depressed company shares to one-third of their earlier peak. Prosecutions have since accelerated, and by February 1999, seven more insider trading cases had been filed in Japan.

Japan is still tremendously lax, however, and the image of insider trading data in Japan is that whatever executives do happen to offer up on their forms merely piles up in some government storage room—unread. And if this isn't what is actually happening, it might as well be. Japan has the appearance of well-developed insider trading laws, but they are, in effect, a mirage. This is too bad.

Everything seems to be in place, but the political will to take the last steps of enforcing insider reporting and releasing the data doesn't seem to be there. Still, this highly important capital market is also on the short list of candidates that it's hoped will develop useful insider trading data in the near future.

GERMANY

The law governing insider trading in Germany is the Securities Trading Act (Wertpapierhandelsgesetz—WpHG) of July 26, 1994, promulgated as Article 1 of the Second Financial Market Promotion Act. It became effective in January 1995 and made insider trading a criminal offense. Seven months later the first German was convicted of insider trading. In that case Harald Kronseder sold shares in his company just before it announced the existence of international trading problems that caused a 40 percent drop in the value of its shares.

The case against Herr Kronseder was apparently overwhelming—as it must have been to succeed as a criminal action. Enforcement of insider trading laws is generally much easier when authorities are able to bring a civil action instead of having only criminal sanctions to rely on. The principal reason is that the burden of proof required to successfully maintain a civil suit is much less than that required for a criminal prosecution to succeed (essentially the difference between "preponderance of the evidence" and "no reasonable doubt").

Countries with somewhat more advanced insider trading laws—such as the United States and France—give regulators the option to advance a civil instead of, or in addition to, a criminal suit. By choosing to make insider trading a criminal rather than a civil offense, Germany may have seemed to be coming down hard on illegal insider trading while, in effect, making it less likely that enforcement would be successful.

In any case, there seems to be little progress in Germany toward mandating disclosure of legal insider trades that could help investors— very surprising given the importance of its financial markets to the European Community's economy.

HONG KONG AND THE REST OF ASIA; RUSSIA

A Hong Kong newspaper reported that when a company director learned the government was serious about prosecuting insider dealers, the director said he would no longer be able to get anyone to sit on his board. Historically, Hong Kong has been one of the most robust markets in Asia—second only to Japan. Unfortunately, it is also one where illegal insider trading has long been an accepted part of the financial landscape. Hong Kong's Securities and Futures Commission was only established in 1989 and active enforcement began in 1992. In 1998 Hong Kong announced the creation of three additional posts to deal with insider trading, and it also beefed up its judiciary in anticipation of more insider trading cases. The relatively new enforcement of insider trading laws can only help, but Hong Kong's efforts still have a long way to go to level the playing field for noninsiders.

Surprisingly, Taiwan seems to be moving in a regulatory direction opposite to that of other nations. In the mid-1990s, Taiwanese regulators were investigating nearly a quarter of the companies listed on its exchange on charges of insider trading. But before much justice could be done, Taiwan's Securities and Futures Exchange Commission (SFEC)—Taiwan's counterpart to the U.S. Securities and Exchange Commission—was stripped of its power to investigate insider trading. Although the SFEC can still impose fines on companies and individuals suspected of breaking exchange regulations, Taiwan's Finance Ministry now oversees insider trading investigations. The Ministry appears to be less able to see such abuses, even though they are rampant.

Mainland China's financial markets are likewise affected with a substantial amount of insider trading, but, surprisingly, China's government has shown more will to punish. As early as 1994, a Chinese securities brokerage firm was fined $230,000 and had its profits confiscated for buying shares in another company on the basis of insider knowledge of a pending bid. Still, buyer beware is the rule of thumb here.

The same goes for investing in India. The Bombay Stock Exchange, the largest exchange in India, is run largely by its member brokers. It is these same member brokers who have been repeatedly criticized for alleged insider trading, ignoring accounting rules, and generally not treating average investors fairly. This clubby atmosphere is likely to continue for some time.

Russia seems to present obstacles to foreign investment that may be significantly greater than almost anywhere else in the world. As a recent newspaper article about Russia put it: "Some say it's now impossible to distinguish between the government and organized crime."[2] Since the dissolution of the Soviet Union, organized crime in Russia is larger and more complicated than the usual organization of underworld mobsters. It is "a three-way alliance of officials, businessmen, and gangsters reaching into every level of society and the economy." The Russian Interior Ministry estimates that organized crime controls 40 percent of the economy—a figure considered by others to be too con-

---

2. "Russian Mob Gaining Unprecedented Power," *Sunday Star-Ledger,* September 5, 1999, p. 33.

servative. Because corrupt officials and gangsters work with these criminal businesses to obtain "insider deals," it's a safe bet that regulation of insider trading is not on the top of most government officials' lists.

LATIN AMERICA

No useful insider data is generated south of the U.S. border either, but the main capital markets there at least appear to recognize the importance of bolstering confidence in their markets by trying to address insider trading abuses.

Mexico and Chile are considered to have relatively fewer abuses than other countries in the region. Legislation introduced in Chile in 1998, whose main goal was to give investors a fair return on their investments, specifically targets insider trading. Such regulations are only the first step in the normal process of developing laws that mandate disclosure of legal insider trades, however, and investors should not hold their breath expecting more progress anytime soon.

Argentina is also trying to improve the poor reputation of its capital markets in an attempt to accelerate the inflow of foreign capital. It passed legislation that legally defines insider trading and provides heavy fines for market manipulation. Practically speaking, however, insider trading is common in Argentina because few brokers consider it immoral or an offense—an opinion prevalent in most of the world's developing countries.

Chapter 12 AT A GLANCE

1. The worldwide trend appears to be toward more regulation of both illegal and legal insider trading activity. The merger of regional and international stock exchanges could speed this trend.

2. Only Canada, England, and Australia have data on legal insider trades that investors may gain access to.

3. France and Japan have the potential to develop useful data before other markets do.

13

Where to Get Insider Trading Data: Traditional Methods

OVERVIEW

Perversely, the insider disclosures that were meant to level the playing field for individual investors have only given institutional investors another leg up on the little guy over recent decades. Since the advent of computers, commercial data providers have been able to deliver more timely insider data to deep-pocket investment firms. By the time the masses have gotten the information, these institutions have already traded on it—which isn't what legislators in 1934 had in mind when they mandated disclosure of insider data. But it's a free market and legislators can't control the information once it's released in the SEC's public room (discussed later this chapter).

Fortunately, as technology has developed further, insider data has finally become affordable to individuals as well as institutions. Cheap computing power has made the PC more of an appliance than a luxury, and the rapidly developing Internet is the cheap distribution system that can deliver insider data to these in-home terminals. This new, large market of wired individual investors is too tempting for institutional providers of insider data to ignore. They are allowing some of their information to be redistributed over the Internet and pricing it lower to attract volumes of these hungry users. Data that cost $250 per month a couple of years ago now only cost $250 per year. An increasing amount of the data is also becoming available free. This trend of increased affordability and timeliness is likely to continue but is already at a point that allows individuals affordable access to the same insider information most institutions receive.

The Internet is clearly the best place to get your insider data at this time, and it is likely to become an even better source in the near future. This statement could be made for many other types of investment information as well, and any individual investor who doesn't have a computer with Internet access is at a disadvantage to those who do. The amount of free or affordable financial information on the Internet is remarkable and getting still better very quickly. Any active investor who looks at a keyboard as a menial device and the Internet as a big time waster is truly an anachronism, and Chapter 15 tells you where on the Internet you should be looking for insider data.

The traditional methods of distributing insider data still exist, however, and deserve mention. I begin by reviewing the mother of all insider data sources: the Securities and Exchange Commission. I then highlight the various service bureaus that have traditionally served the institutional market.

THE SECURITIES AND EXCHANGE COMMISSION

The SEC has three outlets for the insider data it collects: a printed publication, EDGAR (an electronic database that is accessible via the Internet), and the public room in its Washington headquarters, where the forms actually enter the public domain. Because Form 4s, Form 144s, and other insider filings are collected first by the SEC, and part of this bureaucracy's job is to disseminate the information, it makes sense to think the SEC is the best place to get insider data. This may have been the case decades ago, but it is certainly not true today.

The fact that the SEC is no longer the best source for insider data is not wholly its fault, however. Money from institutional investors and the advent of computers have created faster channels for Form 4s and 144s in particular. As long as there are deep pockets that will pay to get their hands on insider trading data before the masses, commercial operations will work hard to meet this demand.

For the SEC to keep up with commercial providers would be very costly; and unlike its free-market competitors, the SEC has no hope of recovering these costs. Institutions pay through the nose for the data precisely because paying such a high price allows them to trade on the information before individual investors can. If the SEC did invest resources to become the quickest and most flexible provider of Form 4 and Form 144 data, it could hardly begin offering this important information to the highest bidder as commercial providers do. Because the SEC is a federal government institution with a mandate to protect John Q. Investor, it would be forced to offer fair access to the data.

The large and unrecoverable costs of making full use of today's technology to collect and redistribute insider data explain why the SEC's EDGAR project is likely to be a step behind commercial providers for many years to come. It also means that for the foreseeable future the people who see such important information first will continue to be the people who can pay for it.

Though none of the SEC's outlets is the definitive place to get insider data, you should be aware of their existence. The SEC's electronic database, EDGAR (which stands for the Electronic Data Gathering, Analysis, and Retrieval system), is particularly worth getting acquainted with because it is the evolving avenue. The other two avenues are more important for familiarizing you with how insider data has—and does—reach the public domain.

The *Official Summary*

The *Official Summary of Security Transactions and Holdings,* a monthly tome, is the only comprehensive source of insider data from the SEC. First published in 1936, for decades it was also *the* place to get insider data. Today, however, computers, electronic databases, and the Internet have made the *Official Summary* more useful as a doorstop than an investment tool. Oddly, with all the advances in printing technology, the *Official Summary* is actually published less frequently now than it was in the 1930s. The time lag of the transactions that are included has also increased, and even though the number of filings has increased tremendously over the past 60 years, the ability to manage information has increased too.

The *Official Summary* understandably went from semimonthly to monthly in the 1940s, when World War II gave both the U.S. government and the investing public more important things to worry about. But it's obvious that the political will (and federal dollars) to maintain the relevancy of the *Official Summary* in the face of growing computing power never materialized.

To illustrate how untimely the book is now, a Form 4 transaction published in the latest *Official Summary* hit free Internet-based services at least three months ago. Quite a lag. Although insiders may be early in their transactions, too many situations exist where time is of the essence to rely solely on the *Official Summary* for data. With subscriptions now costing $166 per year, the *Official Summary* is hardly free either. Nonetheless, the U.S. Government Printing Office will be happy to take your order at 202-512-1800.

For those in the neighborhood, a collection of the summaries is available in the SEC's library at 450 5th St., Washington, D.C. The library is one flight below street level and open to the public weekdays between 9 AM and 5 PM. Bring a picture ID and park your car in a commercial lot. You're more likely to win any number of state lotteries before finding a free parking space around the SEC building.

Researching past transactions in this manner is time consuming, however, and unnecessary considering that Internet-based databases going back at least four years are now so affordable.

EDGAR (Electronic Data Gathering, Analysis, and Retrieval System)

The SEC's EDGAR system for filing and retrieving documents electronically should eventually provide individuals timely access to all insider data filings, but just when is difficult to say. It is mandatory to file Schedule 13Ds and 13Gs on EDGAR, and this free database is the source of choice for these insider filings. Unfortunately, the most important streams of insider data—Forms 4 and 144—are only filed on EDGAR voluntarily now, and only about 5 to 10 percent of insiders do so. Forms 3 and 5 are also voluntary for now, and the SEC has not set a date when EDGAR filing of these four form types will become mandatory.

EDGAR began as a pilot project in 1984 with a few hundred companies volunteering to file through it. Deemed a success, the computer system as it stands now was ostensibly completed in 1992, and the mandatory filing of 10-Ks, 10-Qs, Schedule 13Ds, and Schedule 13Gs was phased in from 1993 to 1996. Though it's an incomplete source of insider data, what is on EDGAR is useful. Accessing EDGAR through the Internet at <www.sec.gov>, you can type in a company's name and see the occasional Form 4 or Form 144 listed right next to the 10-Q and 10-K documents that are mandatory. Clicking on the hyperlinked heading brings up the entire form.

Many larger companies have set up the EDGAR filing process for their insiders, and if you're investing in Dow 30 stocks only, this database can help you. For the vast majority of companies, however, EDGAR has no Form 4s or Form 144s. Microsoft and SonoSite (whose full insider history is presented in Figure 6.4) have no Form 4 data in EDGAR. And even when a company does have some of these filings, you can never be sure they present a complete record. Compare EDGAR's Form 4 history for Yahoo! in Figure 13.1 with the company's full history in Figure 3.4; there's hardly anything on EDGAR. EDGAR is similarly skimpy with General Electric's Form 4 history, and the list goes on. Investors do benefit from being able to view the full details of the few

---

FIGURE 13.1 EDGAR's Form 4 History of Yahoo! (Nasdaq: YHOO)

Results of EDGAR Form Search

For more information about TEXT, HTML, and PDF files, please click here.

Your query: **yahoo**
Your search had **140** hits.

Date Filed	Forms	CIK Code	Company Name	Format
03-31-1997	10-K	1011006	YAHOO INC	[text]
03-12-1998	10-K	1011006	YAHOO INC	[text]
02-26-1999	10-K	1011006	YAHOO INC	[text]
03-30-2000	10-K	1011006	YAHOO INC	[text] [html]
04-29-1999	10-K/A	1011006	YAHOO INC	[text]
08-14-1996	10-Q	1011006	YAHOO INC	[text]
11-14-1996	10-Q	1011006	YAHOO INC	[text]
05-15-1997	10-Q	1011006	YAHOO INC	[text]
08-06-1997	10-Q	1011006	YAHOO INC	[text]
10-30-1997	10-Q	1011006	YAHOO INC	[text]
05-15-1998	10-Q	1011006	YAHOO INC	[text]
07-17-1998	10-Q	1011006	YAHOO INC	[text]
11-13-1998	10-Q	1011006	YAHOO INC	[text]
05-17-1999	10-Q	1011006	YAHOO INC	[text]
08-16-1999	10-Q	1011006	YAHOO INC	[text] [html]
11-12-1999	10-Q	1011006	YAHOO INC	[text] [html]
04-14-2000	10-Q	1011006	YAHOO INC	[text] [html]
12-17-1996	10-Q/A	1011006	YAHOO INC	[text]
01-16-1997	10-Q/A	1011006	YAHOO INC	[text]
01-21-1999	10-Q/A	1011006	YAHOO INC	[text]
01-21-1999	10-Q/A	1011006	YAHOO INC	[text]
04-07-2000	3	1011006	YAHOO INC	[text] [html]
03-10-1999	4	1011006	YAHOO INC	[text]
03-10-1999	4	1011006	YAHOO INC	[text]
03-10-1999	4	1011006	YAHOO INC	[text]
03-10-1999	4	1011006	YAHOO INC	[text]
03-10-1999	4	1011006	YAHOO INC	[text]
03-10-1999	4	1011006	YAHOO INC	[text]
06-10-1999	4	1011006	YAHOO INC	[text]

Form 4s filed on EDGAR, but its lack of comprehensiveness makes EDGAR a third-rate source for the most important form investors use to gauge insiders' sentiments.

The Public Room

The most novel place to get insider data is from the SEC's own Public Room located on the ground floor of the SEC's main building at 450 5th St., Washington, D.C., and accessible by anybody with a picture ID during regular business hours. This is where all the insider forms are released to the public, and, if you have the time and patience, you could be the first one to see that the chairman of a company you've invested in has made an enormous purchase or sale of the company's shares. You could also end up being considered a very ugly tourist.

The Public Room is where numerous service bureaus have posted employees to photocopy all documents, so the data can be typed into a computer database. These databases are the timely but expensive sources of the data that institutional investors have been subscribing to for years from organizations such as Thomson Financial Networks, Primark, Vickers Stock Research, and The Washington Service. (These big boys are described later in this chapter.)

You certainly have as much right to the forms as service bureau employees, but grabbing the paper before them would be foolhardy. The stack of documents is a bit of a mess when it is plunked down on the receiving table in the Public Room, and the people from the different service bureaus actually work together to sort it out. You'd do better to work with them too or wait until after the sorting is done. No original documents can leave the Public Room, but photocopiers are available to duplicate the forms once it's your turn to take them. Copies cost 26¢ each, plus tax.

Although it may seem clever to get your own data in the Public Room, the novelty of being the first on your block with the data would soon wear off. After spending all your time collecting the forms, you won't have time to analyze them. It's much more cost effective to simply buy the data from an already established service.

If you have dreams of building your own insider data empire, you may want to think again. Besides the time and photocopy costs of getting the data from the SEC, the data input burden is tremendous. Interpretation is required on a portion of the documents, so it calls for a team of higher-quality data input personnel. And even if you do hire qualified, cheap data input people, they will be overworked for one week of the month and underworked the rest of the time because the majority of the forms are filed around the tenth of each month.

And if you think optical character recognition is the answer, forget it. The forms are hardly uniform in the quality of information entered into the blanks, and many are filled in by hand.

SERVICE BUREAUS

Service bureaus are the businesses that thrived as the evolution of computers sparked demand from institutional investors to get hold of the insider data filed at the SEC as soon as possible. It is these service bureaus that have the stable of data input people turning the scrawl on the paper Form 4s into a proper electronic database.

Service bureaus are also where many institutional investors still get their data. The reasons some institutions continue to pay a surprisingly high amount to service bureaus for insider data is that the bureaus are— or are perceived be—quicker than the cheaper Internet-based distributors of the data. Some value-added tools are also supplied by many of the bureaus that analyze the data as well.

In some aspects of the data, service bureaus can boast a slight edge in timeliness over Internet sites—but the edge is narrowing. Already, any time difference is certainly not worth it to individuals to pay the institutional-strength price that service bureaus charge their clients. Also, more and more sophisticated tools for using insider data are being distributed on the Internet as well. And the fundamental quality of the data is the same as it is generally the service bureaus that supply the raw data to the Internet sites!

A service bureau, in the sense in which we are using the term, is a company in the business of locating and providing information for a fee. What makes service bureaus different from the newsletters, magazines, newspapers, and Internet sources of information about insider trading activity that we will examine in the chapters that follow is that service bureaus provide what we think of as raw data. Newsletters, Internet sites, and other sources with which we may be more familiar buy and format that raw data to produce information that is more meaningful and therefore more useful to many investors.

Although literally dozens of firms can be classified as service bureaus and provide important services in researching government records for clients, many of them are set up to do research in response to requests from individual clients. Often, their clients are law firms interested in having a particular document or subject researched.

Among the slew of service bureaus are a handful that have made the collection and subsequent distribution of the SEC's insider data a focused part of their business. Four such firms stand out: Primark, Vickers, Thomson Financial, and The Washington Service.

The Washington Service
1850 M Street, NW
Washington, DC 20036-5803
202-778-1380
<www.washserv.com>

The Washington Service has been providing information to institutional clients since 1970. Insider trading data are only a portion of this company's total business—but a valuable part. The three insider-related products offered by The Washington Service are:

1. EZ-Edgar
2. Insider Trading Service
3. Rule 144 Stock Service

Because there is no published rate card for these services, institutions generally contact the company directly to negotiate fees.

EZ-Edgar. This service provides a reformatted and easy-to-read copy of each SEC filing by e-mail to Washington Service customers, who can view the documents as well as print or store them using word-processing software. By using this service, customers can also transfer important financial information to a spreadsheet and apply various criteria to make the information more meaningful for each customer's particular application. Although the documents can be ordered as needed, customers can also establish a watch list, and copies of any SEC filings concerning companies on the list will be automatically e-mailed to customers within minutes of their release by the SEC.

Insider Trading Service. The Washington Service provides timely open-market Form 4 information on all U.S.-listed and over-the-counter (OTC) companies that are required to file with the SEC. Option-related Form 4 purchases are *not* included in this database, reflecting the fact that they are less significant than open-market transactions. Subsequent open-market Form 4 sales, however, do carry an "o" notation to indicate they are related to option purchases.

The decision by the Washington Service not to type in the details of option-related Form 4 buys seems to be a matter of profitability. Option-related buys are less valuable bits of information, yet take the same number man-hours to input in a database. Placing an "o" next to the related Form 4 sale relays the important data while saving on input costs. With fewer forms to input, The Washington Service also seems to get some open-market transactions to its customers before competing services do.

A major draw of Washington Service's Insider Trading Service is the availability of Canadian and U.K. insider data. As Chapter 12 relayed, insider data from other countries may not be as detailed and timely as U.S. insider data, but it is certainly good enough to look at.

The Insider Trading Service is available to customers in several formats, including the following:

- Electronic access
- Weekly reports of significant insider trading activity
- A customized monthly watch service
- A customized weekly industry insider report

Rule 144 Stock Service. As discussed in earlier chapters, holders of restricted stock must file a Form 144 disclosing their intention to sell. This service provides a daily display of all of these Form 144 filings as well as 60-day histories for specific companies.

Primark Financial Information Division
5161 River Road
Bethesda, MD 20816
800-846-0365
<www.primark.com/pfid/>

Known as Disclosure, Inc., before being purchased, Primark offers an Insider Newswire and Insider Interpreter as part of its Global Access product. Setting up a Global Access account starts at $2,000, but you need to call the company to negotiate the exact fee.

Insider Newswire. This is a database of Forms 4 and 144 that can be delivered online by way of Global Access in about as real time as possible. In fact, SEC filings made in the morning are available to Insider Newswire customers on the same day before the market close. Afternoon filings are posted later that day. Although the timeliness of this information is important, the customer's ability to manipulate it so that it becomes meaningful is even more important.

Although Insider Newswire filings are updated daily, the database covers a full rolling one-year period. The records included in the database are these:

- Insider name
- Company name
- Transaction type (i.e., buy or sell)
- Date
- Number of shares traded (or in the case of 144s, proposed shares)
- Share price
- Broker
- Remaining shares held—both directly and indirectly—by the insider after the transaction
- Insider address
- Insider telephone number

In addition, Newswire provides its customers with company and industry alerts. For example, if the customer was interested in learning about insider trading activity in a certain company or industry, he or she could arrange to be alerted as soon as insider data that meet the criteria were posted. These alerts are sent by e-mail or stored so that customers can review them at their convenience.

Insider Interpreter. This performs a different, but complementary, function; although it is also updated daily, its approach is historic. Customers can export the data directly to a spreadsheet program, such as Excel, and search the data for insider trading activity from January 1, 1996, to the present. In addition, rather than being limited to Forms 4 and 144 as is the Newswire, the Interpreter contains all of the data on Forms 3, 4, 5, and 144 for the period.

The records included in the Interpreter are the following:

- Insider name
- Company name
- Company address
- Company telephone number
- Transaction type
- Transaction date
- Number of shares traded

- Share price
- Option grant
- Option exercise
- Option expiration date

Customers log on to the service, select the content module they want to search, and can expect to receive the results of their search in just a few seconds. For both the Newswire and Interpreter, customers can search the database using multiple criteria. You can search the database by the following criteria:

- Company name
- Insider name
- Industry
- City
- State
- Date range
- Transaction type

In addition, customers can customize the results screen so they see only the information they consider relevant, and they can establish the order in which the data items appear.

Thomson Financial Networks (First Call)
1355 Piccard Drive
Rockville, MD 20850
888-818-2027
<www.insiderwatch.com>

Thomson Financial Networks bought well-known insider data provider CDA/InvestNet and has begun offering CDA's data to institutions under its First Call brand name.

Insider Trading Monitor. This Internet database (accessible at <www. insiderwatch.com>) is an historic database that includes all insider trading information since 1984. The large amount of historical data is powerful and very useful for researching the track record of individual insiders. The database is accessible by individuals as well as institutions, but the price tag for unlimited access is too rich for the average investor. Once again, there are no list prices for this service; you must put on your negotiating hat and call the company. More affordable Internet databases (with less history) are described in Chapter 15.

Updated daily, the Insider Trading Monitor allows its customers to track and print out a specific insider's trading history or all of the insider trades for a particular company in a given time period—as well as query the database for other information.

The information included for each insider transaction includes the following:

- Trader's name
- Trader's title
- Type of trade (e.g., whether an option or open market)
- Number of shares traded and the price
- Trader's remaining holdings

Transactions that the company's researchers consider to be outside the norm are identified, and customers are alerted to these transactions. In addition to being alerted, the researchers may also provide information that has been uncovered about the company. Insider activity about which an alert is provided may have been identified because of its volume or transaction price or because it involved multiple transactions or represented a significant reduction in the insider's holdings.

For an additional negotiated price, subscribers to Thomson's Insider Trading Monitor can also access its Management Notes and receive e-mail or fax alerts.

Management Notes. This is a print publication that presents detailed fundamental research on companies experiencing significant insider activity, and both long- and short-selling investment ideas are presented.

Thomson's weekly print newsletter, *Insider's Chronicle* (discussed in the next chapter), has similar research but in less detail. Its price is much lower, however.

Watch list fax alert. This provides an alert to customers by fax or e-mail about any significant insider trading activity in companies included in each customer's portfolio.

Signal II. This is a product available only to institutional investors, and its cost is based on the amount of money a firm has under management. For institutions with less than $500 million in assets under management, the cost is $1,000 per month.

Updated weekly, Signal II grades stocks based on insider trading activity from a +2 (indicating a strong buy recommendation) to a −2 (indicating a strong sell recommendation). Values in between these two extremes are simply weaker recommendations of a buy or sell, while a 0 is neutral. A sixth value—a 99—is also possible to indicate that Thomson believes there is insufficient data to make a recommendation.

Vickers Stock Research Corporation
226 New York Avenue
Huntington, NY 11743
516-423-7710
<www.argusgroup.com>

Vickers, known for its weekly print newsletter *Vickers Weekly Insider* (discussed in the next chapter), makes its extensive insider database available to institutions on a negotiated basis.

Part of the Argus Group of companies, Vickers has data going back to 1986 and gathers Form 13F, Schedule 13D, and Schedule 13G data as well as Forms 3, 4, 5, and 144. The firm does not have its own branded avenue for releasing data to institutions, but it has been more active than most institutional data providers in licensing its data to resellers. It is the provider to many of the Web sites that have sprung up to deliver insider data to individuals.

Chapter *13* AT A GLANCE

1. The SEC's monthly print compilation of insider data is too delayed to be useful.

2. EDGAR does not have comprehensive Form 4 data.

3. Service bureaus are generally too expensive for individual investors.

14

Where to Get
Insider Trading Data:
Print Sources

Because of an inherent time lag in receiving information from printed sources when compared with Internet-based and other electronic services, it doesn't make sense to rely on print sources for raw insider data. Besides being less timely, space limitations keep print materials from being comprehensive as well.

Investors should consider how the publication adds value to the data, however, via research recommendations, special screens of insider data, or other types of compilations. If a publication offers quality and reliable value-added research, investors should feel comfortable paying for it.

NEWSLETTERS

The Insiders
2200 SW 10th Street
Deerfield Beach, FL 33442

Published Bimonthly
$49—One Year
800-442-9000

The Insiders is published by the Institute for Econometric Research, which also publishes ten other investment advisory newsletters. By subscribing to one or more of its newsletters, you automatically become a member of the Institute.

The newsletter rates every publicly traded stock from 0 to 10 depending on its insider activity. Any NYSE, AMEX, or OTC stock that is not listed in the newsletter is rated neutral or near neutral, that is, it has a 4, 5, or 6 rating. According to *The Insiders,* any stock rated 10 or 9 is an immediate prospect for purchase. Similarly, any stock rated 0 or 1 is a candidate for sale.

The Insiders' ratings are not based just on sums of basic insider trading statistics. They take into account most of the rules of thumb used to determine the relative importance of insider trades described in Chapters 3 through 6. These rules include:

- Buying is more heavily weighted than selling.
- Open-market trades are more significant than other trades.
- Clusters of activity are more significant.
- Unanimity in clusters of activity is more significant.
- More recent trades are weighted more heavily than older trades.
- A stock trading close to where insiders traded adds significance.
- The titles of the insiders trading are taken into account.
- Larger trades are more significant.
- Initial purchases and final liquidations are considered less significant.
- Trading within the company's industry is also taken into account.

In addition to giving a rating to each of the listed stocks, each issue of *The Insiders* includes a short article on stocks that the editors consider especially noteworthy as well as various insider barometers. The insider barometers are intended to assess the bullishness or bearishness of the market as seen through the eyes of insiders.

Subscribers also receive "Hot Line Updates" each Friday via e-mail that help to keep the insider trading information current.

Insiders' Chronicle
1455 Research Blvd.
Rockville, MD 20850

50 Weekly Issues and 4 Insider Summaries
$315—One Year
800-488-3908

Insiders' Chronicle is a weekly newsletter produced by First Call, a Thomson Financial Company, that looks at the trading of insiders from a number of perspectives. Although it provides additional intelligence when compared with some other information sources, it may require somewhat more digging to uncover its diamonds. Let's examine the kinds of insider information that it offers on a regular basis.

Buy side activity. This column looks at a number of companies that have experienced significant insider buying activity. The company's researchers identify the companies experiencing the most relevant insider buying and research them. From that research, those top few companies that appear to provide the greatest investment opportunity are featured.

Sell side activity. This column is similar to the buy side activity column except that its focus is on those companies that have had significant recent insider selling activity.

Weekly buy/sell report. For investors who want the numbers, a companion piece to the two columns discussed above is the weekly buy/sell report. This report is a tabular one that offers, in spreadsheet fashion, various important statistics for each of the companies discussed in buy side activity and sell side activity. This particular report allows the reader to make his or her own evaluation of a company's stock based on some of the important company statistics.

Largest insider trades. *Insiders' Chronicle* lists the 15 companies with the largest insider purchases and the largest insider sales based on the dollar amount of the trades and listed from the largest to the smallest. In addition, it lists the number of insiders responsible for the trades.

Industry rankings. When the insiders in an entire industry are buying or selling, it usually means that something important is likely to happen in that industry. The industry rankings section of *Insiders' Chronicle* ranks industries on the basis of the number of insider purchases *minus* the number of insider sales. For example, an industry in which 50 insiders purchased and 30 sold their shares would have a sector ranking of 20 (50 − 30 = 20). Similarly, if there were 50 sellers and 30 buyers, the sector would receive a ranking of −20.

The sell-buy ratio. In the way the industry rankings indicate the bullishness or bearishness of insiders toward a particular industry, the sell-buy ratio does the same for the entire market. It gives the number of insider buys and insider sells—in terms of both the number of trades and the number of shares traded—for each of the five preceding weeks and the total for the five-week period.

Insider rankings. The insider rankings segment of *Insiders' Chronicle* shows the top 50 and bottom 50 companies in the S&P 500 ranked by the net number of insiders buying or selling. The company ranked number one in the top 50 is the company whose insider buyers outnumber its insider sellers by the greatest number over the most recent 90-day period. In the same way, the company ranked number one in the bottom 50 is the company whose insider sellers outnumber its insider buyers by the greatest number over the most recent 90-day period. In addition to the company name and its ranking, the insider rankings section provides the net number of insiders and the net volume traded.

Insider trading. By far the largest section in *Insiders' Chronicle,* the insider trading section lists the Form 4 trades on the New York Stock Exchange, the Nasdaq, and the American Stock Exchange during the most recent weeks. Listing the companies alphabetically, it indicates

- the number of shares bought and sold;
- the dates and prices of the transactions;
- the name of the insider effecting the transaction and his or her title;
- the 12-month stock price range; and
- the net number of bullish or bearish insiders in the company during the 90-day period.

144 filings. This section of *Insiders' Chronicle* alphabetically lists the Form 144 filings made in the most recent week that were considered significant by the *Insiders' Chronicle*'s researchers.

13D filings. This section of *Insiders' Chronicle* lists those 13D filings during the previous month that were considered of significant investment interest. The section shows both increases and decreases in holdings of large stakeholders and lists the company name and type of security traded along with other relevant information.

In addition to all of this information, *Insiders' Chronicle* has a brief article in each issue. Perhaps the article focuses on what an investor might want to look for in the coming month, or it may offer observations of current insider trends or some other information that the editors believe may be of interest to its readers.

Vickers Weekly Insider
226 New York Avenue
Huntington, NY 11743

51 Weekly Issues
$176—One Year
800-645-7715

Vickers Weekly Insider newsletter provides a combination of raw insider trading activity data, company evaluations based on insider trading, an assessment of the market's bullishness or bearishness, and a narrative commentary that helps provide a more complete picture of the market as seen through the eyes of its insiders. Its indexes, ratios, and commentaries—while conveying a substantial amount of meaningful information—will probably be easily understood by the average reader.

Company indexes. Each index is in alphabetical order by company name and rates each company's insider transactions for the last six months, assigning a positive or negative numerical rating to the company. A positive rating indicates that insiders are buying, whereas a negative rating generally indicates the opposite. The rating reflects a number of factors, including:

- The number of buy and sell transactions recorded for each company
- The percentage change that occurs in an insider's holdings with each sale or purchase
- The unanimity among the company's insiders (all of the insiders buying or all selling is a stronger indicator)
- The dollar value of the transactions ($250,000+ transactions are given more weight)

In addition, when there is a trend reversal in a company—that is, when the rating moves from a positive to a negative or vice versa—the reader is notified. Index ratings between +5 and −5 are considered neutral and are not listed.

Insider index rankings. Although the alphabetical nature of the Company Indexes makes it simple to find any particular company, determining the companies that have received the highest or lowest ratings could be a chore. The Insider Index Rankings section of *Vickers Weekly*

Insider resolves that problem to some extent by listing, in declining order, the ten most liked companies by insiders and the ten least liked based on their Company Index Ranking.

Sell-buy ratios. The ratio of insider sellers to insider buyers is a measure of the bullishness or bearishness of the entire market. *Vickers Weekly Insider* tracks these transactions and provides a one-week ratio and an eight-week ratio along with a note explaining the meaning of the ratios.

Eight-week sell-buy ratio vs. Dow industrials. This is a graphic presentation of how insiders felt about the market based on their trading activity overlaid on the Dow Jones Industrial Average over the last 13 months. It shows the correlation of insider activity to the stock market.

Form 4 transactions. *Vickers Weekly Insider* lists the Form 4 filings for the previous week that involved at least 500 shares and at a stock price of at least $1 per share. To help make this alphabetical listing more meaningful for the investor, certain transactions are excluded. Excluded transactions include stock dividends, gifts, private transactions of less than 10,000 shares, and shares acquired by exercise of options or participation in compensation, savings, and thrift or bonus plans.

Portfolio valuation and performance. Two ten-stock model portfolios are maintained by *Vickers Weekly Insider,* and their weekly valuation and performance are compared with the Dow Jones Industrial Average for the same period. The investment decisions for both portfolios are based on insider transactions. Each portfolio's holdings are shown along with the dates of purchase, purchase price, and latest close for each of the stocks held.

Stocks most actively bought by insiders. A listing of the 25 companies whose stocks have been most actively purchased by insiders in the past three months is provided.

Stocks most actively sold by insiders. A listing of the 25 companies whose stocks have been most actively sold by insiders in the past three months is also provided.

Commentary. This is a 500-or-so-word narrative that highlights insider activity thought to be significant and its relation to the market and its performance.

The Insiders' Opinion
Wall Street Strategies, Inc.
P.O. Box 29429
Richmond, VA 23242

Monthly
$150—One Year
$85—Six Months
$35—Three Months
800-266-2517

The Insiders' Opinion takes a different approach from most other newsletters. Rather than providing a wealth of data about a large universe of securities, *The Insiders' Opinion* is devoted principally to an examination of five or so companies whose stocks are recommended for purchase.

The newsletter's stated objective is to discover and recommend low-cap stocks that have the greatest potential for above-average appreciation based on insider trading activity, technical analysis, and fundamental analysis. In fact, the editor states that *The Insiders' Opinion* is the only newsletter that encompasses these three areas of research. The newsletter's evaluation takes the following factors into account in its recommendations:

- Insider trading activity
- Fundamental and technical strength
- Momentum
- High relative strength
- High earnings-per-share rank
- High industry group rank
- High return on equity
- A forecast of significant earnings gains

Fundamental analysis. The editor refers to earnings per share as the basic ingredient of the company's fundamental analysis. Emphasis is placed on earnings growth, earnings-per-share (EPS) rank, and estimates of a company's projected EPS. A company's return on equity (ROE) is a basic indicator of a company's ability to increase its earnings per share.

Technical analysis. The recommendations that appear in *The Insiders' Opinion* reflect, in part, an analysis that may employ up to 30 technical graph indicators and 20 stock market performance indicators.

These stocks are measured against their industry as a whole, and then the industry groups are compared with market indexes to identify the strongest stocks.

After a recommendation touches on the important insider, fundamental, and technical criteria that caught the analyst's interest, the investment opinion provides a 12-month price objective and a suggested stop loss.

In addition to the specific buy recommendations in each issue, the newsletter includes a follow-up and review section in which recommendations made in the previous six-month period are briefly revisited. The information included in this section includes:

- The price and date of the initial recommendation
- The subsequent stock price high
- The current stock price
- The current recommendation—to buy, hold, or avoid

Although the reader may not be entirely familiar with all of the statistics and technical indicators that accompany each recommendation, it's likely that the majority of them will be understandable to most investors. In addition, the more directive nature of *The Insiders' Opinion* may appeal to investors who don't have the time or inclination to sift through and evaluate the wealth of information on many more securities that may be available through other sources.

Jack Adamo's *Inside Track*
Phillips Publishing, Inc.
7811 Montrose Road
Potomac, MD 20854-3394

Monthly
$295—One Year
800-211-6362

It's hard to argue with success, and Jack Adamo's *Inside Track* has experienced some of it. From November 1996, when he began to make information about insider trading activity available through *Inside Track,* through June 1999, the editor's recommendations have averaged gains of 27 percent on ten-month average holding periods. Adamo's approach, however, may not appeal to everyone.

Recommendations. The recommendations appear to be thoroughly researched fundamentally as well as from an insider point of view. Adamo looks at industry considerations, talks with management, and generally undertakes all the methods one would expect of a proper analyst.

The main difference with the presentation of the research is one of style. While some may find this newsletter's writing to be chatty and accessible, others may find the informal style too full of superlatives.

Notes on previous recommendations. Significant events that impact companies previously recommended are reported in the section on previous recommendations. This section might include information concerning changes in companies' earnings per share, operating cash flow or other news affecting the companies, and the actions being taken by the management in response. Each note concludes with a recommendation, which might be "Buy ABC Company up to $25."

Comments on the portfolio. Like many newsletters, *Inside Track* maintains a portfolio of about 25 previously recommended stocks. In a manner similar to the section on previous recommendations, the editor lists each of the stocks—along with its ticker symbol and the exchange on which it is traded—and gives a brief two- or three-sentence update.

Web site and hot line. *Inside Track* subscribers can use the Internet to log on to the *Inside Track*'s Web page. Typing in <www.adamoinsidetrack. com> will take subscribers to the *Inside Track* home page and into the insider information provided. In addition, subscribers can hear Jack Adamo's weekly hot line by dialing into *Inside Track*'s special number.

NEWSPAPERS

Newspapers used to be extremely important to the distribution of insider data to the public in the 1930s and 1940s, but they no longer are. The two remaining papers that have any useful information are *Barron's* and the *Wall Street Journal.*

Barron's, a tabloid-style newspaper published on weekends, carries tables of selected insider transactions under the headings of Recent Filings and Largest % Changes in Insider Holdings. Transactions in the table of recent filings list the top ten most significant open-market buys and sales over the past week in terms of the percentage change in holdings they represent and are screened to omit trades by insiders who are not officers, trades in shares under $2, and trades of less than 100 shares. After similar screening, the table showing the largest percent changes in insider holdings lists the top ten companies in terms of the total change in the total percentage of insider ownership over the latest six months.

The *Wall Street Journal* carries similar tables as part of its Inside Track column on Wednesdays, but if investors are really interested in this data, they can get it on a more timely basis on the Internet at <www.InsiderTrader.com> (reviewed in Chapter 15). The *Wall Street Journal*'s Inside Track column focuses on a specific company or industry experiencing significant insider trading activity or on an issue related to insider data. The column is more news oriented, however, and not usually geared toward generating new investment ideas.

Though interesting enough for present subscribers of these publications to glance at, investors certainly shouldn't count on obtaining any unique or action-oriented insider information from either source.

MAGAZINES

Although *Fortune, Forbes,* and *SmartMoney* each has occasional articles that address insider trading, only *Individual Investor* has a permanent column devoted to analysis of stocks that have insider trading activity. *Individual Investor,* published monthly by Individual Investor Group, Inc., at a U.S. newsstand price of $2.99 (two-year subscriptions for $34.95), has a menu of offerings that appeal to the sophisticated investor as well as the novice—and most folks in between.

In addition to worthwhile feature articles that may address the financial health of a major corporation, or any other topical issue of interest to investors, *Individual Investor*'s format includes several other important sections. It offers regular columns and departments, a segment devoted to mutual funds, a segment—appropriately entitled The Educated Investor—that may be of particular interest to the novice investor, and a section called The Screening Room that provides material of interest to investors who want to watch the insiders.

Part of The Screening Room is Insider's Edge, a column that presents two new investment ideas derived from analyzing insider trading activity. These are fundamentally researched ideas presented in a very accessible writing style. This column also contains a buyer's guide that lists companies with the largest dollar value of insider buys over the past month; it can give readers a starting point for further research on their own.

If a reader is already subscribing to *Individual Investor* for its good general treatment of subjects of concern to investors, Insider's Edge is an interesting and informative column that provides value at no additional cost. Whether it is sufficiently informative for an investor, looking for information about insider trading activity on which to make stock purchases is another matter. Information in the buyer's guide can be obtained in a more complete and timely way on the Internet and in newspapers, and the column is not a proper newsletter that maintains a portfolio of recommendations. There is also no guarantee that a recommended stock will be followed up with analysis in the future.

Chapter *14* AT A GLANCE

1. No periodicals have comprehensive insider data.

2. Choose your newsletter by virture of the value-added data and research it delivers.

15

Where to Get
Insider Trading Data:
The Internet

The Internet is clearly the best place for investors to gather insider data for use in their investment process and is the main reason this book is being written at all. The Internet's accessibility and affordability are what has generated the demand from individual investors that has brought down the price of insider data.

The quality of the free insider data available now on the Internet can be said to have properly leveled the playing field between individual and institutional investors so that the original intent behind Congress's mandating the data in the 1930s is once again being fulfilled. The quarter-of-a-century or so leading up to 1996, when institutions relied on expensive technology to use insider data for getting yet another leg up on individuals, has passed. Computers are now cheap, and the Internet is the cheap distribution mechanism for getting the data to the mass market of PC owners. The playing field will only become more level with time as the remaining insider data still being charged for are eventually being given away for page views and ad revenues.

I have already discussed EDGAR, the SEC's own Web-based insider data source (see Chapter 13), as well as sites that service bureaus use for granting their institutional clients access to the data (also Chapter 13). Now let's look at where most individuals are, and should be, getting insider trading data.

I'll start with some of the best-known Web sites, even though they are not the best places to go if you are serious about using insider data in your investment process.

MASS MARKET WEB SITES

Just about every online investor has heard of and used Yahoo! Finance (located at <www.finance.yahoo.com>). This is the finance channel of that ever-expanding aggregator of Web content—Yahoo! Although this search engine cum Internet empire doesn't really add value to the data it aggregates, it has served its public well by bringing together good-quality data to a single area, thus saving investors time when they're doing basic research. The same can be said of the finance channels of the other major web portals: Excite.com <www.excite.com/money>; Quicken. com <www.quicken.com/investments>; and Microsoft's Money Central <www.moneycentral.com>. The Web site property of *SmartMoney* magazine <www.smartmoney.com> also has decent free insider data.

I am lumping all these well-known sites together for the simple reason that they all basically offer the same data: 12 months of detailed Forms 3, 4, and 144 histories. Through the portfolio features on most of these sites, investors can also receive alerts of insider activity on stocks they are following.

The layouts of the histories differ between the sites, but the data fields invariably include:

- Name of the insider
- Insider's relationship to the company
- Transaction type
- Shares traded
- Price or price range of the trades
- Date or date range of the trades
- Total holdings of the insider
- Notation if holdings are directly or indirectly held

All of these sites (except SmartMoney.com) spell out the transaction types in plain English, which would seem beneficial, but using words like *Given as Gift* instead of some easily understood code actually makes for a slightly messier presentation to this viewer's eye. The fact that they also use the term *Planned Sale* to indicate Form 144 transactions is particularly unfortunate. Form 144s are more complicated than the term used (as explained in Chapters 1 and 7) and could confuse neophytes.

Of the portals, Intuit.com and Excite.com have better layouts. (The layouts of the data are actually the same on these sites because they were related on a corporate ownership level.) They managed to put all the data fields on the basic results page, whereas MoneyCentral, Yahoo! Finance, and SmartMoney.com require an extra click to view an insider's total holdings and direct/indirect notation. MoneyCentral doesn't even list Form 4 and Form 144 transactions on the same history. It should be pointed out, however, that Yahoo! Finance and SmartMoney. com have Form 3 (initial filings) data, while the others do not.

Oddly, none of these deep-pocket Web presences have bothered to allow their insider data to be searched by an insider's name. This is extremely important for analyzing an insider's trades across all of the companies in which he or she is considered an insider. Doing so gives clues to which holdings the insider thinks are relatively better values. Even though insider names are hyperlinked on all of the ticker-generated insider histories on these sites, clicking them only isolates the insider's trades at one company.

Comparing the sites according to which has the most timely and accurate data is not particularly relevant. All the Web sites mentioned in this chapter receive the raw data from one of the four service bureaus reviewed in Chapter 13. Yahoo! and SmartMoney.com license data from Thomson Financial Networks; Intuit.com and Excite.com license from Vickers Stock Research; and MoneyCentral.com, from Primark. All of these original sources are excellent, though each will have its own inevitable errors in a small percentage of the data because of the imperfect nature of the reporting and data input process.

If this were 1997 instead of past the millennium, the insider data on all these mass market sites would be considered groundbreaking in their detail. Now, however, such data are very much a commodity item. And though decent enough for following stocks you already own, they provide no real capability for using the data to find new investments.

WALLSTREETCITY

Free Services
Basic Services—$9.95 monthly
Full Services—$34.95 monthly

WallStreetCity has at least as good free insider data histories as the portals reviewed above in terms of the layout and amount of data returned. And of all the sites on which insider activity is just a portion of a larger financial channel, WallStreetCity.com has also done a good job adding value to the data (which it receives from Vickers Stock Research).

Its adding value to the data stems from the fact that Telescan, the company behind WallStreetCity.com, is a technology firm that has applied its high-end database applications to its insider data. The result is good value-added tables and price charts that integrate insider data. Alas, though, the company's powerful screening tool doesn't make the best use of insider data. Telescan's tools are unique enough, however, that InsiderTrader.com (reviewed later) and CNBC.com (the Web presence of the well-known business news TV channel) have licensed them for their Web sites.

ProSearch

ProSearch is the powerful and proprietary search engine that gives WallStreetCity its excellent screening capability. Insider data is just one of the numerous criteria that can be screened using ProSearch, and combining the data with fundamental and technical criteria *should* have been a very useful tool with which to prospect for new investments.

Unfortunately, ProSearch doesn't allow users to screen on important specifics of an insider's trade, such as the number of shares traded or even if it is an open-market trade.

On WallStreetCity's home page, free canned insider ProSearch screens are accessed through the Search for an Investment link off its home page. On this page you can generate lists of the top and bottom 25 companies in terms of the quantity of insider trading activity.

The problem with the ProSearch screens of insider data is the same as that with any quantitative ranking of insider data. I have mentioned numerous times that insider data should not be viewed as a technical indicator because of their numerous qualitative aspects (e.g., are the trades open market, how well has the insider traded in the past, is a stock's price rising or falling when insiders trade? etc.) that must be reviewed to assess significance.

On the free insider screens I've seen, the sheer number of trades is the basis for their ranking. Looking at the insider histories of the top companies with high insider buying, I found that most of the trades being included in the ranking were not open-market Form 4 transactions. Furthermore, the size of many of the transactions was small both in terms of the number of shares and the dollar value of the trades. No wonder that the chart at the top of the table illustrating "How well has this search been working?" showed it not just underperforming the market but losing money!

The free high insider selling list generated by ProSearch was equally disappointing, being chock-full of high-tech, high-flying companies with insiders cashing in options. The chart at the top of this table illustrating "How well has this search been working?" showed these stocks outperforming the market—the exact opposite of the results that proper analysis of insider selling would garner.

Anyone applying the simple rules of thumb from this book would know that these particular free screens are not useful, but neophytes looking at the results would be forgiven for concluding that it is insider trading data itself that isn't useful. This is a shame. With all of Telescan's keen technical staff, it would seem a relatively easy step to program ProSearch to screen the insider criteria more specifically—at least in the subscriber-based sections of the site that charge $9.95 per month and $34.95 per month. One hopes the company will fix this shortcoming in the future, for the back-testing feature of ProSearch available to $34.95-per-month subscribers would be excellent to use on a more robust insider search function. At this time, however, it is not worth paying for this function if insider research is your main focus. The free stuff will do.

Other free insider tools on WallStreetCity include insider price charts and industry rankings. Incorporating insider trading as one of the indicators on this site's price charts makes for an interesting visual tool.

Industry Rankings

A more useful tool is the industry rankings generated via WallStreetCity's best and worst tables. Users can create rankings of industries or companies within industries based on numerous criteria—one of which is insider trading activity. This screen returns the top and bottom 25 companies or industries based on the selected criteria.

I have already harped on the problem with insider ranking of individual stocks but found the industry rankings more appropriate as the option-related transactions and other "noise" in the data tended to offset themselves when rankings are aggregated by industry.

The results pages of the insider-based industry rankings (see Figure 15.1) includes a nifty visual cue indicating undervaluation or overvaluation according to insiders. Other useful stats are also included on the

FIGURE 15.1 Best Industries in Terms of Insider Tracking Data

Industry Group Insider Trading

Select an Industry ▸   Insider Trading ▸

Portfolio Insider Trading   05/08/00 - 9:12 a.m. Eastern

Symbol	Insider Rank	Net Insider Trading	#Buys	#Sells	#Exercise of options	3Month Change
PORTFOLIO	STRONG SELL ——— STRONG BUY	-2769.0	3471	6240	3702	-0.1%
Machinery/containers/metal	STRONG SELL ——— STRONG BUY	2	4	2	0	2%
Publishing/books	STRONG SELL ——— STRONG BUY	4	4	0	0	2%
Finance/leasing	STRONG SELL ——— STRONG BUY	5	8	3	2	1%
Home/household products	STRONG SELL ——— STRONG BUY	6	15	9	3	1%
Home/office/equipment	STRONG SELL ——— STRONG BUY	3	7	4	3	1%
Conglomerate	STRONG SELL ——— STRONG BUY	6	8	2	1	0%
Machinery/flow control filtration	STRONG SELL ——— STRONG BUY	13	17	4	12	0%
Banks	STRONG SELL ——— STRONG BUY	351	509	158	139	0%
Banks/savings & loan	STRONG SELL ——— STRONG BUY	46	68	22	15	0%
Basic/steel-iron/major integrated	STRONG SELL ——— STRONG BUY	6	6	0	0	0%
Broadcasting/catv	STRONG SELL ——— STRONG BUY	7	9	2	2	0%
Broadcasting/radio	STRONG SELL ——— STRONG BUY	6	24	18	3	0%
Building	STRONG SELL ——— STRONG BUY	5	6	1	2	0%
Chemicals	STRONG SELL ——— STRONG BUY	31	57	26	25	0%
Chemicals/coatings-paint-varnishes	STRONG SELL ——— STRONG BUY	5	7	2	3	0%
Electronics/household appliances	STRONG SELL ——— STRONG BUY	11	12	1	10	0%

table, which is a decent place to start finding new investments based on insider transactions. Clicking the hyperlinked industry name with the best insider ranking brings up the companies within the industry. Reviewing the insider activity company by company is the necessary next step in your research process. Finding the company with the best insider trading profile in the industries with the best insider trading profiles should lead to profitable investments.

THOMSON INVESTORS NETWORK

Free Services
Full Membership—$34.95 per year
Insider Trading Premium Package—$19.95 per month
<www.thomsoninvest.net>

Thomson Investors Network is the retail outlet for the financial data of Thomson Financial Networks (the institutional data provider reviewed in Chapter 13). This site is excellent for free insider-related commentary and research but not for free insider data.

Although insider information is only a portion of what this site focuses on, there are prominent links on its home page to both an insider Tip of the Day and Stock of the Day by Bob Gabele, a well-known and well-respected personality associated with insider trading information. As you would expect, the Stock of the Day is more fully researched and written about than the Tip of the Day, and clicking either exposes another subnavigation that contains a link to further insider commentary called Insider's Periscope. The Periscope is a handy verbal review of insider trading activity over the past week that Gabele has deemed significant.

Also on this subnavigation is a link to the *Insiders' Chronicle,* which gives subscribers to this print newsletter (reviewed in Chapter 14) access to the product over the Internet.

Full Membership

The basic company profiles provided through <www.thomsoninvest. com> contain only a one-word quantitatively generated insider rating of positive or negative. To get any real insider data, you must subscribe. But even with a subscription, there is only one year of detailed Form 4 data. Other nice value-added items include a price chart with the insider data graphically represented, a list of the top insider owners of the stock, and a list of the top institutional holders (i.e., Form 13F filers). While there is certainly some value in bringing all these tables together, users can get all of these data free on other sites.

Insider Trading Premium Package

The site does do a good job on the research and commentary side of the equation, and if you are thinking about subscribing to the *Insiders'*

Chronicle newsletter, you might as well do it through this Web site. For $19.95 per month you get access to the *Chronicle* online and access to the reports that full membership allows. With so much free research on the Internet, however, you really have to like the newsletter to justify the $239.40 per year for its monthly fee.

INSIDERTRADER.COM

Free Services
Member Services—$49.95 yearly
Premium Services—$17.95 monthly (in addition to $49.95/year)
Institutional Services—$249.95 monthly or $2,000 per year
<www.insidertrader.com>

On most Internet sites, insider data is just a section (or afterthought) of a broader base of financial information. InsiderTrader.com has taken the opposite tack. It focuses solely on insider data and research, so it is not surprising that this niche site has the most to offer investors interested in using insider data in their investment process. Its free histories have more data better laid out than other free histories, and it also adds value to the data in numerous ways.

InsiderTrader.com was the first to offer free, comprehensive insider data on a timely basis when it was started in June 1996. The site was purchased by Individual Investor Group in December 1998 but remains its own stand-alone Web site. This site provides the insider data on a co-branded basis to IndividualInvestor.com; Hoovers.com; Edgar-Online. com; and CompanySleuth.com, among others, and receives its raw data from both Vickers Stock Research and The Washington Service (both of these firms were reviewed in Chapter 13).

Free Services

InsiderTrader.com has free stuff for investors just following stocks they already own and investors interested in finding new investments. Features include:

- Two-year histories of open-market and option-related Form 4 transactions, Form 144 filings, and Form 3 data (Histories can be generated for a specific company or a specific insider.)

- Monthly insider histories of open-market Form 4 and Form 144 data that give a bird's-eye view of insider trading activity going back to June 1996
- Daily e-mail alerts of the above transactions on a portfolio of up to 50 stocks
- Daily screens that combine insider data with price action or fundamental criteria to generate new potential investment ideas
- An archive of the daily screens
- A daily list of filings that appear to be filed late
- New stock recommendations each week generated from insider data
- A weekly column that highlights companies with interesting insider activity
- A stock market indicator based on graphing aggregate insider transactions in conjunction with well-known market indexes (reviewed in Chapter 11)
- Summaries of Form 13F (institutional holdings) data for the past four quarters, along with details of the top ten institutional holders of the stock in the most recent period
- Screens that point out companies with the largest changes in the number of institutional investors and percentage of institutional ownership
- Insider industry rankings and price charts (from Telescan)

That InsiderTrader.com has two years of insider data in its free histories instead of the usual one-year histories most sites offer makes these histories better than all but those on InsiderScores.com (which also has two years) by virtue of sheer data volume. What really makes these free histories better than all others, however, is their functionality.

Besides being searchable by company name or ticker, users can also search by an insider's name. Furthermore, the insider name search returns the transactions for all the companies in which the person is considered an insider. The same occurs when you click the hyperlinked insider name in the ticker symbol and company name–generated insider histories.

There are more insiders than you might think that have large cross-holdings or directors who sit on several boards. As explained in Chapter 5, reviewing an insider's activity across all of his or her holdings can give investors a good idea of what the insider thinks the relative value of his or her various holdings is. If you see an insider selling shares in one of the companies they file Form 4s for, while buying shares in a different company, the insider is definitely letting you know which stock he or she thinks is a better investment.

The free monthly insider histories are unique to InsiderTrader.com. They combine all the Form 4 buys that were filed during a month for a company on one line, and the same is done for Form 4 sales and Form 144 transactions. Although they are less timely than the detailed histories on this and other sites, and specific insiders' names are replaced with just the titles of the traders, the data goes back to June 1996. This makes the histories an excellent source for getting a long-term view of insider trading at a company. And if you know that the chairman (represented as a C on these summaries) at a firm you're researching hasn't changed in the past few years, you can easily figure out the specific name of the insider.

The daily screens and weekly review of interesting insider activity are useful for suggesting new stocks to investigate. There are anywhere from 5 to 20 stocks highlighted in each of these features.

If you want more in-depth research, there is also the Insider Weekly Pick. The track record of these recommendations is excellent, but there is no free follow-up analysis, so you have to decide for yourself when to sell.

The daily list of late filers (dubbed the *Table of Shame*) is novel but not of much investment importance. There also seems to be room for some "noise" in the data, so users should investigate a little further before calling a company on the list to chastise the late filers.

The Form 13F summaries are very worthwhile, however. Institutional sponsorship is very important for a stock to perform well, and these summaries give a four-quarter bird's-eye view of a company's institutional ownership history. Most institutional holdings summaries only look at two quarters. The four quarters of detailed Form 13F data listed for the top ten institutional owners of a stock is also more information than is given away on other free Web sites.

The insider industry rankings have the same effective use here as was described previously on WallStreetCity. Similarly, the price charts with insider data graphically represented are pleasant, even though they are not critical for researching new investments.

InsiderTrader's market indicator assesses the bearishness or bullishness of the market as seen through the eyes of insider traders. The site compares the number of companies with insiders indicating open-market buying and selling during a particular week or month and presents the information as a percentage. If there are more companies with buyers than sellers, the indicator is positive; if there are more companies with sellers than buyers, the indicator is negative. For a full review of this market indicator, refer back to page 126 in Chapter 11.

Member Services

The main value of subscribing to member services is the online newsletter, but there is also another layer of value-added tools for researching insider data.

The full menu of added features at this level of subscription includes:

- An online newsletter (also called the *Buy List*) that offers fundamental analyses of stocks with insider buying and ongoing updates of the recommendation until a sale is advised
- Weekly insider data summaries sorted by transaction value for identifying potential new investments
- Interactive screening of the weekly and monthly summaries for companies with specific fundamental and price action criteria
- A listing and brief commentary on companies that InsiderTrader. com is considering for inclusion on its buy list
- A listing of the 20 largest insider transactions (buys and sells) over the most recent week *by hands-on executives*
- A listing of the 20 companies with the largest net buying and selling by insiders as a percentage of the company's outstanding shares
- E-mail alerts of insider trading in a portfolio of up to 100 stocks

Newsletter. This feature is what makes InsiderTrader's subscription-based services unique. It is the only place on the Internet where insider-based recommendations are updated continuously until a sell recommendation is given. The online newsletter lists in tabular form all the stocks it presently recommends investors buy (see Figure 15.2). A stock can be demoted to a hold, and the analysts at the site also tell investors when to sell the position. All closed positions are listed separately, and all of the research is also available to review.

The newsletter takes advantage of the Internet's timeliness of delivery by updating its recommendations as soon as possible after new news unfolds—usually within a day. Price targets and stop losses are clearly indicated, and the entire archive of original recommendations and research updates is logically accessible.

There is no official dollar-denominated portfolio whose performance can be analyzed, but the newsletter has had more winning recommendations than losing ones, and the winners have gained more on average

---

FIGURE 15.2 InsiderTrader.com's Buy List

InsiderTrader's Online Newsletter

Click company name to read original recommendation. Click date in the Latest Update column to read the most recent follow-up research, and to thread your way back through any previous updates.

Buy List

Company	Ticker	Rec. Date	Rec. Price	Yield At Rec.	Target Price	Stop Loss	Latest Update	4/5/00 Price	% Gain (Loss)	Current Rating
Tyco International	TYC	3/9/00	42.38	0.12%	53.00	35.00	3/14/00	46.56	9.9	Buy
Ameritrade	AMTD	3/1/00	20.31	-	30.00	10.00	3/8/00	17.63	(13.2)	Buy
Cendant (2)	CD	2/29/00	17.13	-	22.00	14.00	3/29/00	17.88	4.4	Buy
Pinnacle Entertainment (2)	PNK	2/16/00	16.94	-	25.00	19.00	4/4/00	20.63	21.8	Buy
NetManage (2)	NETM	2/14/00	6.75	-	10.00	3.00	4/4/00	4.75	(29.6)	Buy
Safeway	SWY	2/1/00	37.94	-	50.00	30.00	3/16/00	46.25	21.9	Buy
Seitel	SEI	1/19/00	8.31	-	15.00	6.00	3/3/00	7.44	(10.5)	Buy
US Express (3)	XPRSA	12/17/99	6.56	-	10.00	4.75	3/15/00	8.88	35.4	Buy
Hasbro	HAS	12/15/99	17.75	1.35%	25.00	13.50	3/23/00	16.88	(4.9)	Buy
Windmere Durable (2)	WND	12/15/99	14.88	-	25.00	12.00	3/17/00	14.31	(3.8)	Buy
Sovereign Banc (2)	SVRN	12/8/99	7.75	1.25%	11.00	5.00	4/4/00	7.25	(6.5)	Buy
Callaway Golf	ELY	2/24/99	11.13	-	20.00	10.00	3/29/00	15.38	38.2	Buy
eGames	EGAM	1/14/99	2.56	-	6.00	1.50	3/24/00	2.06	(19.5)	**Sell**
Weirton Steel (2)	WS	7/28/98	2.94	–	12.00	6.00	4/4/00	6.94	136.1	Buy
Main Street	MAIN	6/25/98	3.44	-	5.25	2.50	3/3/00	3.00	(12.8)	Buy
Ampex	AXC	5/18/97	5.75	-	10.00	2.00	2/11/00	2.75	(52.2)	Buy

Holding Pen

Company	Ticker	Rec. Date	Rec. Price	Yield At Rec.	Target Price	Stop Loss	Latest Update	4/5/00 Price	% Gain (Loss)	Current Rating
PSS World Medical (2)	PSSI	12/15/99	9.97	-	12.00	5.00	2/29/00	7.41	(25.7)	**Hold**

Closed Positions

Company	Ticker	Rec. Date	Rec. Price	Latest Update	Sell Price	Total Return	Sell Date
B/E Aerospace (2)	BEAV	12/13/99	6.63	3/13/00	7.50	13.1%	3/13/00
Tricon Global	YUM	8/11/99	37.50	2/24/00	26.00	(30.7)%	2/24/00
Hollywood Park	HPK	10/26/99	16.69	2/11/00	17.00	1.9%	2/11/00
Aeroflex	ARX	11/12/99	8.75	2/10/00	26.31	200.7%	2/10/00
SonoSite	SONO	7/28/98	6.75	2/8/00	25.00	270.4%	2/8/00
Parexel	PRXL	12/15/99	11.31	1/19/00	15.00	32.6%	1/19/00
Midway Games (2)	MWY	11/30/99	20.94	1/18/00	18.00	(14.0)%	1/18/00
Cendant	CD	5/20/99	18.88	1/3/00	26.25	39.0%	1/3/00
Saul Centers	BFS	1/2/98	18.00	1/3/00	14.00	(4.8)%	1/3/00
Bombay (2)	BBA	10/28/99	3.75	12/17/99	4.62	23.2%	12/17/99
Action Performance	ACTN	10/20/99	19.69	12/15/99	13.00	(34.0)%	12/15/99
Concord Camera	LENS	9/16/99	8.69	12/14/99	19.50	124.4%	12/14/99
Ventana Medical	VMSI	10/6/99	18.19	12/7/99	25.31	39.1%	12/7/99
Columbia Sportswear	COLM	10/28/99	19.69	12/7/99	17.00	(13.7)%	12/7/99
Lone Star Tech	LSS	4/14/99	14.94	11/16/99	25.25	69.0%	11/16/99

than the losers have lost. In two-and-a-half years since InsiderTrader. com started delivering research in May 1997, it had 49 profitable recommendations and 43 unprofitable picks. The average winner appreciated 51.5 percent, and the average loser was down 31.3 percent. The average holding period of the newsletter's closed positions was just over six months.

Insider histories sorted by transaction value. InsiderTrader's weekly insider histories are unique to this site and have the same format as the previously mentioned free monthly histories. A main value-added feature of member services, however, is the ability to view both the weekly and monthly histories in one big file, sorted by transaction value (see Figure 4.1 on page 46 for an excerpt).

These files are time-efficient tools for finding new investments. In just five to ten minutes a week, you can scan the latest list of weekly data sorted by transaction value and easily make a list of the most interesting clusters of recent insider activity. The weekly summaries only have open-market transactions, so the noise in the data is minimized, and the largest dollar values on top allow you to stop looking when the dollar value falls under significant levels.

With a short list in hand, you can check out the detailed insider histories to assess the overall significance of the trades using the methods described previously in this book. Stocks that make the grade can then be analyzed according to their fundamentals. This whole process can also be undertaken once a month with the monthly insider data.

Radar screen. Analysts at InsiderTrader can save you even the short amount of time it takes to review the weekly histories sorted by transaction value. They go through the process described above to generate the commentary in the weekly radar screen. In one paragraph, the analysts describe the interesting insider activity and also various fundamental and valuation criteria that make the stock worth looking at more closely. This weekly commentary is the same as that in the free weekly review, but it is made available to subscribers two days before it is given away.

Interactive screening. The screening capability on InsiderTrader is not as sophisticated as WallStreetCity's, but it does return results that are at least as valuable. There is no back-testing capability, however, and the number of criteria with which to combine insider data is much more limited. Still, the fact that the screening is of the weekly data—

which only capture open-market trades—helps reduce the number of companies with insignificant insider histories from being returned, which makes InsiderTrader's screening tool particularly useful for starting the process of finding new investments. Most of the free daily screens on the site are actually static pages generated from this screening function.

Largest trades. There is little question about size mattering when applied to insider trading, so this screen would appear to be useful for finding new investment ideas. These largest trades are broken down into two categories: (1) largest individual trades by transaction value and (2) largest trades as a percentage of outstanding shares. The listing of largest individual trades includes the largest 20 buy and sell transactions effected by individuals over the previous week. The category of largest individual trades includes only the trades (both buys and sells) made by insiders with hands-on responsibilities in the company, so the trades of beneficial owners or outside shareholders are not considered. Furthermore, in the listing of buys, only open-market purchases are considered, so option-related buys are excluded. All sales, however, are considered, even those preceded by purchases incident to stock options.

A subset of the largest trades feature is given away on a delayed basis as one of the daily screens. For both paid and free users, however, the list of largest trades is available before a similar list is published in Wednesday's *Wall Street Journal.*

Premium Services

In addition to subscription services, InsiderTrader also provides what it terms *premium services.* These services are available on an unlimited basis to existing member service subscribers but can also be accessed on a pay-per-view basis. The full menu of features includes:

- Four-year insider data histories that include Schedule 13D and Schedule 13G data as well as the Form 3, 4, and 144 data provided in the free insider histories
- A daily download of transactions that were added to the database during the day
- E-mail alerts of insider trading in a portfolio of up to 200 stocks

Although the free insider histories here and on other Web sites list the most recent activity, serious investors may want to consider paying the extra fee for the increased history provided by premium services. It can be very important for assessing the past trading performance of an insider.

SEC rules prevent insiders from buying and selling (or selling and buying) their own company's shares in the open market within a six-month period (see Chapter 2 for more on the short-swing rules). Because of this, the typical one-year (or in the case of InsiderTrader, 13-month) insider histories given away free all over the Internet are not likely enough to properly analyze an insider's track record. The four years of history presented here are much better for this purpose. Also, combining the more institutional information provided by Schedules 13D and 13G data with the insider data is a definite added value.

Daily download. The daily download adds even more value. This is the only place on the Internet (priced reasonably enough for individuals) where users can see details of all the transactions coming out of the SEC on a given day in one file. This file can also be opened in a spreadsheet for further analysis if need be.

This daily chunk of data is useful for serious investors to scroll through to find interesting clusters of insider activity or other details that may make investigating the stock further worthwhile. In this regard, it is the daily equivalent of the weekly file sorted by transaction value available to member service subscribers. Being more detailed and more frequent, this method of prospecting for new investments is more time consuming, but it is also more timely. Stockbrokers will even find it useful for combing through Form 144 data for new clients.

Institutional Services

InsiderTrader's institutional services are a very robust and cost-effective product for analyzing Form 13F data filed at the SEC. Also known as institutional holdings data, the usefulness of Form 13F is explained at length in Chapters 1 and 8. At $249 per month (or $2,000 per year if you pay up front), this service is too expensive for most individuals, but professional investors will recognize it as a bargain. The cost also affords a subscriber all the privileges of InsiderTrader's premium services.

The institutional service is likely to become less expensive in the near future, however, as more Web sites begin to distribute Form 13F data. The reason this data will become more mass market is that it was recently mandated by the SEC that institutions file their Form 13Fs via EDGAR. Enterprising computer programmers have developed methods for breaking down the individual lines of the now-electronic form so that the data can be fed into a database. This is much less costly than the labor-intensive manual input method needed when Form 13F was filed on paper at the SEC.

Price aside, the layout and functionality of InsiderTrader's Form 13F database seems well thought out. The database can be searched in five ways:

1. By ticker
2. By company name (if you don't know the ticker)
3. By the name of the institution filing Form 13F
4. By the contact name at the filing institutions
5. By the date on which the database was updated

Searching by ticker or company name returns four quarters of Form 13F data for the publicly traded company. All the institutions that have owned the company's stock in the past year are listed along with 17 other columns of data, including:

- Type of institution the filer is (bank, insurance company, investment firm, etc.)
- Date of the latest Form 13F filing (which will be a quarter-ended date)
- Current holdings of the institution in the stock you're looking at
- Recent dollar value of the holdings
- Percentage of the stock owned by the institution
- Number of shares traded in the latest quarter
- Percentage change in the institution's holdings of the stock in the latest quarter

Similar data on the three previous quarters is also listed, and the fact that InsiderTrader has four quarters of data is extremely useful for seeing how the institutions have built up their positions over time.

When the name of the filing institution is clicked from the ticker or company search, the result is a page of all the investment positions of that institution over the last four quarters (see Figure 8.2 on page 100 for an example). This is the same output as when you query by name of the institution filing the Form 13F from the home page of the institutional services. The same 17 data fields are produced in this view as for the ticker-based searches, and the four quarters of data are again useful for analyzing the trading patterns and proclivities of the institution.

An added piece of information that professional investors will appreciate is contact information for all the filing institutions. The name of the primary contact at the institution, its phone number, and address are all listed across the top of the page. The name listed is also what is queried when users search the Form 13F database by contact name.

The search by date of when the database is updated is important for knowing what institutions have recently filed their Form 13Fs. These are quarterly reports that must be filed by institutions within 45 days of the end of a quarter. This makes for a bulge in filings around the deadline date, but some institutions file early, others late. InsiderTrader updates its Form 13F database twice a week, and there is always some institution being updated. This useful search tells you which ones were.

INSIDERSCORES.COM

Free
<www.insiderscores.com>

InsiderScores is another excellent Web site devoted solely to the distribution of insider data and research. It has two years of detailed insider histories comparable in layout to any other free data available, plenty of commentary and research, and—best of all—a unique rating system that scores how well an insider has traded a particular stock in the past. Free portfolio alerts of activity are also available.

This site is the retail product of Primark (the large financial data firm reviewed in Chapter 13), and it is headed by Craig Columbus, another well-known and well-respected personality related to insider data. The free commentary and research are organized under four headings: Strategy Filters, Breaking News, Inside the Numbers, and featured story.

Strategy Filters is a periodic column written by Dr. Carr Bettis, a respected name in the realm of academic research on insider trading data. Dr. Bettis relies entirely on quantitative computer models to identify compelling investment ideas—without emotion or additional research. His screens methodically search for the intersection between interesting insider trading data and compelling fundamental or technical factors. Each column focuses on one company, and Dr. Bettis does provide a few paragraphs of useful background on each of his picks.

Several times each day, the Breaking News column highlights trades that InsiderScores deems significant. A couple of paragraphs of background on both the insider and the company also are provided, giving users a good heads up on where further research time could be fruitful.

Inside the Numbers is a periodic column written by Dr. Donn Vickrey, an associate professor of accounting. Typically, one company is featured in each column, and Dr. Vickrey addresses accounting-oriented questions about the company. The insider activity also is mentioned in the context of these very readable articles, which explains its presence on an insider-related site.

Insider Research is a weekly column that provides more traditional, in-depth analysis of a company with significant insider activity. There does not appear to be a mechanism for updates, however, so investors must determine on their own when to sell and how to interpret subsequent news affecting the recommendation. The free insider histories are good primarily for the amount of history they provide (two years), which overshadows your annoyance stemming from the histories' neglecting to combine Form 144 data on the same history.

In a similar vein, the limitation that the insider database cannot be searched by insider name is overcome by the fact that when you click the insider's name in the ticker-generated history, it returns all the trades for that insider in that company going back to 1986! This is the most individual history available free anywhere on the Internet. There is no search that returns the trades for an insider across all the companies at which they are considered an insider, but, again, it seems unkind to complain about this given the amount of history returned once you find out the other companies an insider belongs to from other sites.

Insider scores. It is the namesake feature of this site that makes it uniquely useful. An insider score is generated for each individual insider that ranks how well the person has traded a particular company's shares in the past. Each insider has a separate buy and sell score (assuming that each has done at least one of each transaction) ranging between 1 and 100. An insider with a score of 59 or below is deemed an unreliable indicator and signifies that you should not view future trading that insider does as giving valuable information.

A score of 80 to 100 means that future trades by this insider should probably be mimicked by investors given that this insider's past track record is so good. Insiders in this highest rating bracket are termed 1st Team All-Stars by the site. Insiders that rank between 60 and 79 are termed 2d Team All-Stars, and are also considered valuable indicators when they trade—though not as valuable as the 1st Team, of course.

Important to remember is that insiders have a different buy and sell score. So though someone may not have sold particularly well in the

---

FIGURE 15.3 Insider Scores' History of Jerry Moyes's Insider Transaction at Swift Transportation (Nasdaq: SWFT)

ⓘⒸ Career Snapshot

MOYES JERRY C

SWIFT TRANSPORTATION CO INC (SWFT)

	iSC SCORE	AVG RETURN 3 MO.%	6 MO.%	NUMBER OF DECISIONS
BUY	100	10.66%	25.26%	31
SELL	21	20.77%	19.59%	4

Note: Number of decisions may exceed filings since a "decision" spans a seven day period.

TRANS TYPE	TRANS DATE(S)	SHARES	D/I OWN	PRICE RANGE(S)	MKT VALUE(S)	TOTAL HOLDINGS
B	02/02/00-02/02/00	12,200	D	$11.94-$11.94	$145,638	25.17M
B	01/19/00-01/21/00	10,000	D	$13.06-$13.94	$135,313	25.16M
B	12/03/99-12/22/99	211,400	D	$13.25-$16.00	$3.21M	25.15M
B	10/26/99-10/26/99	15,000	D	$15.88-$16.13	$240,000	24.94M
B	09/02/98-09/02/98	5,000	D	$17.44-$17.44	$87,200	16.60M
B	08/05/98-08/31/98	20,000	D	$17.00-$20.50	$373,360	13.60M
*B	08/04/98-08/31/98	34,000	D	$17.00-$20.50	$623	16.61M
B	06/10/98-06/25/98	416,500	D	$19.41-$21.69	$8.43M	16.58M
B	12/02/97-12/04/97	13,000	D	$27.60-$30.00	$367,625	10.68M
B	11/13/97-11/25/97	92,500	D	$27.63-$28.95	$2.57M	10.64M
B	08/06/97-11/13/97	94,000	D/I	$27.88-$29.94	$2.70M	10.77M
S	12/20/96-12/24/96	1.15M	D	$20.77-$20.77	$23.89M	10.55M
S	08/29/96-08/30/96	47,400	I	$22.14-$22.15	$1.05M	11.70M
S	05/19/95-05/22/95	25,000		$16.75-$16.88	$420,050	13.09M
B	05/03/95-05/03/95	63,400		$15.63-$15.75	$995,862	13.09M
B	04/18/95-04/18/95	5,000		$13.38-$13.38	$66,900	13.05M
B	03/09/95-03/10/95	6,000		$18.07-$18.75	$109,780	13.04M
B	11/03/94-11/03/94	16,000		$40.63-$40.63	$650,080	13.04M
B	10/31/94-10/31/94	10,000		$43.38-$43.38	$433,800	6.50M
B	07/08/94-07/08/94	10,000		$31.75-$31.75	$317,500	4.47M
B	06/24/94-06/28/94	30,000		$32.50-$32.75	$980,000	6.48M
B	09/16/93-09/17/93	15,000		$27.00-$27.00	$405,000	4.43M
B	03/15/93-08/23/93	100,000		$22.00-$28.13	$2.47M	3.07M
B	03/29/93-05/28/93	53,500		$23.00-$26.50	$1.33M	4.40M
B	03/15/93-03/30/93	35,000		$22.00-$23.88	$804,450	3.01M
S	10/23/92-10/23/92	862,500		$19.50-$19.50	$16.82M	2.97M
S	10/23/92-10/23/92	862,500		$19.50-$19.50	$16.82M	4.32M

---

past, he or she may have been a great indicator of when to jump in. Fortunately, the different scores are easily differentiated by being presented in different colors.

I am not usually enthralled with bunching wads of insider data, which are very qualitative by nature, into a single quantitative number, but InsiderScores' methodology seems more reasonable than most. Basically, historical stock performance is monitored for the three-month and six-month periods following every insider's purchases and sales, and the score is generated based on how well the trade correlated with the stock's subsequent returns.

Still, investors should inspect the detailed data history to determine if some noise may have been sucked into the black box that generates these scores. An obvious shortcoming of the methodology is that insiders need only make one trade in the past five years and two trades in the past ten years to be scored. It would be wise to make sure the supposed All-Star that catches your attention has a larger track record than that. But the site itself also smartly advises users not to make investments based solely on its scores.

Chapter 15 *AT A GLANCE*

1. The Internet is the definitive method of receiving insider data.

2. Mass market portals do have basic insider data, but the handful of niche sites specializing in the investment approach offer much more information.

Appendix A

Securities Exchange Act of 1934
Section 16.
Directors, Officers, and Principal Stockholders

a. Every person who is directly or indirectly the beneficial owner of more than 10 per centum of any class of any equity security (other than an exempted security) which is registered pursuant to Section 12 of this title, or who is a director or an officer of the issuer of such security, shall file, at the time of the registration of such security on a national securities exchange or by the effective date of a registration statement filed pursuant to Section 12(g) of this title, or within ten days after he becomes such beneficial owner, director, or officer, a statement with the Commission (and, if such security is registered on a national securities exchange, also with the exchange) of the amount of all equity securities of such issuer of which he is the beneficial owner, and within ten days after the close of each calendar month thereafter, if there has been a change in such ownership during such month, shall file with the Commission (and if such security is registered on a national securities exchange, shall also file with the exchange), a statement indicating his ownership at the close of the calendar month and such changes in his ownership as have occurred during such calendar month.

b. For the purpose of preventing the unfair use of information which may have been obtained by such beneficial owner, director, or officer by reason of his relationship to the issuer, any profit realized by him from any purchase and sale, or any sale and purchase, of any equity security of such issuer (other than an exempted security) within any period of less than six months, unless such security was acquired in good faith in connection with a debt previously contracted, shall inure to and be recoverable by the issuer, irrespective of any intention on the part of such beneficial owner, director, or officer in entering into such transaction of holding the security purchased or of not repurchasing the security sold for a period exceeding six months. Suit to recover such profit may be instituted at law or in equity in any court of competent jurisdiction by the issuer, or by the owner of any security of the issuer in the name and in behalf of the issuer if the issuer shall fail or refuse to bring such suit within sixty days after request or shall fail diligently to prosecute the same thereafter; but no such suit shall be brought more than two years after the date such profit was realized. This subsection shall not be construed to cover any transaction where such beneficial owner was not such both at the time of the purchase and sale, or the sale and purchase, of the security involved, or any transaction or transactions which the Commission by rules and regulations may exempt as not comprehended within the purpose of this subsection.

1. It shall be unlawful for any such beneficial owner, director, or officer, directly or indirectly, to sell any equity security of such issuer (other than an exempted security), if the person selling the security or his principal does not own the security sold, or
2. if owning the security, does not deliver it against such sale within twenty days thereafter, or does not within five days after such sale deposit it in the mails or other usual channels of transportation; but no person shall be deemed to have violated this subsection if he proves that notwithstanding the exercise of good faith he was unable to make such delivery or deposit within such time, or that to do so would cause undue inconvenience or expense.

c. The provisions of subsection (b) of this section shall not apply to any purchase and sale, or sale and purchase, and the provisions of subsection (c) of this section shall not apply to any sale, of an equity security not then or theretofore held by him in an investment account, by a dealer in the ordinary course of his business and incident to the establishment or maintenance by him of a primary or secondary market (otherwise than on a national securities exchange or an exchange exempted from registration under Section 5 of this title) for such security. The Commission may, by such rules and regulations as it deems necessary or appropriate in the public interest, define and prescribe terms and conditions with respect to securities held in an investment account and transactions made in the ordinary course of business and incident to the establishment or maintenance of a primary or secondary market.
d. The provisions of this section shall not apply to foreign or domestic arbitrage transactions unless made in contravention of such rules and regulations as the Commission may adopt in order to carry out the purposes of this section.

Appendix B

General Rules and Regulations Resulting from the Securities Exchange Act of 1934
Rule 16a-1 - Definition of Terms

Terms defined in this rule shall apply solely to section 16 of the Act and the rules thereunder. These terms shall not be limited to section 16(a) of the Act but also shall apply to all other subsections under section 16 of the Act.

a. The term *beneficial owner* shall have the following applications:

   1. Solely for purposes of determining whether a person is a beneficial owner of more than ten percent of any class of equity securities registered pursuant to section 12 of the Act, the term "beneficial owner" shall mean any person who is deemed a beneficial owner pursuant to section 13(d) of the Act and the rules thereunder; *provided, however,* that the following institutions or persons shall not be deemed the beneficial owner of securities of such class held for the benefit of third parties or in customer or fiduciary accounts in the ordinary course of business (or in the case of an employee benefit plan specified in paragraph (a)(1)(vi) of this section, of securities of such class allocated to plan participants where participants have voting power) as long as such shares are acquired by such institutions or persons without the purpose or effect of changing or influencing control of the issuer or engaging in any arrangement subject to Rule 13d-3(b):

      i.   A broker or dealer registered under section 15 of the Act;
      ii.   A bank as defined in section 3(a)(6) of the Act;
      iii. An insurance company as defined in section 3(a)(19) of the Act;
      iv.   An investment company registered under section 8 of the Investment Company Act of 1940;
      v.   An investment adviser registered under section 203 of the Investment Advisers Act of 1940;

vi.   An employee benefit plan or a pension fund which is subject to the provisions of the Employee Retirement Income Security Act of 1974, as amended, 29 U.S.C. 1001 *et seq.* ("Employee Retirement Income Security Act"), or an endowment fund;

vii.   A parent holding company, provided the aggregate amount held directly by the parent, and directly and indirectly by its subsidiaries that are not persons specified in Rule 16a-1(a)(1)(i) through (vi), does not exceed one percent of the securities of the subject class; and

viii.   A group, provided that all the members are persons specified in Rule 16a-1(a)(1) (i) through (vii).

Note to paragraph (a). Pursuant to this section, a person deemed a beneficial owner of more than ten percent of any class of equity securities registered under section 12 of the Act would file a Form 3, but the securities holdings disclosed on Form 3, and changes in beneficial ownership reported on subsequent Forms 4 or 5, would be determined by the definition of "beneficial owner" in paragraph (a)(2) of this section.

2.   Other than for purposes of determining whether a person is a beneficial owner of more than ten percent of any class of equity securities registered under section 12 of the Act, the term *beneficial owner* shall mean any person who, directly or indirectly, through any contract, arrangement, understanding, relationship or otherwise, has or shares a direct or indirect pecuniary interest in the equity securities, subject to the following:

i.   The term *pecuniary interest* in any class of equity securities shall mean the opportunity, directly or indirectly, to profit or share in any profit derived from a transaction in the subject securities.

ii.   The term *indirect pecuniary interest* in any class of equity securities shall include, but not be limited to:

    A.   Securities held by members of a person's immediate family sharing the same household; provided, however, that the presumption of such beneficial ownership may be rebutted; *see* also Rule 16a-1(a)(4);

    B.   A general partner's proportionate interest in the portfolio securities held by a general or limited partnership. The general partner's proportionate interest, as evidenced by the partnership agreement in effect at the time of the transaction and the partnership's most recent financial statements, shall be the greater of:

        1.   The general partner's share of the partnership's profits, including profits attributed to any limited partnership interests held by the general partner and any other interests in profits that arise from the purchase and sale of the partnership's portfolio securities; or

2. The general partner's share of the partnership capital account, including the share attributable to any limited partnership interest held by the general partner.

C. A performance-related fee, other than an asset-based fee, received by any broker, dealer, bank, insurance company, investment company, investment adviser, investment manager, trustee or person or entity performing a similar function; *provided, however,* that no pecuniary interest shall be present where:

1. The performance-related fee, regardless of when payable, is calculated based upon net capital gains and/or net capital appreciation generated from the portfolio or from the fiduciary's overall performance over a period of one year or more; and
2. Equity securities of the issuer do not account for more than ten percent of the market value of the portfolio. A right to a nonperformance-related fee alone shall not represent a pecuniary interest in the securities;

D. A person's right to dividends that is separated or separable from the underlying securities. Otherwise, a right to dividends alone shall not represent a pecuniary interest in the securities;
E. A person's interest in securities held by a trust, as specified in Rule 16a-8(b); and
F. A person's right to acquire equity securities through the exercise or conversion of any derivative security, whether or not presently exercisable.

iii. A shareholder shall not be deemed to have a pecuniary interest in the portfolio securities held by a corporation or similar entity in which the person owns securities if the shareholder is not a controlling shareholder of the entity and does not have or share investment control over the entity's portfolio.

3. Where more than one person subject to section 16 is deemed to be a beneficial owner of the same equity securities, all such persons must report as beneficial owners of the securities. In such cases, the amount of short-swing profit recoverable shall not be increased above the amount recoverable if there were only one beneficial owner.
4. Any person filing a statement pursuant to section 16(a) of the Act may state that the filing shall not be deemed an admission that such person is, for purposes of section 16 of the Act or otherwise, the beneficial owner of any equity securities covered by the statement.
5. The following interests are deemed not to confer beneficial ownership for purposes of section 16 of the Act:

i. Interests in portfolio securities held by any holding company registered under the Public Utility Holding Company Act of 1935;

    ii.   Interests in portfolio securities held by any investment company registered under the Investment Company Act of 1940; and

    iii.   Interests in securities comprising part of a broad-based, publicly traded market basket or index of stocks, approved for trading by the appropriate federal governmental authority.

b.   The term *call equivalent position* shall mean a derivative security position that increases in value as the value of the underlying equity increases, including, but not limited to, a long convertible security, a long call option, and a short put option position.

c.   The term *derivative securities* shall mean any option, warrant, convertible security, stock appreciation right, or similar right with an exercise or conversion privilege at a price related to an equity security, or similar securities with a value derived from the value of an equity security, but shall not include:

1.   Rights of a pledgee of securities to sell the pledged securities;
2.   Rights of all holders of a class of securities of an issuer to receive securities pro rata, or obligations to dispose of securities, as a result of a merger, exchange offer, or consolidation involving the issuer of the securities;
3.   Rights or obligations to surrender a security, or have a security withheld, upon the receipt or exercise of a derivative security or the receipt or vesting of equity securities, in order to satisfy the exercise price or the tax witholding consequences of receipt, exercise or vesting.
4.   Interests in broad-based index options, broad-based index futures, and broad-based publicly traded market baskets of stocks approved for trading by the appropriate federal governmental authority;
5.   Interests or rights to participate in employee benefit plans of the issuer; or
6.   Rights with an exercise or conversion privilege at a price that is not fixed.

d.   The term *equity security of such issuer* shall mean any equity security or derivative security relating to an issuer, whether or not issued by that issuer.

e.   The term *immediate family* shall mean any child, stepchild, grandchild, parent, stepparent, grandparent, spouse, sibling, mother-in-law, father-in-law, son-in-law, daughter-in-law, brother-in-law, or sister-in-law, and shall include adoptive relationships.

f.   The term "officer" shall mean an issuer's president, principal financial officer, principal accounting officer (or, if there is no such accounting officer, the controller), any vice-president of the issuer in charge of a principal business unit, division or function (such as sales, administration or finance), any other officer who performs a policy-making function, or any other person who performs similar policy-making functions for the issuer. Officers of the issuer's parent(s) or subsidiaries shall be deemed officers of the issuer if they perform such policy-making functions for the issuer. In addition, when the issuer is a limited partnership, officers or employees of the general partner(s) who perform policy-making functions for the limited partnership are deemed officers of the limited partnership. When the issuer is a trust, officers or employees of the trustee(s) who perform policy-making functions for the trust are deemed officers of the trust.

Note: "Policy-making function" is not intended to include policy-making functions that are not significant. If pursuant to Item 401(b) of Regulation S-K the issuer identifies a person as an "executive officer," it is presumed that the Board of Directors has made that judgment and that the persons so identified are the officers for purposes of section 16 of the Act, as are such other persons enumerated in this paragraph (f) but not in Item 401(b).

g. The term *portfolio securities* shall mean all securities owned by an entity, other than securities issued by the entity.
h. The term *put equivalent position* shall mean a derivative security position that increases in value as the value of the underlying equity decreases, including, but not limited to, a long put option and a short call option position.

References

The following list of references offers a menu of the generally more recent but important and representative work by knowledgeable authors on the subject of insider trading and subjects that impact it. Although the large majority of listed works are academic in nature and have a very narrow focus, you will find others included that are much more general in nature.

Barrow, R. J., E. F. Fama, E. R. Fischel, A. H. Meltzer, R. W. Roll, and L. G. Tesler. 1989. In *Black Monday and the Future of Financial Markets,* ed. R. W. Kampuis, R. C. Kormendi, and J. W. H. Watson. Mid-America Institute for Public Policy Research. Homewood, IL: Irwin.

Benesh, G. A., and R. A. Pari. 1987. Performance of stocks recommended on the basis of insider trading activity. *The Financial Review* 22:145–58.

Bernhardt, D., B. Hollifield, and E. Hughson. 1995. Investment and insider trading. *Review of Financial Studies* 8:501–43.

Bettis, C. 1995. A test of the validity of friendly takeover rumors. *Financial Analysts Journal.* November-December: 53–57.

———. Potential profitability of insider trading inferred from publicly available insider trading information. Manuscript. Phoenix: Arizona State University West School of Management.

Bettis, C., and J. Coles. 1997. New evidence on insider trading around merger announcements. Manuscript. Phoenix: Arizona State University West School of Management.

Bettis, C., and W. Duncan. Effect of legal sanctions on takeover target insider purchases. Manuscript. Phoenix: Arizona State University West School of Management.

―――. Insider profits and a regulatory dilemma. Manuscript. Phoenix: Arizona State University West School of Management.

Bettis, C., and S. Chang. Insider trading regulations and their implications for internal auditors. Manuscript. Phoenix: Arizona State University West School of Management.

Bettis, C., D. Vickrey, and D. W. Vickrey. Mimickers of corporate insiders who make large volume trades. Manuscript. Phoenix: Arizona State University West School of Management.

Bettis, C., D. Vickrey, and Donn Vickrey. Volume effects of predisclosure information asymmetry: Evidence from insider-trading activities. Manuscript. Phoenix: Arizona State University West School of Management.

Brudney, V. 1979. Insiders, outsiders, and informational advantages under the federal securities laws. *Harvard Law Review* 93:322–76.

Campbell, J., and A. S. Kyle. 1993. Smart money, noise trading, and stock price behavior. *Review of Economic Studies* 60:1–34.

Elliot, J., D. Morse, and G. Richardson. 1984. The association between insider trading and information announcements. *Rand Journal of Economics* 15:521–36.

Gaillard, E. 1992. *Insider Trading, the Laws of Europe, the United States and Japan.* Boston: Kluwer Law and Taxation.

Givoli, D., and D. Palmon. 1985. Insider trading and the exploitation of inside information: Some empirical evidence. *Journal of Business* January:69–87.

Golder, R., and K. Ambachtsheer. 1983. Are some insiders more "inside" than others? Comment. *Journal of Portfolio Management* 10:75.

John, K., and R. Narayanan. 1997. Market manipulation and the role of insider trading regulations. *Journal of Business* 70:217–47.

Kaushik, I., and H. N. Seyhun. 1993. Is there positive feedback trading in the index options markets? Manuscript. Ann Arbor: Michigan Business School.

Manne, H. 1966. *Insider trading and the stock market.* New York: Free Press.

Seyhun, H. N. 1986. Insiders' profits, costs of trading, and market efficiency. *Journal of Financial Economics* 16:189–212.

Seyhun, H. N. 1988a. The January effect and aggregate insider trading. *Journal of Finance* 43:129–41.

Seyhun, H. N. 1988b. The information content of aggregate insider trading. *Journal of Business* 61:1–24.

Seyhun, H. N. 1990a. Do bidder managers knowingly pay too much for target firms? *Journal of Business* 63:439–64.

Seyhun, H. N. 1990b. Overreaction or fundamentals: Some lessons from insiders' responses to the market crash of 1987. *Journal of Finance* 45:1363–88.

Seyhun, H. N. 1992a. The effectiveness of the insider trading sanctions. *Journal of Law and Economics* 35:149–82.

Seyhun, H. N. 1992b. Why does aggregate insider trading predict future stock returns? *Quarterly Journal of Economics* 107:1303–31.

Seyhun, H. N. 1993. Aggregate Insider Trading and Market Timing. Manuscript. Ann Arbor: Michigan Business School.

Seyhun, H. N., and M. Bradley. 1997. Corporate bankruptcy and insider trading. *Journal of Business* 70:189–216.

Seyhun, H. N. 1998. *Investment Intelligence from Insider Trading*. Cambridge: MIT Press.

Sobel, R. 1977. *Inside Wall Street*. New York: W. W. Norton.

Zweig, M. E. 1986. *Martin Zweig's Winning on Wall Street*. New York: Warner Books.

Index

About the Author

Jonathan Moreland is the director of research and founder of InsiderTrader.com, now wholly owned by Individual Investor Group, Inc. (Nasdaq: INDI). Via the Web site <www.insidertrader.com>, Mr. Moreland distributes insider data and also presents his firm's research in an online investment newsletter. He can also be heard Wednesday mornings at 9:10 AM on Business Talk Radio, a nationally syndicated radio program.

Before forming InsiderTrader.com, Jonathan Moreland was the assistant director of research at Individual Investor Group, publisher of *Individual Investor* magazine. One of his responsibilities there was to be the analyst and author of that publication's Insider's Edge and Insiders Out columns.

Mr. Moreland received an undergraduate degree in biology from the State University of New York at Oswego and an MBA in finance from Henley Management College (Henley-on-Thames, England), and he has successfully completed levels I and II of the CFA qualification.